GOD-WALK

GOD-WALK

Liberation Shaping Dogmatics

Frederick Herzog

ORBIS BOOKS

The Catholic Foreign Mission Society of America (Maryknoll) recruits and trains people for overseas missionary service. Through Orbis Books Maryknoll aims to foster the international dialogue that is essential to mission. The books published, however, reflect the opinions of their authors and are not meant to represent the offical position of the society.

Copyright © 1988 by Frederick Herzog
All rights reserved
Manufactured in the United States of America

Manuscript editor and indexer: William E. Jerman

Photo Credits:
cover: "The Indonesian Christ: Jesus Healing a Blind Person"; relief by Samuel Ginting, Karo-Batak Church, Indonesia; photo by Theo Daubenberger; © Vereinigte Evangelische Mission. Permission granted.
p. xvii: photograph © 1949 by Constance Stuart Larrabee. Permission granted.
p. xxiv: "The Misereor 'Hunger Cloth' from Ethiopia," by Alemayehu Bizuneh; © Misereor, Mozartstrasse 9, 5100 Aachen, Federal Republic of Germany. Permission granted.
p. xxv: "The Misereor 'Hunger Cloth' from Peru" © Misereor. Permission granted.
p. xxviii: photographs from *A Road to Walk* © 1987 by Jenny Labalme. Permission granted.

Cover design: Alicia Grant

LIBRARY OF CONGRESS
Library of Congress Cataloging-in-Publication Data

Herzog, Frederick.
    God-walk : liberation shaping dogmatics / Frederick Herzog.
        p.   cm.
    Bibliography: p.
    Includes index.
    ISBN 0-88344-607-3.   ISBN 0-88344-606-5 (pbk.)
    1. Theology—Methodology.   2. Liberation theology.   I. Title.
BR118.H47   1988
230′.01—dc19   87-34792
                                                                                    CIP

In memory of

Pauli Murray
(1910–1985)

and for

Katie G. Cannon
James H. Cone
C. Eric Lincoln
J. Deotis Roberts
Gayraud Wilmore

and all other black theologians
who blazed the trail . . .

Justice is immortal.
—Wisdom of Solomon 1:15

CONTENTS

PREFACE

No easy walk to freedom . . .
Peter, Paul, and Mary

We often grasp more about God on a walk than through a book. We cannot help reflecting on God when we are walking together with the "stranger" Jesus—often hardly recognizable, as with the disciples on the road to Emmaus, or not recognizable at all as with the boy born blind. And whenever we are walking together with people in a common justice struggle, the "stranger" is walking with us. Thus: God-walk.

We soon painfully discover, however, that not all of us have the same mind when we use the word God. So in one respect I perhaps ought to stop right here and not go on writing. The searing pain I feel over how differently people grasp God stays part of me throughout this book. I am also very aware of the many who merely draw a blank when they hear the word God. The futility of referring to God in the presence of countless persons who in our modern or post-modern world experience the absence of God haunts me on every page. What gives me courage to go on is the chance of a common walk through fairly uncharted territory. There is hope in the walk together—occasionally inspiring, always taxing, never dull.

"We've got a road to walk. . . . "[1] Roads have a strange attraction in the South of the United States. People walk them for all kinds of reasons. They also walk them for justice-making. Almost everyone knows about the march from Selma to Montgomery, Alabama. Not everyone knows about the walk in Warren County, North Carolina. The march in Alabama was for civil rights, the walk in Warren County for further civil rights and the rights of all creation. In 1978, when the Raleigh-based Ward Transformer Company had sprayed 31,000 gallons of polychlorinated biphenyl

(PCB) along 240 miles of the state's highways, the Warren County population was 64 percent black. By 1982 the state had selected a disposal site in the highly black county.

The people of the county, black and white, started walking together to resist the destruction of their environment. Yet PCB is still being dumped almost everywhere in our inhabited world where civilization pushes ahead. The Rhine (a busy waterway in the news in 1986 because of the Swiss chemical spill) already is full of PCB. Obviously it is being carried into the North Sea, soon to be another Dead Sea. The crime done to our roads, waterways, and byways is immeasurable. There is no more urgent task for us today than to rediscover God-walk.

The "thought-results" of walking together with Jesus have been drawn together in the Christian tradition, doctrines, and teachings—time and again expounded in various ways through catechists, bishops, ministers, nuns, professors, and a host of volunteers in Sunday schools. This book intends to be no more than a textbook in Christian doctrine, though concentrating on one basic point: that the genesis of any Christian thought lies in God-walk. In other words, *Christian reflection always grows out of a social location—out of discipleship in a context of conflict.* Unfortunately many of us manage to ignore or repress the conflict.

Some dogmatics texts still begin from the premise that theory provides guidelines for walking in the world—for action. The project of *liberation shaping dogmatics,* by contrast, is premised on the inescapably conflictual context where praxis precedes theory. Dogmatics now is shown to arise out of God-walk. Praxis gives rise to thought. Here is a turning. It differs from the more orthodox view of the *creed shaping dogmatics,* or the more modern (liberal) view of *religion shaping dogmatics.* We are working on a *new paradigm.*

Obviously we often bring theory to the situation. But its ideas are here all put through the wringer of praxis. The core thought-process in praxis always begins from scratch. So there was great wisdom in describing in the Christian scriptures the budding life and ideas of the early church as the *praxeis,* the Acts of the Apostles, in other words, their God-walk. What is more, the early Christians were first of all called people of the "Way" (Acts 9:2; 19:9,23; 22:4; 24:14,22).

As we see ourselves as links in a chain that begins with primitive Christianity, we cannot escape facing the crisis of the modern world—discovering how God walks with us into the crisis, offering us a new way of life. Along the way we encounter our human limitations as well as the healing power of self-limitation that Jesus embodies. We also see a new view of Jesus beginning to evolve, along with new community, new teaching, and new doctrinal formation, all growing out of the new praxis in small communities involved in the justice struggle. In this preface, besides introducing a few searchlights on these topics, I also pay tribute to the people whose walk has supported my own. We all get shaky knees sometimes. We all occasionally walk off in the wrong direction. Therefore solidarity and the mutual accountability we struggle for are crucial.

The Power of (Self-)Limitation

The Jesus of the road is key today because he teaches us limits of human control within which *alone* the engine of historical change can move history on constructively. Just like Jesus in his short life, we cannot walk forever and we can only walk so far. Jesus did not cover "a lot of turf." Instead, he concentrated on the creativity of his interactions with people and nature. Rather than doing everything, he did a few important things. In our world today, besides facing the "limits of growth" we also face the limits of goodness. We can do good only in fairly small ways. If we reach beyond them, we inherit the whirlwind. Jesus' God-walk invites us to accept our human limits voluntarily. The people who walk through the following pages very concretely have taught me the power arising from self-limitation.

The forces unleashed when we deny the "limits of growth" and of human capacity are frightful. For what is threatening us from the future is a plague of unspeakable death. Countless beings in ocean, air, and on land have already been destroyed or are on the verge of destruction. Death is sneaking up on us. We thought it could never happen. We thought we were good—very good. Modernity seemed to promise heaven on earth, but what is now threatening us appears like hell on earth—living death.

The history of technology is the story of the magician's apprentice who forgot how to limit the magic power usurped from the master. It has often been stressed that not all things should be done that technology can do. Yet technology still makes more things than are healthy for us. We do not know how to stop the destructive magic. We do not even know how to get our bearings among all the magical gadgets we are bombarded with. Precious resources are wasted on controlling and destroying at the expense of human needs.[2] The task is how to find the power to set limits. Population explosion in many parts of the world accompanies technological expansion. Take only Nigeria. There is the possibility of doubling and even tripling the population within a few decades. It boggles the imagination when one thinks of what overpopulation will do to the dignity of human life on this planet.

Healing Power

Just as lack of limitation brings destruction, so Jesus' self-limitation often brings healing. There are several ways in which the walk together with Jesus might set free healing power. This becomes evident as we discover God's character anew and human character as well.

1. We cannot help discovering *God's character* in a new way, since walking together with Jesus gets us into conflict over who God is. The current crisis over the reality of God is almost unparalleled in modern times. Language inflation has set in. The theological formulas have lost their cash value. While there are all kinds of amateur Nietzsches running around trumpeting that God is dead, the practical atheism underlying the pseudo-spirituality of our Orwellian world—East and West—is worse yet.

To get a good perspective on our predicament in terms of doctrinal language we might look back to the third and fourth centuries. One way to grasp our situation today is to see ourselves on the road toward a new Chalcedon. If a new ecumenical council should be called in the foreseeable future—as many hope and pray—it would first of all have to pay attention to new christology. This book can offer only a glimpse of the direction in which we need to walk to find healing. As we walk, a new vision wells up in our souls from which new teachings get shaped that add to the healing of our lives. As healing comes, we will no longer primarily be concerned with the true God/true man dispute that preoccupied the age of Nicea and Chalcedon. Instead we will focus on Jesus as refuge and refugee, person and non-person, for Jesus' person embraces also all who have been rejected as persons, the marginals and the poor.

Thus far, the incarnation too often has been interpreted as just another expression of God's omnipotence. Instead, we need to see that it is precisely God's choice of self-impoverishment, of deprivation, that embodies self-limitation. God chose not at all to be omnipotent in the popular sense.

This understanding of the incarnation does not in any way entail that we think less of God, but rather that we need to think more highly of human life. By living and walking among us, God reaffirms the dignity of each person as also the sanctity of all nature.

The cover picture from Indonesia suggests God's healing walk through the world—a liberating walk. This is not a picture of mere charity. As we all know, justice is part of the context without which the picture is not complete. The blind man was not healed by sheer divine fiat, but by the Jesus who shared in the impoverishment— and thus the limitations—of human life. So it is not the healing itself that is the main message of the picture, but the *context* of self-limitation God chooses for embodying the divine character. And note the bird—just visible on the tree at the right edge. It is an ecological context. All creation shares in the divine self-limitation and sings its praises. "Thou art worshipped knowingly or unknowingly by all creatures capable of loving" (St. Augustine). We too can sing:

> O Master, from the mountainside,
> make haste to heal these hearts of pain;
> Among these restless throngs abide,
> O tread the city's streets again.

O *walk* the city's streets again. This stanza from a well-known hymn also emphasizes the strong connection between walking and healing. It pertains also to the trees on the cover and *their* hearts of pain—suffering acid rain, for example. Many trees can no longer "sing for joy" (Ps. 96:12).

2. We discover *human character* in a new way. Walking the roads of the South I often thought that people walking for justice here

were sometimes closer to other walkers all over the world than they were to sisters and brothers sitting in nearby precinct halls or church pews. To be human is to be in solidarity with your context of pain. The significance of the walking couple (p. xvii)—an African woman with her husband, a Methodist minister—also lies in the *context* of the struggle in which they walked, their social location. The picture was taken in Natal in 1949 when yet greater oppression was looming on the South African horizon. They walk in hope, as Constance Stuart Larrabee, the photographer, likes to put it. Even so, they were also walking toward the inferno of hunger and war threatening the people on the African continent as a whole, in Latin America, and elsewhere. The proud women who walk through many of Larrabee's photographs of South Africa[3] also walk through the pages of this book as I try to hear their voices. As the world becomes ever more interconnected in a global village, the webs of oppression tighten their grip on people everywhere, seeking to destroy especially those who continue to walk upright, who will not bend their knee before the idols of power. By now it is clear why the women of *Sweet Honey in the Rock* point to the links between places of struggle like Wilmington, North Carolina, and Capetown and cry out in their songs: "Chile, your waters run red through Soweto," and "the waters of Chile fill the banks of Cape Fear." In walking together, sharing the pain of the world brought about by our inhumanity to each other, we inhere within each other more than ever before. We can become a corporate selfhood of resisting pain. Recognizing this is the first step of releasing the healing power of God-walk. I have learned this especially from the women of the walk.

People of Healing

Over the years my life has increasingly been shaped by the healing power of partners and friends and also strangers who share the walk. Chile is present in Sergio Torres and his friends, South Africa in Allan Boesak—and Steven Biko, no longer with us. I remember the jailcells of the Wilmington Ten—and I think of Benjamin Chavis. I remember Warren County in 1982, and I think of Leon White. The places of pain are countless, and yet always peopled with persons valiantly resisting pain, injustice, and death.

On the walk others often seemed to form a wall of protection around me so as to make the pain bearable, a pain that for me is also an intellectual injury. Here José Míguez Bonino, Lee Cormie, Mary McClintock Fulkerson, Gustavo Gutiérrez, Robert T. Osborn, Sharon H. Ringe, Letty Russell, and Susan Thistlethwaite were at the right place at the right time to channel the hurt creatively—occasionally unbeknown to them. Listening to Etta B. Edwards sometimes made me forget the injury-altogether.

The configuration of the walk was in constant flux. Ron Johnson faithfully "pastored" me in all the turmoil the walk is part of. J. C. Cheek forcefully kept the needs of the black church before me. Paul Douglas persisted in his clarion call not to surrender the local church to our junk culture. Louis H. Gunnemann made sure we kept the dynamics between church tradition and church polity clearly in focus. M. Douglas Meeks brought the East-West conflict into creative tension with the North-South conflict. Frederick R. Trost contextualized these concerns time and again in a "diocesan" grass roots accountability without which justice in the church would be dead. Grant S. Shockley and William C. Turner helped me remember the black/white conflict as a national challenge beyond the walls of the church.

Part of the flux in the configuration of the walk was also an occasional step outside my own denomination, the United Church of Christ, to join in efforts of Presbyterian friends, often headed by Edward Huenemann, a most adamant walker. Robert McAfee Brown's unflinching opposition to the national security state for me was the pace-setter. Paul Lehmann kept insisting on biblical empowerment without which I could not have kept up with the pace. Gayraud Wilmore was sterling in reminding us of the contribution of black theology in singularly channeling such empowerment on our North American continent. I also will never be able to forget Covenant Presbyterian Church of Durham as wayside station since the days of the Civil Rights struggle, especially Clara Thompson standing by when the going got tough.

As the pattern of the walk became clearer, I began to grasp how a new spirituality was at work. New teaching around which the church can make sense in mutual accountability is emerging from the new praxis.[4] I hope that this book will contribute to these dynamics of accountability as church members wake up to their social location. My *Justice Church* (1980) already tried to lay the groundwork for the mutual accountability dynamics. David L. Watson has challenged me time and again to embody this new spirituality in covenant discipleship and prayer/contemplation groups.

Learning the healing spirituality involves the basics of walking together with Jesus in the justice struggle. This has to be clear lest we reach for too much. Alice Walker expresses it in a short story where an old black woman is thrown out of a white church she dared to enter for worship. Jesus meets her on the church steps where a few burly Christian men had dumped her. All Jesus says is: "Follow me." Jesus and the black woman then start walking down the road together: "When they passed her house, forlorn and sagging, weatherbeaten and patched, by the side of the road, she did not notice it, she was so happy to be out walking along the highway with Jesus. . . . "[5] Walking along the highway with Jesus brings joy as the core of the healing spirituality. It was joy at the center that I learned from the partners, friends, and strangers on the walk. In this sense they all are people of healing.

I also dare not forget those forerunners I came to know on the walk only by "tradition." Two names will have to represent all of them. Dorothy Day is very much at the center of a course I teach, for years already, on prayer and contemplation. Her picture on her autobiography walking through the woods keeps haunting me in my own walking.[6] In this context I need to mention also John Wesley, who is equally responsible for much of this walking business in my life.[7] The picture of Wesley preaching in the fields graces one of the doors in our home. Yet immediately the historico/self-critical method goes to work. Do we learn from Wesley real single-heartedness in regard to the oppressed? His vision calls forth creative re-vision.

I need to stress that there is a fierceness to all this walking that keeps tempering the joy. Gayraud Wilmore recently again reminded us of the hardly visible progress we have made on the walk as whites taking black thought into account. We have not as yet oriented dogmatics and the whole enterprise of ministerial education in the "universal consciousness of injustice" in which black theology is grounded.[8]

Speaking to the Living in the Language of the Dead?

We certainly can no longer speak to the living in the language of the dead (Holly Near)—if we want ourselves and others to become aware of our blindness. We need to use very transparent contemporary language rooted in the altering of consciousness. I had to learn this especially because of my social location which, among other things, includes a university. The healing power of God's justice cannot be imprisoned in the language of the past, despite the attraction of past language for us professors. Because of the new praxis we will have to learn a new language.

Do not trust a thought discovered while sitting in your chair (Nietzsche). It takes not only the whole person to think boldly; it takes the walking of the whole person. Luther thought, *pecca fortiter*, sin boldly. I wish he had said, *cogita fortiter*, think boldly—on your feet. Only thus will we be able to discover the genesis of a Christian thought also in our day and begin to speak the language of the living. Social location is all-decisive for *liberation shaping dogmatics*. Today the term social location is often viewed as new-fangled, invented by liberation theologians. Yet it is actually nothing new. We have used it in the South even in academic discourse for years.[9]

Of course everything depends on what we do with the term. God-walk as social location involves God's justice struggle in the struggle of the poor. In terms of my social location in the South, I will occasionally be asked what happened to the explicitly black orientation of my *Liberation Theology* (1972). It is precisely the continuing search for a teaching doing justice to the black experience in North America that leads me to use new metaphors which help us grasp how different relationships of power constitute and reinforce each other. Even my own language would become a language of the dead if I kept on using the old terms and metaphors over and over again.

The Warren County struggle against PCB-dumping mentioned earlier shows how these power-webs work: the power of whites over blacks, the power of industrial capitalism over the poor and our natural resources, and the power of state bureaucracy over citizens in a country that is still on the way toward full democracy. The web of oppression can be traced in various parts of the globe in the interlocking of the power structures. One of the great challenges we face is the need to discover the new metaphors or wisdom words that grow out of the praxis grounded in our vision of the underside of history. From the black/white non-encounter of the past decade we ought to have learned why we can't wait.

Since it is mandatory to speak in the language of the living, if we want to move forward at all, occasionally I feel constrained to shout at others walking in what I consider dangerous directions: "Watch out, there's treacherous terrain ahead!" In the uproar I found community not expected. I need to mention John B. Cobb, Jr., and Peter C. Hodgson, who both have been more gracious about my shouting and interfering than I deserved. I might still appear to be shouting at them and others even in this book, for example, at Tom Driver, John Macquarrie, or Schubert M. Ogden. *Peccavi.* I have sinned. We are all mutually accountable for the earth and each other. As Wesley thought, we need to watch over each other in love. So I won't apologize for obstinate shouting. I will just no longer speak to the living in the language of the dead.

Resisting Empire

One of the major metaphors we can no longer escape is empire. When we are in the midst of empire we do not notice it—usually. Yet our dogmatics is crucially dependent on it. We serve the state. We support our culture. We support it even in our critique. Liberation theology in this context is no more than a hermeneutical focus. We have apotheosized theology for too long. It has become an idol. Theology is not the be-all of Christian thought. It is merely a means to an end rising up from discipleship—God-walk. Liberation theology is certainly not a system. If it ever would become a system it would destroy itself. Accountable teaching—growing out of God-walk and focused in liberation theology—means resisting empire as idol: resisting what today competes most with God. We have to say no to every missile and bomb, every hamburger produced from cattle fed by grain robbed from the lips of a hungry child,[10] and to the destruction of the rain forest. What about us as evil empire?

Liberation theology is often scored as one of the overbearing generative theologies that worship only a small slice of the total theological material. Nothing could be further from the truth. It is a hermeneutical focus taking into account the historical process we need to describe. But how difficult to describe the bird in flight! As its method, liberation theology here can use nothing but the historico-critical method. Yet it first always needs to turn upon itself—as we discover ourselves in the midst of empire. So it functions ultimately as historico/self-critical method. It is not the text that is to be critiqued primarily, but the interpreter in context, and the text only in view of the self-critique. On this basis we inescapably also struggle with the socio-critical and psycho-critical dimensions of method.

What would happen, asked Albert Schweitzer at the beginning of our century, if theology were not dismantled and reassembled from the ground up every hundred years or so?[11] Fortunately a useful kind of reconstruction of Christian language is already taking place as some people begin once again to seek forms of expression that constantly emerge anew from concrete struggles. Wherever base communities arise, the new language already begins to grow in the church.[12]

The whole struggle against empire as idol makes for a peculiar kind of argument we are not too familiar with. We need to begin with the hypothesis that we still can discover something new: "Discovery is not a step of logical thought, though the end-product is tied to logical form" (Albert Einstein). There are occasional leaps of thought in this book. The new thing does not burst upon us as "a step of logical thought." Liberation theology begins as the poor begin to listen to each other before God. Liberation theology continues as we listen to the poor before God.

As newness emerges, once in a while it gives rise to oxymorons. It is the difficulty of being in the midst of empire and at the same time struggling to be at an absolute distance from it that keeps our walk—and thought—from being always steady. Our leaps of thought are also brought on by our rejection of any hegemonic solution. Everything we do is in *via*, on the road. There is no one answer to our search, except the (continually changing) walk itself. The road is not preordained. That is why I try to avoid the words *must* or *should*. If we were not blind, we would see what is at the inside of history or the heart of creation. The first step toward healing our blindness is the rejection of the rigid expectations of state and culture, so we can direct our gaze at the innermost reality of things. There is not some goal we *must* reach, some rule we *should* follow. Instead, there is the innermost reality that God walks, and walks with us as we take the risk of walking.

We are not at the end of the walk as yet. In a dialectical way, we begin anew to appreciate our pilgrim heritage. To be a pilgrim in 1988 is to take a God-walk. It is almost the opposite of the original American pilgrim walk. The first pilgrim story ended up in conquest, people owning the land. God-walk is merely a quest. Liberation theology thus becomes the new *theologia viatorum*. We are pilgrims for the sake of pilgrimage. We do not own the land.

In view of these dynamics, those who are looking for a theology of the Holy Spirit might find some beginnings here. For we are always confronted with the Holy-Spirit-Jesus as we share in the eucharist—and from our eucharistic walk develops the talk. Said the great-grandmother of one of my students: "If you can't walk the talk, don't talk the talk." That's a woman who knew what she was *walking* about.

Unblinding Reason

What is Jesus doing now? This is the key question arising from this book. Our response depends on what God allows faith's vision to see. Faith is at bottom nothing but reason awakened to its true character. Ultimately theology and philosophy are not too different. We are all challenged to find our vision of the underside of history as the inside of history. The Ethiopian hunger cloth (p. xxiv) tries to make that point.[13] It made a lasting impression on me when I compared it with the 1965 Salvador Dali painting, *Perpignan Station* (in the museum across from the Cologne cathedral), in which Jesus behind a thin transparent veil of reality on the underside of history, undergirding and sustaining human fate, as it were, passively hangs on the cross forever. In the Ethiopian hunger cloth Jesus is "trampling out the vintage where the grapes of wrath are stored"—a quite different view of the underside of history. The gold ground indicates God's involvement in history in thorough presence. (Unfortunately the hunger cloths could not be reproduced in color in this book).

Some of the earliest pictures of Jesus are images of the shepherd.

Ethiopian Hunger Cloth

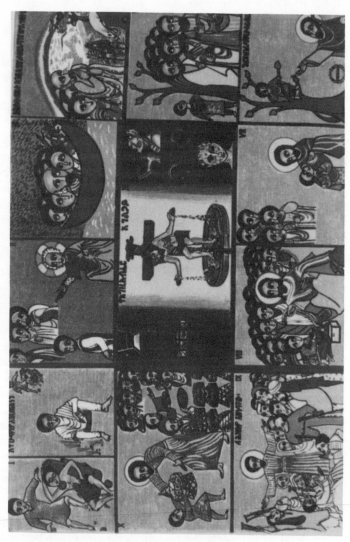

Peruvian Hunger Cloth

They reflect a vision of the life of Jesus. It was only in the Middle Ages that a fascination with his death became so strong that finally Jesus seemed to be nailed to the cross forever. Certainly there is a divine suffering Jesus yields to. Yet, on balance, there is also his life as countervailing all injustice. As Jesus continues to suffer, sharing the torture, hunger, want, and sickness all around him, injustice is being pressed down like the grapes of wrath (as on the Ethiopian hunger cloth).

It is exactly in visions of the inside of history that we retain God's mystery. We know that the pictures have to collapse, in the end, in order that their full power may break forth. But we need to pray for these visions and then work on them until reason finds its deepest identity.[14] Probably closest to *God-Walk* is the Peruvian hunger cloth, the work of a base community in Santiago de Pupuja, which named the cloth "As Christians on Our Way." Bible, foot, and hand are the central images. The *Bible* is the new pair of glasses that helps us to walk (*foot*) and labor (*hand*) as we proceed in God's own walk and feel God's right hand (p. xxv).

Our reason has blinded itself so as to be unable to see its innermost dynamics. In fact, it does not want to see its inside. It is this unreasonable theological rationality that keeps us, for example, from really listening to black theology, so forthrightly expressed by James H. Cone and others.[15] It is the same blindness that has kept us from opening ourselves to the Jewish liberation struggle, now so movingly articulated in the work of Marc H. Ellis.[16] Slavery and the Holocaust are irrevocable events that reason time and again needs to fathom at the inside of history lest we forget. We also cannot forget the conquest of both continents in this hemisphere with the American Indians still victims and their powerful and subtle spirituality ignored or sentimentalized.[17] Christian theology is reluctant to have its eyes opened and to take on past infamy, because its systematic principle seeks to control the divine and provide an answer to every question. Recently a few theologians have stopped using systematic theology as description of concerted Christian reflection.[18] Yet only with the feminist insistence on just language have we noticed how much "systematic theology" belongs to the oppressors' vocabulary. In order not to be enslaved by the system I have tried to keep the Bible ever before me. (Translations, where not otherwise indicated, are partly my own, partly derived from the RSV rendered in just language.)

I have also kept Marxist social analysis before me. Trying in social analysis to face American conquest, slavery, and Hiroshima, there is, however, little point in remembering them without struggling with the causes of the infamy and resisting their continuing effects. In the midst of all the pain suffered by the innocent, Auschwitz stands out all by itself. German people as Christianized people callously denied their intimate link to the people of God. Any shaping of Christian dogmatics today has to be inescapably confronted with it. Lest we forget. It has to come through loud and clear: Never again.

It is not surprising that God-walk frequently is rudely disrupted—as the pictures from Warren County (1982) indicate (p. xxviii). There is no *neat* way for the basic vision to emerge among us today. Marc H. Ellis appeals to Irving Greenberg's powerful dictum that after the Holocaust "no statement, theological or otherwise can be credible if it is not credible in the presence of burning children."[19]

The picture of children in Warren County protesting the destruction of creation reminds us that our credibility is at stake. Yet children can teach us even more: with the lightness of a child's heart we need to keep suffering and action, passivity and activity, the gift and the effort, in creative tension. Only thus will we get our act together. Being mindful of our human limitations, we rediscover laughter—Easter laughter.[20] In *The Name of the Rose*, Umberto Eco makes laughter the secret a fiendish person tries to hide. It is the secret of the whole book. If the power of laughter were fully known, no pope could prevail, no authoritative structure, no empire. If reason were unblinded, "laughter would be defined as the new art, unknown even to Prometheus, for cancelling fear."[21]

Laughter expresses the incongruity of our most fervent efforts at God-walk—our discovery that it is God who enables us to walk— "to will and to work" (Phil. 2:13). Henry David Thoreau knew something about walking as a gift: "It requires a direct dispensation from Heaven to become a walker. You must be born into the family of Walkers. *Ambulator nascitur, non fit*."[22] For God-walk, well, you need to be born again, or, in my language of *Liberation Theology* (1972), you still need to become black. Otherwise you will not see Jesus—refuge and refugee.

Reflecting on the dialectics between gift and effort, I am well aware that no such publishing venture as this book could do

without a support structure, both gift and effort. I need to thank the Orbis staff: Catherine Costello, Geraldine C. DiLauro, Eve Drogin, Bernadette B. Price, and Hank Schlau, for wise counsel and sterling cooperation. I am grateful to William E. Jerman for his careful editing labors. Over the years of walking these pages through the typewriter, I also have been blessed with a superb "secretarial infrastructure" at Duke Divinity School: Gail Chappell, Mary Chestnut, Sarah Freedman, Frances Parrish, Tammy Smith, and Shelby Wallen. We also cannot be grateful enough for our housekeeping staff that keeps our shop spruced and humming: Irene E. Burrus, Johnny Emanuel Holland, Lear Lee, Lugenia R. Parker, Evelyn Mae Smith, and Dora Blackwell Watson.

All the while, my closest and dearest companions have been my wife, Kristin, and our daughter, Dagmar. Our walking (and working) together often generated sparks that occasionally "set fire" to my pages and made me start all over again. The book is better for their caring input, notably Kristin's editing. These two surely know what they are *walking* about. For us all, the basic dynamics prevail: "We still have a road to walk."[23] So, "Rise and Walk" (Matt. 9:5).[24]

Notes

1. Jenny Labalme, *A Road to Walk: A Struggle for Environmental Justice* (Durham, 1987), 6.

2. John B. Cobb, Jr., *Process Theology as Political Theology* (Westminster, 1985), 120ff.

3. Constance Stuart Larrabee, in collaboration with Alan Paton, *Go Well, My Child* (Washington, 1985).

4. *Covenant Discipleship Quarterly,* 1:3 (April 1986), 4f.

5. Alice Walker, *In Love and Trouble: Stories of Black Women* (New York and London, 1973), 86.

6. Dorothy Day, *The Long Loneliness* (San Francisco, 1981).

7. Howard A. Snyder, *The Radical Wesley* (Downers Grove, 1980), has been extremely helpful in my recovery of Wesley. As to the overall implications of a Methodist framework for a possible church praxis I was instructed by Howard A. Snyder, *Liberating the Church* (Downers Grove, 1983). At the same time I have learned equally much from the countervailing voices as, for example, brilliantly summarized by Thor Hall's inaugural lecture, "Tradition Criticism: A New View of Wesley" (University of Tennessee at Chattanooga, 1987).

8. Gayraud Wilmore, "Foreword," in Theo Witvliet, *The Way of the Black Messiah* (Oak Park, 1987), viii.

9. Dennis M. Campbell, *Authority and the Renewal of American Theology* (Philadelphia, 1976), 95.

10. Frances Moore Lappé, *Diet for a Small Planet* (New York, 1971). Still the classic in explaining the nutritional chain between the Third World and our eating habits. See also Frances Moore Lappé and Joseph Collins, *World Hunger: Ten Myths* (San Francisco, 1979).

11. Albert Schweitzer, *The Quest of the Historical Jesus* (New York, 1948), 333.

12. Sergio Torres and John Eagleson, eds., *The Challenge of Basic Christian Communities* (Maryknoll, 1981). The volume carries a crucial essay by James H. Cone, "From Geneva to São Paulo: A Dialogue between Black Theology and Latin American Liberation Theology," 265–81. Here decisive issues are addressed: Do the poor speak for themselves or do others incorporate them into their schema?

13. Reviving (in 1976) a medieval tradition of shrouding the altar with a cloth at Lent, the Roman Catholic *Misereor* group in West Germany put out at least five such cloths—from Haiti, India, Peru, and this one from Ethiopia, besides a reproduction of a medieval cloth. The artist of the Ethiopian hunger cloth is Alemayehu Bizuneh. The Peruvian hunger cloth also very much reflects the point of *God-walk*. Women and men in a village in southern Peru put it together under the heading: "Christianokuna Nampi Kanchis." The Quechua words say: "As Christians on Our Way" (see p. xxv). The cloths have to be read "clockwise," beginning in the upper left-hand corner.

14. In regard to the very human drive for vision unspoiled by civilization, we can learn much from the American Indians who struggled with our hemisphere long before Europeans tried to Christianize these shores. "Native understanding is predominantly experiential, i.e., based on visions, rather than theological; the situation is reversed in Euro-American culture" (Jordan Paper, "The Post-Contact Origin of an American Indian High God: The Suppression of Feminine Spirituality," *American Indian Quarterly*, 7 [Fall 1983], 12). See also Sam D. Gill, *Native American Religions: An Introduction* (Belmont, Calif., 1982); and by the same author, *Native American Religious Action: A Performance Approach to Religion* (Columbia, S.C., 1987).

15. Once again in James H. Cone, *For My People: Black Theology and the Black Church* (Maryknoll, 1984). I was very much helped in sorting out the whole Euroamerican framework of these issues by two dissertations: Elizabeth Barnes, *Theological Method and Ecclesiology: A Study of Karl Barth's Doctrine of the Church* (Duke University, 1984); and Sheldon Sorge, *Karl Barth's Reception in North America: Ecclesiology as a Case*

Study (Duke, 1987). See also Benjamin A. Reist, "Dogmatics in Process," *Pacific Theological Review,* 19:3 (Spring 1986), 4–21.

16. Marc H. Ellis, *Toward a Jewish Theology of Liberation* (Maryknoll, 1987).

17. The key theological reflection on the infamy is still Vine Deloria, Jr., *God is Red* (New York, 1973).

18. An excellent case in point is Gabriel Fackre, *The Christian Story* (Grand Rapids, 1984).

19. Marc H. Ellis, *Toward a Jewish Theology of Liberation,* 90.

20. Conrad Myers, *The Comic Vision and the Christian Faith* (New York, 1982), 9–21.

21. Umberto Eco, *The Name of the Rose* (New York, 1984), 578.

22. Carl Bode, *The Portable Thoreau* (New York, 1947), 594. In a different vein, a somewhat similar point is made in Nhat Hanh, *A Guide to Walking Meditation* (Nyack, 1985). Walking is a universal "sixth sense," as it were. In walking we draw closer to God.

23. Jenny Labalme, *A Road to Walk,* 28. For a long time already it has struck me as strange that we often "traverse sea and land" (cf. Matt. 23:15) to find the poor when they are on our doorstep or in our backyard. See Michael Calhoun and Tom Harris, *Poverty and Hunger in the Midst of Prosperity: A Growing Crisis in Durham* (Durham, 1987). Copies available from Michael Calhoun, 53 Green Mill Lane, Durham, North Carolina 27707. We do not have to walk very far to discover the justice struggle.

24. Walking (*peripatein*), often translated as "following," "leading a life," or "conducting oneself," in the Christian scriptures always indicates a way of life, an ethos: "Walk as children of light" (Eph. 5:8). *Walking* is a good expression for coming to terms with the elementary Christian stance in the emerging global consciousness. The *new paradigm* of Christian thought is evolving from medieval consciousness and modern consciousness superceded by *global consciousness.* The elementary move in global consciousness is often expressed in the phrase: "Think globally, act locally." Yet it is all based on trying to answer the question: What is God's social location today? There may be those who will insist I should have used the term "Exodus" more centrally. Yet the liberation encounter between Jews and Christians is only in the very beginnings. "Exodus" did not belong centrally to my Southern story. In liberation shaping dogmatics we are experiencing theology as *self-critical reflection on actual praxis.* I need to remain true to what went on in our praxis. The answer to the question of God's social location today will move us eventually much closer to Israel's Exodus story. Whether the actual *liberation dogmatics* will become an Exodus dogmatics, who knows? For now, it is not labels that count, but the walk.

In many instances I wish I had advanced further. Only in a few places was I able to break through the iron bars of thought. I was able, for example, to press on to the oxymoron of the poor Messiah—a breakdown of normal dogmatic speculation. The work of Rosemary Radford Ruether, from *Faith and Fratricide* (1974) through *Sexism and God-Talk* (1983) and beyond, was of great help, as was Susan Thistlethwaite's and Letty Russell's, and that of other feminist theologians. But I am still in the early stages of processing the wealth of their insights. I still have to concentrate on my Southern social location with a justice challenge with which I have not as yet come to grips. On another level, I have not dealt with foundationalism and deconstruction, or the pluralism of world religions. Another book is necessary. I also did not mention many other "walks" people undertook for justice, in print as well as in life. Think of Mahatma Gandhi and his salt march (1930)—another God-walk. I am overwhelmed by all the "walking" among thousands of people for justice, peace, ecology, animal rights, etc. Especially in the midst of the black struggle I learned that *the primacy of Scripture is the primacy of God's vulnerability in impoverishment.* Yet there is many a lacuna left in the book. Mistakes will appear, and misjudgments. Meanwhile God is still *walking* in the garden, our beautiful planet earth, asking all of us: "Where are you?" (Gen. 3:8f.)

INTRODUCTION

Social Location and Method

With our recent sense of having been catapulted into the global village, a small planet with limited resources, we have experienced a shaking of the foundations of modern Christian thought. For example, we have begun to doubt that systematic theologies still ought to be written. They were based on the modern Christian assumption that an author is able to develop a sufficient picture of Christian teaching based on a systematic principle that is the author's very own. In our time, this literary operation can have disastrous consequences.

More importantly, Christian existence itself has become questionable.[1] What do we mean by Christian existence today? Does Christianity in the West still contribute anything distinctive to the human enterprise? Or do we merely bunch together modern ethical precepts and religious notions available to human beings everywhere and call it Christianity?

In any case, we discover ourselves caught in a gigantic struggle over the elementary components of Christian thought. I initially thought that the cutting edge of the new situation was new accountability for Christian teaching. The churches again were compelled to take a stand on Christian doctrine. But a more primal issue imposes itself: How does Christian teaching emerge in the first place? How does a Christian thought develop? We are forced also to offer an analysis of the *location* in which we as Christians live and develop doctrine from our life.

We cannot bypass our churches. They communicate Christianity to us. But frequently they also distort it. So a new search for Christian truth becomes necessary.[2] To begin with, new efforts will have to evidence more fully the social location of the churches.

1

Some Christian thought efforts still seek to ground themselves in a Christian culture or civilization. Yet there is at the same time the fact of the vast secularization of contemporary life. The North Atlantic community tends to breed a "junk culture" (*Time*), more so than most of us care to admit. Even in a "junk culture" the phenomenon of religion tends to persist. But it is not the same as the Christian way of life.[3] What do we do with this nominally religious civilization of the West? Some Christians might still be able to play the role of leaven. But we will never again permeate the whole loaf.

We cannot come to understand how a Christian thought emerges and also finally evokes teaching(s) by deciding theoretically on a systematic or dogmatic principle beforehand. At the same time, we need to show what is meant by a systematic or dogmatic principle. We need to consider the options. We need to understand the vast struggle we are involved in as we analyze the options. We have to clarify the reasons why we regard some options as unfruitful. Above all, we have to show how the terms are redefined for us by God's new activity in history.

In Western Protestantism at this time the various doctrinal approaches break down into three main models. The danger of oversimplification is of course always present. Yet the basic differences can be formulated, although there is overlapping in many individual approaches. Some identify with *(neo) orthodoxy*. Some see themselves partly in *liberal* thought, partly in *liberation* thought. Others might want to combine all three. The models are not intended as straitjackets. Yet the clearer we come down on one of them, the more forthrightly we communicate. In two of the models, Christian thinkers mainly work with a deductive logic: in the one, the dogmatic principle predominates (orthodoxy); in the other, the systematic principle rules supreme (liberalism). The third (and most recent) option tries to show how Christian thought originates from discipleship, or from what I usually will call God-walk. By using the somewhat odd phrase "God-walk," I do not wish to do more than call attention to the exact opposite of mere God-talk.

Diagrams necessarily oversimplify. But in the following schematization we can begin to find orientation points for the present dialogue on Christian teaching:[4]

<table>
<tr><td>

I
orthodoxy
neoorthodoxy
dominance of concept
theory-focused

evangelical
conservative
neoreformation

Barth as model?

</td><td>

II
liberal theology
neoliberal theology
dominance of symbol
theory-focused

social-change theolo~v
death-of-God theolog,
existentialist theology

Schleiermacher/Macquarrie
as model?

</td></tr>
</table>

III
eucharistic theology
discipleship theology
liberation theology
feminist theology
black theology
Native American theology, etc.
dominance of metaphor
praxis-focused

the poor and marginal as model

In the tensions among these three options the present truth/ untruth struggle in Protestantism is being experienced, as also in much of Catholicism as well. This becomes clear if one pays attention to the accountability factor in regard to church teaching. One dare not overlook the fact that Madison Avenue teaches, and that Hollywood, the Pentagon, and the White House teach as well. The White House is not only a "bully pulpit." It is also an Ivy League lectern. Churches had better realize that they might not be teaching at all, but merely making room for secular teaching or taking cues from various societal teaching turfs, perhaps adding some religious flavor. What is lacking is accountable teaching.

Crucial for the orientation in the above schematization is the difference between *concept, symbol,* and *metaphor.* As these terms will be used in this book, each stands for a different outlook or basic atmosphere in approaching the subject of Christian thought.

In dogmatics, the *concept* compels us to reconceptualize the world in terms of the basic Christian dogmas. If worked out thoroughly, it approaches a metaphysics—a project that interprets the world on grounds of Christian ideas as the ultimate truth for time and eternity. In modern systematic theology, the *symbol* compels us to transfer all Christian ideas to the wider framework of a philosophically conceived worldview—for example, that of a Spinoza or a Heidegger. In this approach there is always a ground or depth behind the Christian idea that ultimately is the crucial referent to which dogma or teaching has to conform.[5] In liberation thought, *metaphor* makes us appreciate Christian words as energizers of "walking." They do not invite us to metaphysicalize or to ontologize, but to realize the Spirit of God in history and nature as we walk by its power. In a sense we come close here to feminist spirituality, as stated by Carol Ochs: "I wanted to go beyond conceptual systems to the actual experiences that underlay them."[6]

There often is still too much emotion connected with Christian thought. I do not want to exclude emotion; it is an important element in our Christian walk. But there is no reason why religious persons should excitedly get at each other's throats when they choose fundamental premises of thought. We need only to develop a good argument for choosing a particular option.[7]

Our first step in Christian reflection today is to describe our social location. Never do we begin Christian thought in a vacuum, but always in community. The elementary question is where one sees oneself walking together with others in a particular community. Tell me with whom you walk, and I will tell you who you are— a "proverbial" truth when related to the discipleship community.[8] Focusing on social location does not mean concentrating on mere sociality, but being aware of the social dimension of our Christian walk.[9] Finally, we are historical beings and persons or souls as well. So we need to work *historico*-critically and *psycho*-critically even if we are viewing ourselves primarily *socio*-critically. All of these aspects of method imply working self-critically.

The Socio-Critical Dimension of Method

What does it mean to view ourselves *socio*-critically? We most holistically express who we are as Christians individually and corporately in the eucharist. Here we share most concretely in the life of Jesus, the realpresence of God in Christ as God continues to struggle with humankind in history. Jesus coming to us in the eucharist is not merely the crucified Jesus on the cross or the Pantokrator Jesus sitting at the right hand of God, but the whole Jesus present once more to the weary and heavy-laden. Jesus sharing himself with the sick and the poor, the outcast and down-trodden, is with us, as is the Jesus who cared for the sparrow's fall and the lilies of the field.

We have an encounter with Jesus in the eucharist that makes us face the "walking wounded" of the world and at the same time—in the elements of bread and wine—the elements of nature that indus-trialized peoples often belittle or ignore. It is as though Jesus had foreseen the threat of nuclear destruction and ecological disaster as clearly as our blindness to neighbors hungry and destitute. He taught us that the human body broken in the walk with God is one with the elements of the natural world.

The eucharist is the justice meal in which nature and neighbor receive their due. It is definitely also a meal of forgiveness and of reconciliation. The cross is present in the marketplace as in the sanctuary. It ties us together with the "groaning of the whole creation" (Rom. 8:22) as much as with all those in the world struggling for bread, forgiveness, and reconciliation. The eucharist puts us in the context of "the hopes and fears of all the years," the orphan's cry, the woman's oppression, the hunger of the hungry, the want of the poor, and the groaning of all creation. Our social location in the eucharist is inescapable.

The role of the eucharist is especially important because it offers a peculiar opportunity for the marginal person to have a concrete encounter with God in Messiah Jesus.[10] An example is the thirteenth-century devotion to the eucharist as a particularly fe-male emphasis. Francis of Assisi seems to have turned to mystical women in order to learn more about eucharistic piety. Nuns, for example, the Beguines, desired an experience that took the place of the clerical experience. They felt the same commitment in service to Messiah Jesus. Yet it was only in the hands of the priest that Messiah Jesus was able to become incarnate again. Might there not be a similar opportunity for a communicating woman to be that close to Messiah Jesus? In the eucharist women could have union with Jesus, and it could be repeated time and again. They could see in themselves what was crucial to priesthood. They could touch

God. They too could be vessels within which God became incarnate again. The situation of course has changed drastically from the Middle Ages.[11] But the metaphorical power of the eucharist has remained the same. It evokes a vision of equity and of justice-making.[12] It is important to keep in mind that women have insisted on this.

All would be misunderstood, however, were we to overlook the conflictual dynamics of this social location in present-day society. We are not dealing with spiritual beauty culture. The 1984 publication of an Instruction by Cardinal Ratzinger, of the Vatican Congregation for the Doctrine of the Faith, forcefully brought the seriousness of the conflict to our attention again. It is a conflict in the church as well as in society. The Instruction is surprisingly positive in regard to concern for the poor. But it asks Catholics to be concerned for the poor *on its terms*. It vehemently objects to the view of liberation theologies with Marxist sympathies that "only those who engage in the struggle can work out the analysis correctly." The Vatican claims that Christian truth "itself is in question here." In fact, the statement goes so far as to say that Christian truth is here "totally subverted." To explain the subversion, the Vatican statement adds: "There is no truth, the liberation theologians pretend, except in and through partisan praxis." The Instruction argues on the premise that the "ultimate and decisive criterion for truth can only be a criterion which is itself theological."[13]

There is conflict in the church largely because, in view of the social location of liberation theology, the conflict of society (in which the church participates) can no longer be circumvented. In principle, we might agree that some truths could be stated effectively in theory without reference to praxis. The whole issue for us, though, is how Christian truth originates in the first place. In general, Alasdair MacIntyre's view of the dialectics between theory and praxis is well stated: "Every action is the bearer and expression of more or less theory-laden beliefs and concepts; every piece of theorizing and every expression of belief is a political and moral action."[14] Yet we also have to ask whether we can simply apply such observation to the origins of Christian thought in Jesus of Nazareth. We have to look at the event on its own terms.

We cannot see Jesus apart from his own social location, the toils, conflicts, and sufferings through which he had to pass. What emerged in the process were new ideas, new thoughts. Although it is true that countless ideas and thoughts of Jesus can be paralleled in other Jewish teachings of his day, including some teachings of the Pharisees, the notion that God was deeply involved in human toils, conflicts, and sufferings was something new. A sharp profile of this newness is found in the Fourth Gospel where Jesus is accused by his opponents of breaking the Sabbath and calling God "his own Father, making himself equal with God" (John 5:18). The emphasis on theo-praxis makes the difference, as Jesus says: "My Father is working still, and I keep working too" (John 5:17).

This was not a thought that came out of the blue, the abstract, but in connection with Jesus' healing of the man thirty-eight years sick, especially on a Sabbath. Only those who as disciples were involved with Jesus in the struggle could work out the analysis correctly. It took this particular partisan praxis (partisan in the eyes of their opponents) to make the discovery of new truth possible. The criterion for truth here did not come from an abstract theology as in the Vatican Instruction. It was praxis that "guaranteed" the truth—God's own praxis, theo-praxis.

The Historico/Self-Critical Dimension

In this context, the socio-critical view drives us to take into account also the *historico*-critical dimension. It is important that we look at the scriptures historico-critically. Yet it is equally important also to look "historico-critically" at ourselves as Christians. To what does this historico/self-critical method amount?

First of all, we are not reading the texts of the early church as much as the texts are reading us. We need to be shaken in our modern self-security. There has to be a shaking of the foundations, so that we let go of our ego-trips and have God begin to shape our character from the underside of history.

"In Antioch the disciples were first called Christians" (Acts 11:26). That was several years after Jesus' death. Are we today Christians of the same caliber? For three centuries Christians were like the persons mentioned in Acts 11:26. It was the period of primitive Christianity, a time of conflict, persecution, martyrdom.[15] Truth had its price, the price of theo-praxis. God was working in and through the followers of Jesus. As has been said, the blood of the martyrs watered the seed of the church. Ever since, *conflict* has been part of the church/society framework within which the church had to make up its mind on accountable teaching.

By the same token, Christianity has been saddled with a measure of accommodation ever since the time of primitive Christianity came to an end. About 313 C.E. Emperor Constantine associated himself with Chrisianity. Some scholars seriously doubt that he himself ever became a Christian. But it was convenient for him to make Christianity the religion of the empire. The Constantinian takeover implied that what had been an illicit religion (*religio illicita*) become the established religion, the legitimation of Roman mores and power. Ever since we have been more Constantinian than Christian.

We always have to keep this historico-critical "truth" in mind as we find ourselves in social location around the eucharist. We need at least an inner distance from ourselves as Constantinians. The sinister cloud of empire overshadows our sharing in God's realpresence in the eucharist. Alistaire Kee, in *Constantine Versus Christ* (1982), suggests that Constantine probably was not exempt from the human desire to image God in his own likeness. Christians soon began to regard the emperor as part of the divine scheme of salvation. The emperor, "like some interpreter of the Logos of God, summons the whole human race to knowledge of the Higher Power, calling in a great voice that all can hear and proclaiming for everyone on earth the laws of genuine piety."[16] When Constantine was victorious on the battlefield, a monarchical form of government replaced a more pluralistic form. Constantine "grows strong in his model of monarchic rule, which the Ruler of All has given to the race of men alone of those on earth."[17]

Viewers of the May 1985 CBS production on Christopher Columbus (anticipating the 1992 anniversary) will never forget how in 1492 the great admiral of the oceans stepped ashore in the West Indies, planting the cross in the sand, and claiming the new lands in the name of the king and queen of Spain for "gold and souls". For gold and souls! There is a straight line running from Constantine to Christopher Columbus and the Americas. It is the rule of Empire. Souls figure here only in terms of power and gold.

From Constantine on, we have to take the factor of political power into account, and the overt or covert *assent* to power, as we reflect on social location. It haunts us even in democratic societies.

However subliminally, there is a trace of Constantine in all of us. In his day, the human being was viewed as a rational creature, reasonably discerning the legitimacy of monarchy and its laws. The mark of those informed by the Logos on Constantine's terms was to know "how to rule and be ruled."[18] It needs to be underscored: human beings not only know how to rule, but also how to be loyal subjects. They know the value of assent. They play a part in the imperial scheme by being obedient to its laws. Hence to reject Constantine is to reject God.[19] In Constantine's wars, the barbarians are also the enemies of God, not just the enemies of Rome.[20]

What is attributed to God is first attributed to Constantine. Long before his so-called conversion he had determined to become the sole ruler of the empire. The Christian God blessed the project. The church was incorporated into the grand design of empire as an instrument of its unification.

Eusebius tried to present Constantine's values as Christian. But the facts do not support the claim. The emperor's values were wealth, power, and social aggrandizement. They were made to appear as Christian values. Ever since then European history has also been determined by secular values as though they were the values of Christ. The order of Christian values has been inverted. Ideology reigns supreme.[21] In social location at the eucharist, much depends on how we view ourselves historico-critically in regard to our Constantinian value scale. Do we assent to worship as a tool of the powers that be in order to enforce secular power? Or do we let the eucharist distance us from the values of wealth and success, so that we can join the struggle for justice?

The Psycho-Critical Dimension

Here the historico-critical perspective is joined by the *psycho*-critical concern. The "religious arrangement" instituted by Constantine also involved "opium for the people." On the same terms, Christians today easily become spiritual dope pushers. The Constantinian situation in its concrete aspects has changed in myriad ways, but the core dilemma remains the same.

In what way is state or culture using Christianity to legitimate its values? Are we in the religious academy accomplices of the American empire? Do we represent a Christianity of assent? We need to take a hard look at ourselves and at what goes on, not just on the surface, but subliminally in our psyche. What shapes our values long before we make any conscious decision of Christian thought? What does this tell us about how Christian thought originates?

Christian life originated in God-walk, on the road, in the marketplace, by the seaside, and outside a city wall in a criminal's death on a cross. "Disciple" is a word we use for someone who joins in this walk. Discipleship is the first and decisive word for God-walk in Christianity. It covers a way of life. It does not say: What you *do* is what counts. What counts is where your head is and where your heart is. "Where your treasure is, there is your heart also"(Matt. 6:21).

In other words, God-walk means willingness to immerse oneself in life as a whole and to stand where Jesus stands in all walks of life, especially with those whom society tunes out: the invisible women and men, as also the injured creation. That is why the eucharist is so central. Only here do we touch—as it were, bodily—the realpresence of God in history in terms of Christian community.

So it is not activity in general that is called for when we reflect on our social location. It is first of all participation in the justice mission of Jesus. It is eucharistic action. It is immersion in *conflict,* with class struggle at the cutting edge. It is immersion in conflict because Jesus is still caught up in conflict. Jesus' life has not come to an end as yet. It is still going on.

There can be a lot of busy activities in the church. We can take part in them and yet stay very much apart from life as a whole, from the groaning of creation, cloistered away in the sanctimoniousness of the sanctuary. We can miss God's ongoing activity in Jesus completely. In all our busyness we often are no more than "a noisy gong or a clanging cymbal" (Cor. 13:1).

It is misleading to speak of participation in God's ongoing activity as *doing theology*. This cannot but end up in works-righteousness. The presupposition is that there is first a theory called theology. Next we somehow prove it by doing it. This turns things upside down. It is indicative of the increasing irrelevance of theology.

We certainly can practice a talent (voice), or an instrument (piano), or a profession (medicine). We can also practice an idea (being Catholic). But God-walk does not begin with an idea we ought to practice. Christian life is its own creation and referend. The forces that millions of years ago dynamically shaped the whale and the seagull, the eagle and the squirrel, the fir tree and the violet, are still shaping humanity in ever new modes. The human being is still to come—just as we still anticipate the epiphany of the Messiah. Creative forces are surging up from the inside of history. We celebrate them in Jesus' eucharistic presence. Even with regard to the coming of the Messiah we think of the process of growth: "I rejoice in my sufferings for your sake, and in my flesh I complete what is lacking in Christ's afflictions for the sake of his body, that is, the church" (Col. 1:24).

A psycho-critical method is especially crucial in regard to women. Catholicism throughout the centuries has held that women cannot be priests and thus cannot offer the eucharist. Handling and controlling the body (especially the body of the church or Jesus' body) was a privilege of males. There are Protestant groups that hold similar teachings. I already called attention to the fact that in the Middle Ages, when female congregations were at their height and women mystics like Hildegard von Bingen and Mechthild von Magdeburg were—often unacknowledged—among the best theologians, the eucharist became especially important for women. Here they could at least receive and "touch" the power they were not allowed to administer.[22] Gathering around the eucharistic table we remember that exclusion of women from administering the sacrament is a perversion of its reality.

That the eucharist does not only point to Jesus' death but to everything he stood for in his life can best be understood by paying attention to those biblical narratives that bear the same message as the sacramental meal. The story of the foot-washing shows Jesus doing the type of work usually done by servants—in our time generally by women: mothers, maids, nurses. Peter objects to being served this way. He could not envision Jesus doing the work of a slave or mutatis mutandis the work of a woman. Many today still expect women and "lower-class" males or members of other racial groups to be foot-washers and dish-washers. The "body broken for all" that Christians partake of in the eucharist calls attention to such psychological blind spots.

Elisabeth Schüssler Fiorenza has shown that the story of the woman anointing Jesus' head is that of an unnamed apostle who celebrated Jesus' kingship (Mark 14:3-9).[23] Jesus' logion, "what she has done will be told in memory of her," is similar to the eucharistic formula in 1 Corinthians 11:24-25. Mark's story of the woman at Bethany who acted out what Peter had verbalized in his great confession (Matt. 16:16) points to Jesus as God present in the form of the poor and marginalized of this world. The woman anticipates his death and celebrates his life. The psycho-critical method ponders the reasons why Peter and Paul are known to us by their names and their leadership roles, whereas the woman from Bethany is not only nameless, but has been confused with a "great sinner" (Luke 7:36-50), and her story has been used to justify the church's neglect of the poor, always with us.

As Christians we are already "engaged" long before we take the conscious step of formulating thoughts. It is our walk as Christians we need to reflect on before we move to pondering preexistent concepts. Christian thought grows out of this walk. Christian ideas grow out of discipleship. Thus praxis gives rise to thought—theo-praxis, that is. Accountable teaching develops from following "the Way" (Acts 9:2).

We need to begin our conscious thought process by recalling the structure of primitive Christianity. The implications of indwelling the eucharistic presence of Jesus were quite plain:

> The whole company of believers stuck together and held all things in common. They were selling their goods and belongings, and dividing them among the group on the basis of one's need. Knit together with singleness of purpose they gathered at the church every day, and as they ate the common meal from house to house they had a joyful and humble spirit, praising God and showing over-flowing kindness toward everybody. And day by day, as people were being rescued, the Lord would add them to the fellowship [Acts 2:44-47].[24]

God-walk, theo-praxis, is a form of discipleship: "And they devoted themselves to the apostles' teaching and full communion, and to the breaking of bread and the prayers" (Acts 2:42). In Israel, many teachers had disciples. Jesus' disciples rooted themselves in the wholeness of God's human presence in history.

So where are we when our Christian thought originates? Today, too, the breaking of the bread is very much the *center* of discipleship. Here we share in God's own walk in Christ. Thus the eucharistic "breaking of the bread" (Acts 2:42) is much more than a mere ritual sharing of wafers. The realpresence of the center of our community is all-important. Jesus is the bread. The eucharistic action brings not only cross and death, but "a style of religious practice oriented not so much by the word of scripture as by the manifestations of the sacred in image, icon, ritual."[25] On these terms, preaching "as sacrament will join the sacraments of baptism and eucharist."[26] This matter of sacrament has to be pressed even closer to the Bible itself. The scriptures are fundamentally the eucharistic scriptures in that they are rooted in the realpresence of Jesus in the justice meal. Preaching is most genuine when it is sacramental through the eucharistic scriptures in close tie-in with the eucharist embodying in *body*-language what the body-*language* of preaching intends to convey.

The eucharist is both justice meal and peace meal as much as it is forgiveness meal. It offers the Jesus who forgives the sins of all as he shows solidarity with all—especially the poor and outcast. The eucharistic scripture of Ephesians 2 sees Christ as Peace who makes "out of the twain," two former enemies, one new person. In him, enmity no longer exists.

The implications are far-reaching. Where Bultmann and Macquarrie wanted an existentialist interpretation of Christianity, or process theologians a process interpretation, liberation thought takes the struggle of classes, sexes, and races into account affirming the stance of the gospel: "Blessed are the peacemakers" (Matt. 5:9). This is not to surrender to pacifistic ideologies. There is the dire need, though, to oppose the whole history of established Christianity that turned military prowess into a god who usurped the place of God in Christ. It is the need to turn against ourselves as Constantinians. The choice is clear: Christ or empire.

The whole history of empire has been a history of warfare. From generation to generation the notion has been transmitted that wars are needed and the planned killing of persons is justified under certain circumstances. Preparation for killing in a war is considered legitimate. Victors and victims alike as Constantinians have time and again given a religious halo to the god of warfare. With the threat of nuclear holocaust, we detect the lies by which humankind deceived itself for thousands of years.

How do we unlearn the rules of empire? For Christians, the other side of class struggle is soul struggle, the truth/untruth struggle. Just as we can learn the socio-historical dynamics of God's presence in history by listening to the Third World, we become aware of the psycho-historical dimension of Christianity today by turning to the Second World, for example. We have the strange phenomenon in the Soviet Union today of people finding God in the midst of a vast atheism. One convert, now a priest, claims, "I'm not a remnant of capitalism, I'm a remnant of communism." He served in the army, fought in the resistance against Hitler, and worked as a laborer when he found God.[27] He told the communist functionaries that the men of their community were not following the party line, but the vodka line.

It is impossible for us in the West to imagine what it is like not to have God "available" in the media, the public cascades of religious words from politicians, entertainers, and professional religionists. Tatjana Goritschewa, a Russian woman born in 1947, describes her pilgrimage from a child of atheist parents through her conversion and God-walk in communist society, in a context foreign to most Westerners. It is the story of being shadowed by secret police and arrested for speaking the name of God; of psychiatric hospitals, incarcerations, and forced emigration. She becomes aware of the reality of God while praying the Lord's prayer and meditating on it as mantra. As a characterization of how some Soviet citizens view life, she quotes a Russian saying: "You go outside in the street, and everything seems all right. The sun shines. The birds sing. But there is no life."[28] She finds the happiest Russians in the monasteries, of which, in her account, there are about twelve left.

Words almost break to pieces when one tries to describe the clash between the religiously saturated world of the West and the barren soul struggle of the East. A monk named Alexander is ordered to a secret police interrogation. They wonder: Did he actually say that there is no freedom in the Soviet Union? His response: "For me there is freedom only in Christ. Of any other freedom I can only say, if it would exist, I would not have to appear here."[29]

To be rooted and anchored in God, to find freedom through God in Jesus under these conditions, is a dimension of liberation too. It illumines the truth/untruth struggle, the soul-struggle each of us also in the West undergoes. The presence of God in Christ in our lives is not a matter of course. We cannot experience it by listening to the religious verbiage that inundates us. It always is a new event in our souls that comes through personal agony, repentance, and conversion. We express the *psycho*-critical dimension best when we do not let ourselves get caught in the rash assumption that we are already truly grasped by the presence of God in Christ. We need to test ourselves time and again about the price we need to pay, the measure of commitment we invest.

That the social, historical, and psychological perspectives belong together in a human being is something we can learn especially from American Indians. Their traditions do not separate the religious from the political, the psychological, or the medical. The soul is unthinkable in isolation from the Great Spirit as well as its involvement in ancestors, future generations, Mother Earth in all her manifestations, and the socio-political community of human beings entrusted with the care of creation. Our technologized, overrational Western psyche would do well to learn from American Indians the sense of awe in view of a living God who is, in terms of the Johannine Jesus, "working still" and expects human beings to share in the work of creation.

The Options Examined

A new elementary model is emerging from these dynamics. This does not mean that previous models have been utterly erroneous or demonic. But circumstances have changed: "New occasions teach new duties. Time makes ancient good uncouth."

1. Neoreformation thought tends to focus on the *concept*, which provides the mood for orthodoxy and in the United States often turns into neoorthodoxy. In what way does Karl Barth function as a model here? "To that which ought to be valid in the Church as reproducing the Word of God, we give the name 'dogma.' The Church asks and must continually ask itself to what extent that which takes place in Church proclamation corresponds to dogma."[30] The major identity of the church lies for Barth in proclamation, voicing the Word, in the minister's God-talk, in *Rede von Gott*.[31]

The eucharist, for example, in this approach is not the crucial reference point in social location.[32]

2. Liberal thought emphasizes *symbol*, which makes us always look for deeper levels of truth behind the immediate or concrete. Reality is acknowledged. But there is a "deeper reality" yet, to which the immediate and concrete points. The religious person searches for ultimate reality. The "father" of this approach is Friedrich Schleiermacher (1768-1834). Christian doctrines also matter for him, but they are "accounts of Christian religious affections set forth in speech."[33] So what is really going on in Christian thought is "reflection upon religious affections."[34] The basic referent here is religion-in-general. Schleiermacher is far from focusing on discipleship when he seeks to define the social location of Christian reflection. John Macquarrie in our day takes a similar tack when he speaks of theology as the expression of the content of a religious faith. Important here is the word *religious*.

3. Neither neoreformation thought nor liberal thought puts us in immediate touch with the rough and tumble of the church in conflict with society. God struggling for justice in humankind and all creatures is not an immediate focus. Because God's work is not confined to human beings, the ecological dimension is part of the picture. Neither neoreformation thought nor liberal theology emerged at a time when the general public was as sensitive to the ecological threat to God's creation as it is today. By the same token, church/society tensions were assessed in a different light.[35]

In fairness to both neoreformation[36] and liberal thought, we need to note that representatives of these approaches have often plunged deep into the muck and mire of life, and have made tremendous contributions to renewal in church and world. We discover new ways for our time because they developed approaches that sought faithfully to address their time. They invite us to be critical of them, not to follow slavishly in their steps. They want us to think for ourselves. But the development of their thought frequently left out what are for us the most crucial aspects of social location.[37] Here we need to start out in a new direction. The elementary factor of the eucharistic realpresence of Jesus' struggle for justice can help us to reorient ourselves in new church accountability. It would be a farce if, in the justice struggle, we would not do justice to those who opened up the way for understanding our task. But we would also not do justice to them if we were to blur the distinctions between the approach we believe is needed today and previous ones.

We grasp the reality of God not primarily in God-talk, nor in religion, nor in sermonizing on the Bible as such, nor in making God relevant for the modern mind, but in *God-walk*, in what God does in Messiah Jesus by struggling in history for and with all persons, especially the nonpersons we overlook, the persons we are not faithful to as our society conditions us not to see the outcast.[38] There are "invisible people" all around us.[39] There are also invisible fellow creatures we neglect in willful ways. We often view all of nature as simply an object for our use, or even for our manipulation and sheer exploitation.

The notion of God-walk develops in point/counterpoint fashion on the foil of the God-talk emphasis of recent times.[40] John Macquarrie in 1967 published a book with the title *God-Talk*. Within two decades God-talk increased by leaps and bounds.[41] Macquarrie claimed that the religious problem today is "how in human language one can talk intelligibly about a divine subject-matter." For him, "the word 'theology' would seem to be equivalent to 'God-talk.' It is a form of discourse professing to speak about God."[42] The issue for us is whether via God-talk we find access to God in Christ.[43] A Christian recently wondering whether he had made a difference at all during his life finally declared: "There is a ministry of presence. Whenever I was present somewhere with my body, I made a difference." A person can make that claim only because it was first of all God who made a difference in the *body*, and not in talk.[44]

In both the orthodox and the liberal positions we have paradigms that, as in Macquarrie's examination of God-talk, direct our attention to the search for some convincing argument or logic that would make God a reasonable proposition. Argument dare not be excluded. It belongs to the core of Christian thought. But how does Christian thought originate? Perhaps argumentation is here a secondary, not the primary move.

Established paradigms already subliminally shape us, occasionally victimize us. The neoreformation and the liberal models intimate that assent is a major priority. We either give assent to an intellectual world of Christian ideas or to their translation to a more ultimate reality. Here we prove to be Constantinians first of all, expected to make some adjustment to the state of things or to society as it is. Both models have boxed us in with a theory-application scheme wherein the genesis of the theory is not reexperienced and articulated.[45] The emphasis on God-walk introduces a double check.

The entire realpresence of God has to be allowed entry into our shaping of Christian thought, our teaching. Otherwise we do nothing but shuffle words back and forth without requestioning our elementary position as Christians.[46] We are confronted with God's realpresence only when we are completely absorbed in God-walk, in discipleship, and let it work on our own words and ideas as a double check.

God-walk for us begins at the eucharist involving both deed and thought, action and word. Obviously the New Testament community as such is not *the* blueprint for Christian life. The first century C.E. is long past. Yet this does not mean we cannot struggle also today to learn in our churches how to "think on our feet," how to care for losers as well as the lost and the wounded co-creatures of God's creation. So we need to begin time and again by reinterrogating our own discipleship.

"O for a closer walk with God, a calm and heavenly frame." This hymn line expresses the fact that our basic identity as Christians does *not* lie in *doctrine*, which even in Barth can occasionally come through as propositional truth handed down to us from above. Our basic identity as Christians also does *not* lie in *feeling* (religious experience, existential commitment), which even in Schleiermacher occasionally can turn into sentimentally feeling the religious pulse. Our basic identity lies in God's *interaction* with us, God's will to be corporate, to incorporate us into the divine body. If dogma is priority for us, we cannot avoid concept, and thus *abstraction*. If religious experience is priority for us, we cannot avoid symbol, and thus *contraction* of reality in symbol.

At stake in Christian teaching is not pulpit identity (great proclamation, Barth's concern) or religious virtuoso identity (the super-Christian, Schleiermacher's approach), but human identity as just persons, growing out of the apostolic teaching centered in the eucharist, the breaking of bread, and prayer.

The point is to move against the grain of controlling reason where individuals produce themselves as speakers or seekers. We have had a surfeit of electronic church egos. The names of the pied pipers of religion are legion. An unknown person laboring in the kingdom of God does more good than does a well-known TV preacher electronically converting (entertaining?) viewers en masse.

Today we are in a difficult position. The church framework for liberation theology in North America is practically nonexistent. The vacuum is especially obvious in ministerial education. An example is provided by the United Church of Christ. When matters of teaching came to a head in this denomination in 1984, its Executive Council (as General Synod *ad interim*) detected "an explosion of theological expression in our church." The basic interpretation was: "We celebrate this fact and wish to share that news."[47] Although mention is made of the commitment of church members that "has led all parts of our church to pronouncements and actions in social service and social justice" and there is reference to "several historical traditions," there is no analysis as to what the ferment might indicate with respect to identifying the church in the justice struggle. What we get instead is a listing of nodal points in the explosion of theological expression. (1) A number of theological educators want the UCC to be more faithful in word and action. (2) Sixty representatives of the UCC from across the nation call for a new spirituality. (3) A new Council on Racial and Ethnic Ministries (COREM) has been founded. (4) A Committee on Pluralism "is at work on a theological framework by which we may understand the kind of church we seek to be." (5) Involvement with the WCC *Baptism, Eucharist, and Ministry* (1982) paper continues. (6) Several UCC groups have been formed on distinct theological positions—for example, the United Church People for Biblical Witness and the United Church of Christ Fellowship of Charismatic Christians. What will be the outcome of celebrating the theological explosion in the UCC?

Little do we understand as yet that Jesus did not expect his disciples to engage in a theological talkathon. He wanted us to give an account to each other of our convictions, the mainsprings of our actions and lodestars of our faith. Otherwise common discipleship will not come about. The vagaries of an age need to be attended to. Infelicities in church life need to be exposed and opposed. But all this is not possible unless we grasp the dynamics of the history in which we share, the dynamics God personally struggles with. As those dynamics shift, the teaching of the church changes. It does not negate its old teachings, but it adds to them in the light of the new.

Anarchy, absentmindedness, and sleep have a thousand faces. Dryness of the soul comes in countless versions. Valueless decisions abound. No orthodox straitjacket, no creed as such, will galvanize the hopeless. But as we mutually give an account to each other of our Christian mandate, we will again be drawn into the mainstream and the maelstrom of history where God is struggling for liberty and justice for all.

There often is great mystification about what the church is. To be sure, much of it is institution. As any other institution, it needs administration and maintenance. Within the context of the institution nominal Christians are legion. The administration of the church turns into an ecclesiastical establishment. Yet Christian thought time and again in the third option or model mentioned above makes room for discipleship as the church that embodies God's realpresence around the eucharist. The way of going about this is accountable teaching, giving each other an account of the basic data of this realpresence. The task of all reflection and writing in the Christian community is aimed at making disciples again. "Go therefore and make disciples of all nations" (Matt. 28:19) is at the core of what Kierkegaard meant when he said: "Each generation has to be again converted to Christ."

What God-walk is moving toward is *full communion*. We can make clear to ourselves what is involved when we remember Acts 2:42: "They devoted themselves to the Apostles' teaching and *koinonia*, to the breaking of the bread and the prayers." In terms of detail it comes down to perhaps four points: (1) There is always a basic teaching metaphor around which Christians gather, whether it is Messiah Jesus, resurrection, or Trinity, for example. It always grows out of a praxis that has plumbed the depth of God's presence. (2) Praxis is aimed at full sharing of humanity, the *koinonia* of persons. (3) It focuses on the eucharist, the celebration that fires the imagination. (4) In the triad of teaching, *koinonia*, and the eucharist, the new spirituality emerges wherein prayer directs all toward more accountable teaching. The institutional church always needs to be re-formed, re-shaped through the emergence of full communion.

Yet we enjoy the good life (*la dolce vita*). The dynamics of history are of no concern to us. We are afraid, for example, to think of the involvement of Christianity with industrial structures. Karl Marx did not invent the class struggle. But he had the grace to articulate its driving force in history. For the first time religious thought consciously was confronted with the role of class structures:

> One does not set out from what men say, imagine, or conceive, nor from man as he is described, thought about, imagined, or conceived. Rather one sets out from real, active men and their actual life-process and demonstrates the development of ideological reflexes and echoes of that process. . . . Morality, religion, metaphysics, and all the rest of ideology and their corresponding forms of consciousness no longer seem to be independent.[48]

Although we disagree with Marx's atheism, there is no way of escaping the historical reality he describes. That is what God-walk wants to remind us of. The issue now is to discover in what way disciples will face up to economic forces, giving each other an account of the social location in which they find themselves in the global village.

The acknowledgment of class struggle is important because it shows how groups of persons, even nations as a whole, play God with each other. The ruling economic forces are "principalities." In fealty to them we try to "lord" it over others and become instruments of the ruling classes. Certainly sin expresses itself in more ways than one. There is the battle of the sexes, racial strife, and ecological wantonness. But we have to become aware of it especially at the point where we tend to overlook it: in our economic fate.

In its root, sin is usurpation—the human attempt to wrest power from God, personally to play God with our neighbor. On September 4, 1984, CBS presented the film *Broken Promise*, the story of five foster-home brothers and sisters separated from one another. Unforgettable in the story is how the "man in charge," a welfare officer, plays God with the children, especially the oldest, finally sending her off to an insane asylum although she is perfectly healthy and is only struggling for the reunion of her family. There are countless other examples in social structures or the dynamics of the soul where the issue is the usurpation we human beings are involved in as we try to play God and turn God-walk into mere God-talk.

Sin, of course, has to be grasped anew in every age, and it will be sensed differently by master and slave, man and woman, First World Christian and Third World Christian. Describing sin as usurpation does not mean idealizing meekness or yielding to injustice. Such "virtues" have been held up to blacks and women, for example, as "models" of Christian behavior when they were merely convenient tools of domination. Can a slave usurp? The issue is the little turning of the inward "switch" that keeps God out of our life. It is as sinful to yield to injustice as it is to inflict injustice. But whether yielding or inflicting, it amounts to taking away God's right to our lives, God's claim to us, and appropriating it to ourselves. Hildegard von Bingen tellingly described sin as a drying up of our sense of justice: "A person who lacks the verdancy of justice is dry, totally without tender goodness, totally without illuminating virtue."[49] Sin takes away our being attuned to the fullness of life. Because we take away God's right, we shrivel up, we are like a stream that has lost its source. We introduce a "dualism": standing over against God we stand in opposition to God. We now think we are our own source. And we dry up.

As I ponder God-walk at the beginning of reflection on the liberation shape of dogmatics, I sense that God acts as counterforce of human self-destruction and the destruction of the planet, as soul-force and as globe-force. God in Christ embodied in the eucharist works in history, not only in abstract dogma, but in faithful walk—discipleship. Teachings grow out of discipleship and provide its ever-growing enablement as framework of ideas.

In discipleship we first of all embody God as the God of the losers as well as the lost, the God of Moby Dick and of Homo sapiens. Messiah Jesus as God's deprivation, God's impoverishment, leads the way to finding God's presence among the poor as well as the rich, the fish as well as the human biped.

The Truth/Untruth Struggle

Accountable teaching grounded in the teaching of the apostles (Acts 2:42) as enabling framework of discipleship keeps us from closing our eyes to the truth/untruth struggle in our churches. The reality of God in history penetrates to the soul-struggle of each person caught in all the tensions between groups in the midst of poverty and oppression. God-walk is not merely a matter of *caring* (alas, often only by "remote control") for the oppressed in Latin America or South Africa. It is also a matter of *daring*, telling the truth in any matter of human concern right in our own lives and on our own doorsteps as well.

The Breakdown of Marriage—A Case in Point

God-walk also reaches into the increasing breakdown of the family in our society. Does the church know how to deal with it? Hardly. Church members are bewildered about the increasing divorce trends and many tend to move along with the trend. Children are the foremost victims.

Do we ask what God is struggling with here? As early as the mid-1970s the United Methodist Church, semiofficially at that time, brought out an "alternate" divorce ritual. A North Carolina newspaper commented on part of it:

> The couple saying "I do" at the altar may be ending a marriage instead of starting one. The divorce service is part of a new "alternate ritual." . . . It calls for the estranged couple to stand before the minister with the congregation present. Later in the service, the wedding band is transferred from the left to the right hand as a symbol of divorce. "I expect it to be used by quite a few people. I hope the ritual will help people realize they are in no way cut off from the church when they get divorced," says Rosalyn Bentzinger, 52, of Des Moines, who helped develop the service rite.[50]

Self-righteous shock may cry out: How featherbrained can the church get? But it takes caring analysis to find the hub of the dilemma. Because we are still widely Constantinians, the truth/

untruth clash gets to the core of the church itself. According to the ancient principle *lex orandi, lex credendi*, the structure of worship yields the structure of accountable teaching. Worship is an expression of discipleship.[51] Otherwise the kingdoms of this world become the basis of discipleship.

A divorce rite tends to derogate the worship basis of the liberation struggle. Attention is directed away from God's unending struggle for justice in creation. Obviously the task of the church is to minister to the brokenhearted as much as—or more than—to those who by grace and their own volition live in lasting relationships. But in what ways do we *minister* to those who believe they have broken their marriage vows or will have to break them?

It boils down to what Christians present to each other as accountable teaching rooted in eucharistic discipleship. Even if there were an accepted divorce rite in all churches, there is no reason to think that the divorced would feel less cut off or alienated. Rites can quickly turn into corporate cosmetics. A divorce can happen just *because* a church does not faithfully enough minister to a couple before and during marriage, failing to support more lasting relationships when the couple is still struggling for faithfulness. The limits of our attempts are only too clear. Yet Christians cannot throw in the towel right away when two persons have trouble in faithfulness to each other. Marriage counselors can often be helpful. But we cannot turn over our Christian responsibility to "marriage professionals."

Marriage is—among other things—an ecological event. Two Christians covenant to become co-stewards with God in creation—not only, and not always, in procreation. Because class struggle often has a ruler class exploiting nature as well as human beings, the church has to be very much concerned to sensitize women and men to the implications of their marriage vows for creation. Our focus in worship is usually too anthropocentric. The divorce rite increases the anthropocentricity and narcissism of marriage.[52] It misdirects the fundamental focus of Christian worship on God's preservation of creation, and the liberation and reconciliation of all creatures. If husband and wife focus on each other only, they have to despair of their imperfections sooner or later. But if they consider each other physical and spiritual partners in God's struggle for justice in creation, they might not be obsessed with controlling each other.

What can we concretely learn from a divorce rite? The United Church of Christ, in its 1982 test documents for a new book of worship, offered an "Order for Recognition of the End of Marriage" in the *Proposed Services of Marriage*. In the *Book of Worship* (1986) the rite has been moved to the section on "Services of Reconciliation and Healing". In the original form, after a few introductory Scripture verses and words of salutation, the leader says: "We are here to witness an end and a beginning, and share the making of a new covenant. (*Man*) and (*woman*) have decided, after much effort, pain and anger, that they will no longer be husband and wife. They wish to be friends and to respect and care about each other."[53] So the whole liturgy was cast into the mold of a "new covenant" the couple was entering. Who was not reminded of the eucharist as "new covenant" and similar more proper uses of the term? Fortunately the notion of "new covenant" was changed to "new commitments" when the rite was moved to its new place. There still is no indication of how the event itself relates to creation as a whole and God's justice activity. The leader expresses the expectation that the parents will continue to be responsible for their children. Yet one wonders whether the parents would not naturally want to continue to show concern even without such a ritual.

It is difficult to grasp how the *lex orandi, lex credendi* is going to work here. No scriptural pattern for the rite is cited. No precedent from tradition appears. How can we hope to see accountable teaching emerge on the issue? How can we help it along? Or is the divorce rite going to be "tucked away" in our book of worship without any corporate effort of the community as a whole to own what is happening here? Does it emerge from the praxis of the poor? Not at all.

Are we a generation without compass when it comes to the dissolution of marriage? Is the pain over hopes dashed surpassed only by our awful uncertainty about right and wrong? Or is there a fixed point in human relationships against which we could measure our human right and wrong?[54]

The UCC's new *Book of Worship* is a courageous step in the struggle for just ("inclusive") language. It could be a magnificent base for new teaching dynamics to develop. Yet missing is a clear wrestle with what is happening at the inside and the underside of history that would energize our joy in search for a lodestar of human right and wrong. What good can come from becoming value-neutral in our desire somehow to meet the needs of others in a new rite?

"Recognition of the End of Marriage" might soothe the conscience. We do not, however, know as yet where it might make a difference in our care for justice in creation. We cannot underscore enough the vast challenge the breakdown of a marriage presents to Christian sisters and brothers for support, concern, and the sharing of pain. But do we truly care for the divorcing couple unless from the outset of their dilemma we witness to God's struggle for faithful relationships in justice? Much more needs saying. Yet there first of all needs to be a common grasp of the center around which we are empowered to firm up our life. How much is the *Book of Worship* centering, say, the "Order of Marriage" in God's work for a just world? Perhaps marriage itself has not been anchored deeply enough where God is most deeply immersed in human life. There is plenty of emphasis on human love and commitment, but little stress on God's activity.

We occasionally think of divorce even as something creative, to judge from a book title.[55] Yet for our discipleship, creativity first of all needs to be part of the concern for that suffering divorcing sisters and brothers go through when no accountable teaching points to God's justice as lodestar for judging right and wrong. No such teaching seems to exist. Obviously in the process toward divorce, practicalities usually cloud the sky, so that accountable teaching gets sidetracked.

We dare not lay a guilt trip on others. How could we—who are caught up in other or similar dilemmas? The gospel is good news. How will it evoke our greatest potential? We cannot rejoice enough about the effort to develop inclusive language throughout the *Book of Worship*. The great challenge now is to move from there to accountable teaching that articulates the basis of inclusive language in God's commitment to a just life of all creatures.

At the most pristine level of liturgy, there was a justice struggle from the very outset in what turned out to be Christianity. Jesus' own life was wrapped up in it. The struggle was over the integrity of Israel as the people of God. Because of the emergent new teaching, Christianity was separated from Judaism—a tragic development. The challenge is to face it honestly and to deal with it caringly. Our present struggle over a divorce rite is very much part of the pattern of these truth/untruth tensions. At the moment we are trying to treat symptoms and disregard the cause. A book of worship could clarify the social location of struggle over divorce rites. Much could be gained. The *Book of Worship* in a second edition could tie together the great outlay of United Church of Christ commitment, say, for a social challenge like the Wilmington Ten and commitment to "just" marriage.

The fog we get into with "Recognition of the End of Marriage" makes us turn back to addressing the point of marriage. If in the smallest social unit God's struggle for faithful relationships has no appeal, why should society as a whole care? Here is a unique opportunity for all of us to work together on the more creative solution. With our focus on the eucharist, we discover in marriage most concretely God's involvement in history *and* nature. Marriage for the Christian is the place where history and nature coincide in God's creative action. It is the eucharist in the natural realm. If that eucharist is ruptured, God's order of the world is ruptured. So it is impossible to romanticize marriage as a private love affair or to downgrade it as a convenience arrangement.

We are allowed to link marriage and the eucharist closely, even though most Protestants do not view marriage as a sacrament.[56] Intimate human community is at the cutting edge of the historical struggle. It has to become much clearer why so many couples feel a need to celebrate the eucharist at their wedding. What connects the wedding eucharist to God's justice work in creation?

Meanwhile half the world is up in arms because I broke the spell. The bottom line is that we ought not to cast out devils through Beelzebub (cf. Luke 11:15ff.). I struggle against the tyranny of new ritual imported into our lives that is not shaped in concert with the praxis of the poor and has nothing to do with justice.

Class struggle coincides with the battle of the sexes. Whatever justice can be embodied in the smallest societal cell (marriage) can be transferred to the larger social cell (class). The exploitation of women is often worse than class exploitation, for it is done in the closest of human proximity. A church that overlooks this common injustice has no right to glorify marriage or wail over divorce statistics. We have no reason to reverse the Catholic emphasis on celibacy as the "loftier" state by seeing marriage as the only perfect and "natural" state for the Christian.

That there are also many single Christians who are stewards of creation in a full sense does not undo my point about marriage. The single Christian is inescapably tied to God's immersion in all strife. There is no escape from the justice struggle also in the single natural state. In fact, the single state expresses differently, but no less clearly, what eucharistically is the point of marriage: the embodiment of God's justice-bonding and creativity in all dimensions of the natural human state.

A very small difference between the single and the married state lies in the "liberating" possibilities of marriage some persons seem more attuned to than others. Marriage provides a concrete testing ground for faithful stewardship of God's creation. It is a state in which we touch and feel in a most intimate way the gifts and needs of another creature. But do we do it faithfully? Those who choose to be single or are forced to be single by circumstances do not have the same testing ground of faithfulness. They will have others. They may also be kept from the temptation to confuse God and one's partner, or to practice an *égoïsme à deux*. "Let those who are able to receive this, receive it" (Matt. 19:12).

I am not dealing here with marriage or the single state from a secular point of view. Our task is to move toward accountable teaching on the grounds of God's justice struggle. The core of this contribution is the Christian witness concerning (1) God's faithfulness, (2) our bodies as temples of the Holy Spirit, and (3) our task to be stewards of creation. Not only married and single heterosexual Christians will need to measure their conviction in these matters by such biblical insights. Homosexuals will want to do the same.

The tendency of society to bolster creative divorce is tempting the church in divorce rites to offer an ideological veneer, to find excuses that legitimate hedonism, self-adulation, and anarchy.[57] To call attention to creative marriage is to stress how God enlists two persons in the justice struggle in their natural state.

It will be said that marriage issues have no place in dogmatics. Yet the possibility of separating ethics from dogmatics, especially since the Enlightenment, is shown here for what it is: a catch-22. The core of ethics is participation in God's character in history. God's character is most concretely embodied in Christ's presence in the eucharist. Here marriage is first of all a dogmatic issue, a challenge to give an account to God also in our most natural state, as God has become accountable to us in allowing us to participate in divine creativity.[58]

Accountable teaching, as it grows from the eucharist, time and again seeks to reactivate the church as God's people in history and nature by offering the enabling idea-framework for discipleship in society today. Discipleship is thinking on one's feet, as the eucharist is thinking on one's knees.

In order to see how accountable teaching comes about in the struggle of truth with untruth we need to grasp the dynamics of accountability in the church. The matter of marriage and divorce is only one example. (1) We have to distinguish between acceptance of and care for those who feel they are a failure or are guilt-ridden, and the legitimation of failure in a rite especially invented for a particular failure. (2) The church remains a vessel for God in Messiah Jesus to reach creatively into the lives of individual Christians and to evoke the accountability process.

On these grounds we need to make a sharp distinction between (1) *serving* the needs of others, and (2) *changing* the needs of others (as they become capable of sharing in God's own walk). We easily make serving the needs of others—pastoral care—the be-all and end-all of the church. So it is not a surprise when some suggest that it is exactly a divorce rite that can show that the church cares. In fact, a rite in church might even make it comfortable to break a promise and shed some of the guilt. But the rites of the church are not intended to make things comfortable for us. Although the church is certainly not called to give persons a bad conscience, it does have the task of making us form a conscience. Here accountable teaching generates the truth/untruth struggle that enlists us in God's own God-walk. Human needs as such dare not determine Christian truth in terms of expediency.

Criteria for Discerning the Truth

In the everyday struggle of Christian existence, we reflect on these matters within church structures that ought to offer us a few criteria by which to discern and judge Christian truth. Part of the problem with a denomination such as the United Church of Christ is that it has not as yet elaborated the criteria for a framework of accountable teaching. As a consequence, one keeps groping around in a fog. In comparison, the *Book of Discipline* of the United Methodist Church, notably part 2, offers the quadrilateral of scripture, tradition, experience, and reason. To what extent can they function as guides or criteria?

Scripture. For the church the Bible is rooted in the eucharist. The scriptures are first of all eucharistic scriptures. They present in Wordpresence what the eucharist embodies as realpresence. They certainly also present information, divine imperatives, and a goodly amount of narrative, poetry, and song. But at the eucharistic meal they first of all point to God's presence in history.[59] From this perspective, all human relationships become sacramental. So there should be little surprise that we hear said of marriage for example: "A man shall leave his father and mother and be joined to his wife, and the two shall become one flesh. This mystery is a profound one, and I am saying that it refers to Christ and the church" (Eph. 5:31f.). Christian marriage is understood in analogy with Christ's sacramental relationship to the church. We learn of this involvement of God in marriage through God's Wordpresence in the eucharistic scriptures.

Besides the references to marriage, there are many other biblical pointers to our being sacramentally tied to each other within the body of Christ (Rom. 12) in history and among the elements of the cosmos (Eph. 1; Rom. 8). Our willingness to listen is not based here on *sola scriptura*, scripture alone, but on *scriptura prima*, scripture first. In this sense scripture remains *the* rule of discipleship. We indwell the scriptures in God-walk as we indwell the eucharist. They are part of our home in God. Scripture is always the primary criterion of Christian truth.[60] It generates the struggle of truth with untruth. There is no real parallel to this elementary function of the Bible in the church however inapplicable time-bound detail will be.

Tradition. Ultimately, there is no absolute distinction between scripture and tradition. God's walk through history affirms itself eucharistically through scriptural Wordpresence. The scriptures are the Wordpresence of the realpresence. And yet in some sense the scriptures are already the human reception of God-walk as tradition. But the major part of the reception became itself dependent on God's Wordpresence, time and again activated by what we now have as scriptures, so that we have come to think of this reception as tradition distinct from the scriptures. Tradition supports the unique function of the Christian scriptures to show evidence of God's engagement for those who suffer from injustice and guilt. The crucial difference that Messiah Jesus' history has brought about is God's identification with the nonperson. Jesus Christ, by "wordly standards," is a nonentity, part of the nameless "waste" of humanity. "Not many . . . wise according to worldly standards, not many . . . powerful, not many . . . of noble birth; but God chose what is foolish in the world . . . God chose what is weak . . . God chose what is low and despised" (1 Cor. 1:26f.).

Early Christians made the discovery that history looks different from the underside. God does not intend only for the wise to make discoveries, only for the powerful to survive, only for elites to rule. On the underside of history God is shaping new soul-force. Humanity has not as yet appeared fully. God is still shaping the full sense of being human. Turning to the nonperson in special concern, God brings from the inside of history a unique factor into consciousness and human selfhood. It has not all been worked out in God's own deprivation in Jesus, or in the scriptures. Nor has God's self-realization in history always been transparent to tradition. In fact, tradition has often clouded the historical factor of injustice that God wants us to pay attention to.[61]

There is still today a continual process of self-correction going on between the scriptures and tradition, so that we can discover the justice power of both. We are not always aware of it. But as soon as we concern ourselves with either scripture or tradition, we notice the necessary dynamics between them.

The seemingly "far-fetched" issue of marriage in this context is a case in point. The sacramental view of marriage developed in the church during the Middle Ages, because the scriptural mystery (*sacramentum*) of Christ and the church in terms of Ephesians 5:31f. asserted itself time and again in the Christian community. Whereas the Catholic Church on the one hand glorified marriage by making it an official sacrament, while on the other hand devaluing it by emphasizing celibacy as the "higher" state, the Reformation, seeing the irony here, went to the other extreme. It upgraded marriage without granting it the importance of a sacrament and stressed its superior natural value. In both instances the sacramental mystery was partially lost. In "conversation" with this ongoing tradition we today can regard Christian marriage as the joining of a woman and a man for sharing in God's justice struggle—if only, again and again, we delve into and test the scriptural rationale of the various traditions. Marriage for the Christian is never an end of nature in itself, but a unique participation in God's creativity. In these dynamics, tradition functions as a secondary criterion of Christian truth.[62]

Experience. The United Methodist *Book of Discipline* claims:

> This "new life in Christ" is what is meant by the phrase "Christian experience." Such experience opens faith's eyes to living truth in Scripture, informs and guides the Christian conscience in ethical decisions, and illumines the Christian understanding of God and creation.[63]

The basic Christian experience is that of indwelling the eucharistic scriptures. The scriptures are like a home, the place we are born into, the cradling walls we are nurtured in, the rooms we grow up in, a sheltering environment of our daily existence. And yet this home is intensely part of the global village. It is not an idyllic place. It makes us aware of much struggle. There is tragedy. There is also comedy.[64] It is in this indwelling that we are confronted with the nonperson and the poor, the oppressed and despised.[65] Experience, then, also functions as a criterion of discipleship.[66]

Scripture, tradition, and experience merge in the eucharist as criteria of the struggle of truth with untruth. Experience does not stand by itself alone. Making us citizens of the global village, it provides the field for the functioning of the Holy Spirit. Christian experience is always in dynamic tension with the scriptures and tradition.[67] This is why different parts of scripture and tradition are important for different ages. Our *experience* of certain abuses, for example, directs us back to *scripture* in order to change certain *traditions*. We are historical beings. God mediates the divine reality to us through these historical dimensions—even in what seem to be very "secular" experiences. The peculiar historical configuration of God's struggle for the nonperson as part of our selfhood constitutes our "new life in Christ."

Everything else God shares with us flows from it, including

justification, regeneration, and sanctification.

Reason. The *Book of Discipline* stresses that "Christian doctrines must avoid self-contradiction and take due account of scientific and empirical knowledge." Yet experience may well "transcend the scope of reason."[68] Among the four criteria, the function of reason, in many respects, is the "touchy" issue. There is no way to proceed in the God-walk model biblicistically or crypto-fundamentalistically. The God who reshapes our self so that we can grow into a corporate selfhood is not an irrational God, yet cannot be fully comprehended by reason either. *Ein begriffener Gott ist kein Gott*, is an old saying: a God grasped (a God you can lay your hands on) is not God. But there is another side to it. Though reason cannot be eliminated from judging the truth/untruth struggle, it is not a "rationalistic reason" Christians adhere to. It is "con-science reason," con-scientious reason, co-reason. It is reason as it judges together with God the justice of the God-walk.[69] Reason is the monitor through which scripture, tradition, and experience are consistently grasped as criteria and linked to human experience as a whole.

We need to distinguish contradiction, paradox, oxymoron, and verifiability. God-walk cannot want to support irrational "contradictions." "Paradox" is used in Christian thought too much in terms of what is against reason, what contradicts it. It often is a post-Enlightenment cop-out of lazy thought. What we have to note is the oxymoron character of even God personally, for logically contradictory realities are joined in God in a *coincidentia oppositorum* (as, on the human level, expressions like "laborious idleness" or "cruel kindness" are oxymorons). Co-reason in God-walk continually has to cope with what many consider the empirically nonverifiable. It is exactly the task of "con-science reason" (faith as awakened conscience) in God-walk to show that God's presence in the human struggle has verifiability, though not on grounds of sheer empirical data. Ultimately, faith is reason. At the most elementary level, the two coincide. This is the primordial oxymoron the human being lives with.

Reason indicates for Christians how scripture, tradition, and experience, focused in the eucharist, are deeply immersed in the struggle against domination and oppression. They explicate how God stands up for the poor, especially within the context of class struggle. Whose power will prevail? The power of the high and the mighty? Or that of the Holy Spirit—God's power among the poor?

Accountable Teaching in the Truth/Untruth Struggle

God-walk orientation cannot follow the neoreformation model that tends to limit the criteria of Christian truth to scripture and tradition. God's struggle in history is left out. There is mainly struggle over church truth. Dogmatics is for Barth "the testing of Church doctrine and proclamation" by scripture and tradition.[70] The key word is "testing." It is not a question of verification. Of course Barth also concerns himself with experience—as he understands it. "Faith is concerned with . . . the whole of living and the whole of dying."[71] How much wider might one cast the net of experience? Faith here takes in the whole range of experience. But there is no inroad of God in experience on its own grounds. There is no supportive evidence in experience.

In Barth's *Church Dogmatics* there is a long section on the Word of God and experience. Before he comes to it he has already said: "Faith, of course, is also a human experience. . . . But that this experience is the experience of the faith . . . is decided not by the faith but by the Word believed in."[72] What Barth wants to guard against (as he says later when he comes to the discussion of experience directly) is that the Word of God becomes "man's own, a predicate of his existence."[73] Experience as criterion could easily mean allowing the human being to control God. So, for Barth, experience as criterion is ruled out entirely. It is only a testing ground of faith.

What Barth shows is that each generation in the church faces the struggle for truth in a peculiar way. As he saw it, human beings were using Christianity for religious self-adulation, religious narcissism. But the human being cannot control God, not even in terms of the best Christian experience. God personally needs to offer divine truth time and again and cannot depend on human cooperation. For human beings to let experience take the place of the self-evidence of the Word of God would be hubris.

Barth does see the power struggle going on all the time. But he does not make it central in God's own God-walk, God's immersion in the historical struggle and the processes of nature. So class struggle does not even loom on the horizon here as part of his method. We can only hope that we are as faithful to our situation as Barth tried to be to his.

With scripture and tradition as criteria, Barth develops a

straightforward Word of God theology. God is evidenced in the proclaimed Word. Experience and reason can only mislead Christians if appealed to as criteria. Much of what went on in Barth's context supports him in his claim. It was the Hitler time. The beast from the abyss had to be fought. Barth's approach worked.

Is it a possible model for us? Its inner consistency has to be measured in terms of the full dynamics of the primacy of scripture, the support of tradition, with experience as medium, and reason as the clearing house where the other three factors are sorted out in terms of verifiability. Reason as co-reason (or conscience) examines whether the promptings of God in history prove truthful to human fulfillment in justice.

In social location the praxis of God-walk evokes teachings exactly within the dynamics between scripture, tradition, experience, and reason. Personal growth of Christians is always the goal of any teaching effort. But there is also confusion, even anarchy and alteration, in the teachings of the church.[74] There is always a drive toward unity and commonly held ideas (see Eph. 4:3–6) and at the same time confusion about how this drive is to be handled creatively.[75] Teaching on Christian terms makes sense only if all involved feel responsible for giving an account to each other about the hope that is in them.[76] Some might view the ecumenical movement today, with its many bilateral conversations, for example, as doing no more than treading water.[77] But one can also see it more positively, as the beginning of a global accountability process in the church where Christians begin to give an account to each other of the hope that moves us on in the global tasks of the church.[78]

The accountability here concerns not merely the contemporary witness, but also the witness of the mothers and fathers of the church (tradition). The United Methodist *Book of Discipline*, for example, describes the teaching circumference both historically and in contemporary respects.

It is within this overall framework that we begin to appreciate the recurring need to change the model of Christian thought because of changing social locations. The *Book of Discipline* helps us focus the core issue:

Christian experience is not only deeply private and inward; it is also corporate and active. The Bible knows nothing of solitary religion. God's gift of liberating love must be shared if it is to survive. The range of reconciliation must continually be widened to embrace the world and all who are alienated and who suffer. "Christian experience" carries with it the imperative to engage in ministries of liberation and healing in the world.[79]

Ideas are dangerous illusions unless they are rooted for Christians in the God-walk that lies at the base of all Christian unity. Today the ministries of liberation and healing are especially taxing. They raise the question: Does the neoreformation model still function adequately for our day?

Karl Barth as the major representative of this model takes us deep into credal truth and battles against Arianism and Pelagianism, pietism and modernism. Classism, racism, and sexism hardly appear on his horizon. In this context, God's character comes through not in the justice struggle, but as divine sovereignty in control of human destiny or as triumph of grace. Today we have discovered the central challenge of justice. To give the nonperson as well as every neighbor their rights is not only a societal concern. Even the issue of the "divorce rite" took us deep into the justice struggle. Thus the present experience of discipleship also functions as a criterion of the truth/untruth struggle.

Without downgrading the Reformation, we view it today from an angle different from that of neoreformation times. Centering worship almost exclusively on the Word, the Reformation contributed to a pervasive rationalism of faith:

> The *sola-fide* doctrine is closely aligned with the centering of faith on *God's Word* and, in terms of personality structure, on the reorientation from the sensuality of Catholic sacrament focus to the dominance of a word-regulated activity in the sermon, a shift that in the acts of culture revolution takes hold of all areas of the religious and cultural worlds.[80]

These words of Alfred Lorenzer describe a process, begun in the Reformation, where language formulas increasingly contribute to the development of a definite subjectivity of the human being that is dependent more on an educational *Weltanschauung* than on an elementary encounter with the mystery of the world.

Today we are questioning not proclamation itself, the preaching of the Word, but its distortion since the Reformation. The Enlightenment having intervened with its "gift" of rationalism, the typical Protestant worship service has become completely disconnected from sacrament and has turned into a glorified lecture event. On these grounds it makes sense to say that Protestantism aims at "the educational process of personality formation in individuals."[81] I shall return to these issues in greater detail. Suffice it to say here that today we aim much more at the sacramental process of justice formation in creative corporate selfhood.

The Authority of the Scriptures

I ask once more: How does Christian thought emerge?[82] From the eucharist with its eucharistic scriptures, human beings receive the power to move in God-walk. Here Jesus draws us into the social location of the poor, the walking wounded and nature wounded. In view of the lowly and of the abused creation, the scriptures struggle over faithful relationships between nations and races, managers and workers, human beings and animals, friends and enemies, and also between marriage partners: "Husbands, love your wives, as Christ loved the church and gave himself up for her" (Eph. 5:25; cf. Matt. 5:32). The scriptures are never merely "out there" for us—in a vacuum, as it were. We always indwell the scriptures or they indwell us in our God-walk. In this way they prove their authority.

Authority

Authority is what authors us in our God-walk. Authority here is what brings our Christian thought and action, our identity in Christ, into being. The Bible is not primarily the eucharistic book on the beautified altar, but the eucharistic book of the streets and the shacks—the places Jesus frequented. It derives its power as Wordpresence from the realpresence of God in Messiah Jesus in the justice-meal. Its most germane location is the huts of the poor.

It was not written primarily to be the object of scholarly, objective, and detached analysis in the Divinity classroom.[83] Authority discussions in the Divinity guild today often suffer from a distant point of entry. The Bible is viewed as an object, unique, to be sure, but nonetheless a piece of literature among many others.[84] But the primal function of the Bible is its power, which, together with the realpresence of Messiah Jesus in the eucharistic meal, brings the corporate Christian community into being.

We indwell the scriptures as home and as roots. They do not straitjacket us in literalism. They are a living environment or part of a living organism like roots are part of a tree. What brings us into being as disciples is not a normative understanding of every word of scripture, but the eucharistic event constituting us in God-walk.[85] We experience Messiah Jesus through the Word that makes us just in the meal. The Hebrew scriptures author us insofar as they witness to this event in the foundational promise. The Christian scriptures continue the authoring in invoking the fulfillment of the promise in the eucharist and calling us as congregation to think on our feet and on our knees.

Discipleship as Focus of Scripture

Scriptural authority in social location with the poor does not involve immediate applicability of any text to any church situation. It always focuses in the offer of our new identity in the poor Christ and his immediate disciples.[86] It is not for the Christian to say: "Let us open the book of Genesis—chapters 1 and 2 contain a universally applicable doctrine of creation, chapter 3 has a universally valid doctrine of sin." What creation is for the Christian is known in discipleship as we follow the poor Jesus in solidarity with rejected human beings and with the lilies of the field.[87]

Biblical Language as Eucharistic Language

The Hebrew scripture writers knew well how to distinguish between poetry, chronicle, and history, though not with our modern historico-critical tools. They were not confused when it came to the exact meaning of their words. They said exactly what they wanted to say. Similarly also the authors of the Christian scriptures knew the limitation of their all too human words and the function they served in discipleship. By the power of the Holy Spirit they let their words turn into energizers; "The kingdom of God does not consist in words (*en logō*) [God-talk], but in power (*en dynamei*) [God-walk]" (1 Cor. 4:20). Consider an illustration. When I say "water," what do you see? A lake? When I say "dam," what do you visualize? Earth piled up holding back the water? When I say "turbine," what image comes to mind? Coils? But when I say "electricity," what picture appears? The images that words convey are not operative in this case. Here we do not "see," but sense immense power—electricity. By the same token, the scriptures evoke power. But they do it in the spirit of the eucharist. They communicate the realpresence of God in Messiah Jesus among the losers and the lost of this world. The whole range of Christian thought grows out of it.[88]

The Justice Claim of Biblical Language

As long as we battle over what heaven looks like or how to measure the inner-trinitarian dynamics, we have not grasped what is at stake. The core reality is the self-offering of the imageless God as justice in the form of a human person. It involves a claim: we do not belong to ourselves, but to God. It appears in terms of the Christian scriptures from the synoptics through the book of Revelation. We are to sense the justice due every neighbor and every creature (Matt. 5:21f.).

The point of the language of the Christian scriptures is to articulate the making of disciples. Why disciples? God in Messiah Jesus enables a new community to stand up for justice among unjust structures. The class struggle centers around this issue, too. It is over this issue that the truth/untruth struggle flares up time and again today.[89] Christian worship confronts this issue when it sings:

> Once to every [soul] and nation
> comes the moment to decide
> *in the strife of truth with falsehood*
> for the good or evil side.

Strife of truth with falsehood over God's justice is today the context of discipleship. Accountable teaching develops as the

Christian community is pressed against the wall to give an account of the truth of justice against all untruth about it. It is not imposed on us as intellectual superstructure that all need to assent to. It grows naturally out of discipleship. Discipleship gives rise to accountable teaching. Praxis gives rise to thought.

The issue of authority today comes down first of all to the question of social location. Without agreement on beginning in a definite social location we can keep talking about authority endlessly and not come to any conclusion.[90] Focus on method and criteria in regard to authority point to the same dynamics: the power-flow from scripture to tradition to experience to reason, with scripture holding the primacy, is a dimension of it.

Yet even all this remains utterly theoretical or abstract unless we see it feeding into accountable teaching—something many of the North American Protestant denominations and, in its own way, the Catholic Church are not attuned to. Christian truth is still too much viewed as deposited truth handed down to be memorized. As a consequence, we never consider the full weight of scripture as it impacts tradition, experience, and reason in determining our social location, evoking the need for us to give an account to each other of the hope that is in us. As the class struggle in the West and between the nations, especially North-South, becomes more tense, the need for accountable teaching becomes increasingly self-evident.[91] The truth/untruth clash cannot be disregarded.

Lest all this be misunderstood in a humanist fashion or identified with the liberal theology approach, it ought to be underscored that authoring through the Bible in the struggle for truth makes no sense unless it is in social location centered in the eucharist—its proper power setting. The Bible is not primarily bedtime reading or morning devotional material, and certainly not just literature for scholarly research, but *eucharistic* word in connection with breaking the bread and drinking the cup. Whatever *method* evolves from it, it is *eucharistic* method. Under these visible elements, the bread broken, the cup shared, we receive Word-power to be disciples. As the Word works together with the elements, the event becomes the elemental sacrament of discipleship.

Lest this still be misunderstood as somewhat privatistic or pietistic religion, we need to see authority through discipleship extended to the world as a whole. What is true of Messiah Jesus in the eucharist pertains to all persons, and to creation as a whole. Authority in the Christian community begins with God's faithful justice struggle, offering a broken body for all. There are two points to be made:

1. What we see God doing in Messiah Jesus we trust God is doing in the world everywhere. Authoring through the scriptures here means: the poor belong to God. The poor are not justified *in themselves*. As Gustavo Gutiérrez says, we are not on the side of the poor because they are good, but because God is good. The eucharistic scriptures say: "Blessed are you poor" (Luke 6:20). Theirs is the new realm of God—because God struggles or rules in a unique way—as only disciples know. Our identity lies with what God does in taking sides with losers. They have no one but God to stand up for them. This basic social location is equally important for our relationship to creation. Only those who understand the underside of history can sense the underside of nature—"the groaning of creation" (Rom. 8:22).

2. Sin is seen either as *usurpation* (infringing on others' rights; unauthorized, arbitrary arrogation of power; arrogating unto oneself God's authoring), or as *dryness* of the soul (the opposite of being alive to every living thing, the opposite of soul-force, thoughtless submission to injustice, blind accommodation). Sin proves a lie here—we pretend to have power when we actually have none or we give in to fake authority. Persons so attuned easily "fall asleep" (Matt. 25:5).

The authority question is turning more and more into the social location question. How does God make clear to us that God is real? A tempting answer in modern times has been to point to the leap of faith. Yet the first thing that happens in Christianity is that someone says, "Follow me." "Move." Our questions are stopped, our words fail, and God-talk ceases, so that before the leap of faith there is the leap of *shock*. Our words die in our mouth. We are at a loss for words. We are speechless. This is not something negative. Silence begins communication with God. The first Christians, women and men, belonged to "the Way" (Acts 9:2; 19:9; 19:23; 22:4; 24:14; 24:22). "Follow me" (Matt. 4:19). That is clear enough. "Immediately they left their nets and followed him" (Matt. 4:20). And they were on the Way.

We do not get any dissertation on God's existence by posing a question like: What do you have to say for yourself on the subject? Face to face with the reality of God, we do not begin with the remark: "There is no perfect answer." We are certainly not on the level of philosophical talk. Jesus commands: move, relocate, change the territory. We cannot understand God in Messiah Jesus just anywhere.

What is at stake at the *beginning* of Christian thought is moving, not "faith-ing." A completely different sensibility is introduced. This claim tells us: I am moving you out (out of the "guild," for example). We get a different location, a social location. No safe haven anymore, with our boat securely anchored. We are drawn into the muck and mire, into encounters outside safe locations, outside the "city wall," outside academia.

We now have to come to terms with a claim (not a law): "Whoever has done it to the least of these has done it unto me" (Matt. 25:40). It is not primarily a matter of revelation (disclosure), or transformation (social change), but of captivation (enlistment): "I have called you by name, you are mine" (Isa. 43:1). The initial struggle of Christian thought is the coming to terms with this "enlistment." In a new social location, it is enlistment in God's justice struggle.

We have to offer a rationale for all of this "moving." What do these claims entail for history as a whole? Cross and resurrection are an incursion upon our history. Where we fail in the justice struggle, God on the cross and earlier in Israel as suffering servant already suffers for us to forgive, and in the resurrection injects the hope for the passing away of all suffering and death: "God will wipe away every tear from their eyes, and death shall be no more" (Rev. 21:4). Again, praxis gives rise to thought. The claims of captivation, forgiveness, and hope evidence God. This is the way God encounters us. Luther asks in the Larger Catechism: "What does it mean to have a God?" He answers: "What you put your heart in and trust, I say, that is really your God."[92] This dynamics of captivation (enlistment), justification (forgiveness), and animation (resurrection) is what underlies the shaping of human beings as Christians. It is what author-izes us as Christians.

The significance of Christian authority depends very much on one's angle of vision. Many Christians still object to the emphasis on God's identification with the poor in the justice struggle. "Why,

God is to be found in all kinds of places." No, not in Jesus. God in Messiah Jesus chose to walk the lonesome valley in order to enable us to see all things from the standpoint of the world's dire need. For the redemption of the world we are not primarily helped by the bird's-eye view that sweeps up the panorama of the world in vast dimensions and neglects detail. God of course encounters us everywhere. But we need the painstaking attention to God's pain, the groaning of God, and the groaning of the whole creation. Even though activists are pointing out the needs of the world—hunger, the threat of ecological death and nuclear death—there is little change of overall sensibility. Why does the human race continue with business as usual? The vision from below, from the underside of history, offers the power not merely to see things and persons differently, but also to treat them differently.

Formative Process toward Accountable Teaching

Treating things and persons differently may mean one thing to society in general, and something else to the church. In society, it often does not get beyond holy anarchy or laissez-faire pluralism. The ecological challenge, for example, is felt by a wide range of persons and groups. Does the church have to relate to it? Here we have to keep in mind that God places us in a special social location, not just anywhere. We dare never forget: the church is always in conflict—creative, not destructive conflict. We are members of the *ecclesia militans*. It expresses itself in different ways at different times.

Borrowing a thought from Arnold Toynbee, Harvey Cox has pointed to the overall civilization conflict in which the church shares:

He held that as any world civilization reaches senility a creative "internal proletariat" appears. This germ cell, usually inspired by a religious vision, becomes a fetus that grows within the larger body politic but is sufficiently independent of it to survive. Eventually it provides the spiritual core of the succeeding civilization. . . . It suggests further that to gain some insight on what to expect next, we concentrate not on the brontosauri but on the small, more agile marmots we might otherwise overlook.[93]

It may well be that some Christians already function as the "internal proletariat" of our civilization. They certainly do so, for example, in some Latin American countries, in Poland, and in South Africa. The black church has done so in the United States. The sharp profile of the class conflict in some instances is still missing. Yet what one needs to see is that today there are principalities and powers that own our lives— installing more nuclear weapons and triggering the ecological death of creation. In another context I have stated the issue more succinctly:

> There are those who own the means of production for making Pershing IIs and other mass murder weapons. There are those who do not own these means of production. When it comes to ownership, the situation is in principle the same in the Soviet Union as in the United States. Only a radical change in ownership of the means of production would stop the arms buildup. The means of production have to be in the hands of all the people for making peace products and not weapons of war. The time is far off. But the goal is clear. Whether one talks about the owners as a ruling class or gives them some other label, the owner class and those who do not own the means of production are antagonists in harsh conflict.[94]

By no means do churches across the board see this issue clearly. We do not expect them to see everything the way the Divinity Schools see it, or some individuals in the Divinity Schools. Yet there is much searching going on in the churches. Uncertainties have arisen. Self-contradictions are being noticed. There are puzzlements about the teaching of the church. But few thus far know how to work with this new phenomenon doctrinally.

The Power of Traditions

The best way to get hold of the present situation is to view what is happening as a formative process toward new teaching. What happened during the first two or three centuries of the church on the way to Nicea happened every so often again. Christians early had to make up their minds together as to what the person of Jesus really meant for the life of the church. The early centuries struggled over the ontological role of Jesus. In the Reformation, we see Christians struggle over his justification role. Today the church is caught between the awakening to a new age and the death throes of an old one. It is not immediately clear as yet what core issue the churches need to address. Powerful forces try to control our lives. New teachings in the church seek to address the world power conflict, the class struggle, the race clash, or the battle of the sexes. Why so many altercations about the new teachings?

The function of tradition is usually the core issue involved.[95] Too often it is viewed as a straitjacket that demands nothing more than intellectual assent.[96] As a consequence, some Christians demand that denominations not require creeds as framework for ordination or similar occasions. Neoorthodoxy did not help much in solving the basic issue, because it did not clarify the transition from scripture to creed. The relationship between the authority of the two remained unclear.[97] Because the scriptures usually were not anchored in the eucharist, the tradition started to function as a "free-floating" authority base.[98] In Barth's *Dogmatics in Outline*, a reflection on how tradition grows out of experience is lacking. A person might still be satisfied that scripture springs from revelation, but would not wish to acknowledge that tradition springs from revelation. Did neoorthodoxy ever radically ask whether tradition might grow out of discipleship?

From Creedal Teaching to Accountable Teaching

The importance of church teaching impresses us as we become conscious of standing in tradition. It is also tradition that mediates to us the importance of the scriptures. Thus scripture and tradition confront us interdependently in the experience of the moment. Scripture, tradition, and experience lend themselves as criteria because scripture as well as tradition communicate God's truth as they convict us of truth in our discipleship. The scriptures do not impose concepts on us, but energize our God-walk. Tradition *corroborates* this energizing influence. Scriptures appear meaningful as they in Wordpresence corroborate God's realpresence in the eucharist and in history. This is a mutual validation process, though the scriptures, as we indwell them, always are primary in evoking new understandings and decisions. Most objections to tradition as a criterion are reactions to a hierarchical and patriarchal concept by which popes, bishops, and synods impose creeds as straitjackets on human minds. This concept produces a creedal teaching that does not allow a *formative teaching process* to take place in the church. It seems to assume that persons have to be inculcated or inoculated with truth. It misses completely the dimension of *mutually accountable teaching* lying at the root of character formation in spite of patriarchal perversions. We are again learning the historical dynamics involved.

What is going on today is somewhat similar to what transpired during the first four or five centuries c.e., before the creeds were solidified. There was a long process of Christians giving an account to each other of their teachings about God, Christ, and the Holy Spirit. During the Reformation and the following one or two centuries a somewhat analogous process took place. In the early Catholic Church it was an issue of the closeness of Jesus to God, represented by the catchword *homoousios* (sameness). In the Reformation, the challenge was God's closeness to the human being represented by the word *justification.* Today the concern is God's closeness to history in the struggle for *justice.* Thus the traditions today are being examined for their *justice* power. Accountable teaching in the church develops as God's justice struggle is being examined. God-walk compels us to analyze, for example, how we relate to politics and economics. Are we using our commitment to Christ merely to legitimate our life politically and economically? Or does Christ open a way for critical spirituality?

No Need for "Centrist" Creeds to Check Experience

The issue of accountable teaching is not to develop a mainline or centerline position or to find the lowest common denominator. Consensus is not an end in itself in the church. The function of creeds is not to develop a "centrist" base, but to remind us that the appeal to experience *as such* is not enough. Theo-praxis has to be the starting point and ultimate court of appeal. There is nothing in creeds that expresses a middle-of-the-road or centrist location. All they want to do is energize the formative teaching process.

John Macquarrie makes experience the starting point. He claims that, unless theology has its roots in experience, it "deals in abstractions and becomes a mere scholasticism."[99] Experience is here not directly tied to discipleship. The struggle between truth and untruth makes no difference to speak of. Class struggle is nowhere near. Experience for Macquarrie is *participation in a religious faith*, Christianity being one of the "varieties of religious experience" (William James). At the very outset of Macquarrie's theology there is the *theoretical* starting point that Christianity as a religion has elements in common with all other religions:

> Running through the many varieties . . . there may be discerned basic elements common to them all. In the community of faith, there is met what seems to be a quest inherent in the very constitution of our human existence. The quest is met by the opening up of the dimensions of the holy, which is experienced as addressing, judging, assisting, renewing, and so on.[100]

Macquarrie, in a vast religious sweep, is here reflecting on Christianity as a religion, integrating it into humankind in general:

> In the broadest sense, then, it is the experience of existing as a human being that constitutes a primary source for theology; not just explicitly religious experience, but all experience in which a religious dimension is discernible. This was implied in my remark that faith meets "what seems to be a quest in the very constitution of our human existence." But this remark implies further that although it is only in experience that we become conscious of the quest, the roots of the quest are, in a sense, prior to experience since they belong to the very structure or form of human experience.[101]

Karl Barth takes sin so much into account that he can think of it only in terms of *total depravity*, but Macquarrie hardly considers sin at the outset and views it more as *estrangement* from the ground of life, an estrangement that can be corrected. No "centrist" creedal position will improve matters between Barth and Macquarrie. The point is to grasp the dynamics of a teaching process counteracting Christian thoughts that stay in the realm of mere theory. Indwelling the scriptures mediated through the tradition we are enlisted in God's justice struggle. Here we learn that through sin the *very structure of human experience* has been tampered with and is still being tampered with. In Barth's view, sin is *separation*. God is totally distant from the individual. God's task, then, is to establish contact with the human being. Bible and tradition proclaim that initiative of God. But our own discipleship situation in this view is not crucial for God's interaction with us. Experience is surely not in the picture as criterion. In Macquarrie's more existentialist view, sin is *alienation*. Our estrangement from the ground of life expresses itself in various forms. Obviously, here we are asked to reflect on experience. But the experience of sin is in Macquarrie not necessarily related to the experience of the discipleship community. It is more a private "falling out."

I have stated before that for God-walk sin is either *usurpation,* an arrogation of power, or it involves a drying up of soul-force, a silent submission to injustice. Here we need to reflect on the specific experience of discipleship as countering the temptation to rule over others or to permit such a rule. What kind of situation does scripture place us in when appealing to Messiah Jesus? Before scripture leads us to creeds—important as they are—or to religion on Macquarrie's broad scale, it invokes in us discipleship. Scripture itself requires a measure of our experience to demonstrate its authoring power. But "centrist" creeds that want to harmonize various strands of tradition are not authoring experience as a matter of course. The social location of our experience has to be kept in mind. We stand in the midst of the struggle against all manner of powers and principalities.

From Liberal Analyses to Liberation Analogies

The most difficult move for many North American Protestant theologians is the parting of ways with theological liberalism. Obviously the first need we all feel is to begin with ourselves in making clear what Christianity means. But liberal theologians have often made a kind of virtue out of this need, offering a general religious starting point for Christian reflection when scripture and tradition call our attention to a different experience, God's realpresence in historical conflicts, without neglecting personal struggles. For the maintenance of empire, the military-industrial complex of the West has developed the most subtle security system the world has ever seen, but with tremendous attrition in the world's poor and our natural resources. God in Jesus places the divine shoulder to the wheel of history at the point of greatest need. Together with God we here look at human destiny from the underside of history. This is especially the case if we see the eucharist as the social location for beginning any Christian reflection.

Macquarrie starts with general human selfhood, something that does not actually exist. This way we initially do not pay attention to human selfhood in Messiah Jesus. For Macquarrie, scripture comes alive in the context of present experiences of "the holy." Tradition also stays very much within the broad religious notion of "the holy." So does reason. In this position there is no direct wrestling with the formative teaching process in the church. It becomes an issue of starting with a preconceived philosophical principle, in this case an existentialist angle. Macquarrie "plugs into" experience, scripture, tradition, or reason very much in terms of what seems preferable to him at the moment. If he begins much of the time with experience, it is the first among equals.

But in the social location of the eucharist, do not the scriptures have the *primacy*? No formative teaching process emerges if one proceeds in keeping one's religious options open, choosing one time from experience, the next time from tradition, and so forth. God's immediate interaction through the eucharist is left out. It takes us in a different direction and calls for a different approach.

The *scriptures* as God's Wordpresence at the eucharist evoke God-walk, discipleship. *Tradition* confirms this authoring power. We are compelled to look for the underside of history, class struggle, the truth/untruth clash, and all the conflicts in the church that have yielded greater human dignity. *Experience* sifts the values of the past, reflecting on the exploitation and power factors involved in discipleship as well as on the factor of personal guilt. Just as we are stewards of tradition in this critical sense, we are also critical stewards of creation. The shaping of accountable teaching comes through the living process of scripture authoring our new life, confirmed by tradition in socially critical experience. *Reason* is the checkpoint where this process is arranged for communication, consistency of argument, and transparency of understanding.

Reason here is not autonomous reason, but co-reason, reason illumined by the Holy Spirit, seeking to think together with God, shaped in the context of discipleship. So is it reason at all? It is certainly not arbitrary reason, self-propelled reason, reason as a law unto itself. It is part of praxis seeking justice. It revolts against intellectual anarchy. It is not the kind of reason that figures out how to make the biggest profit or build the biggest bomb. Its logic is shaped by what God is doing in Messiah Jesus in history. And yet it checks the evidence of God's activity in terms of what human beings know about justice and liberation. It looks for analogies of God's liberation in all acts of justice among humankind. It does not analyze a general human condition and then use its findings to explain Christianity in religious terms. It takes God's own walk seriously and moves from there to those evidences in history that bear out God's justice activity. They are never the same as God's own "evidence." But reason expects them at least to be analogous.

Accountable teaching does not have any neat formula for arranging scripture, tradition, experience, and reason in sequence. But it shows that these factors work together in a particular empowerment of human beings. In the dynamics of the empowering process, *scripture* functions as the rule of God-walk, *tradition* as its source, *experience* as the medium, and *reason* as its double-check.

Autonomous Reason and Base Communities

The formative process toward accountable teaching is not an abstract end in itself, but takes the place of what we consider autonomous reason. The self-orientation potential of the human being through reason is a great gift we despise only at our own peril. But in sin, reason is always mixed with unreason, rationality with irrationality. God's countermove in God-walk stymies unreason, but not reason. It is beautiful for the human being to be self-determined. Yet on the level of self-direction sin causes much confusion, anarchy, and self-destruction. The oppression of our neighbors, their exploitation, all the misery on the underside of history, is too much due to misjudgments of autonomous reason. So we cannot rejoice in its mere agency. Autonomous reason is self-inflated and self-deceptive. In theo-praxis we need to find a way that reason, as co-reason together with God, does not surrender an ounce of its sharpness and integrity, and yet does not usurp either God's integrity or that of our neighbor.

Sin in many respects is merely autonomous reason unable to be anything but usurping reason. Or, instead of soul-force powerfully moving the historical process, the timbre of the soul in sin is dryness. Persons shrivel up; in fact, fall asleep (Matt. 25:5; Eph. 5:14). They let injustice happen to themselves and others. When we today speak of conscientization, we speak of a high state of wakefulness, an alertness that is the exact opposite of the dryness in which the soul shrivels up.

The state of alertness and wakefulness is a corporate state. It occurs when persons become mutually accountable to each other in that they lift out the basic dimension of God-walk for each other. They do not give each other a bad conscience or a good conscience, but a sensitive conscience, the co-reason in which we argue together with God the justice of the divine case. Here lies the core of discipleship.

There is much discussion today about base communities. In most respects, there is no particular mystique to them at all. As discipleship communities in primitive Christianity developed into the church as an institution, dry rot soon set in. Mutual accountability turned into church maintenance, accountable teaching into patriarchal church administration and hierarchical magisterium, the official teaching office. In every generation the process of the administration of Christianity takes over, so that the church as institution remains viable. In that situation Kierkegaard's dictum is apropos: every generation has to be converted again to Christ. The ossification or bureaucratization of the institution is inescapable.

Today's base communities are counterchurches, liberation churches, groups of Christians who counteract autonomous reason as a usurping factor by introducing the mutual accountability factor. They fight dry rot of the soul, intensifying prayer, contemplation, and personal commitment. Obviously base communities take on different shape and form in the Third World than in the First

World. But they all tend to root themselves in the eucharist, take Bible study seriously, examine tradition critically in terms of the option for the poor, and shape experience within the dynamics of these factors, so that reason knows what it needs to doublecheck.

1

THEO-PRAXIS

In God-walk the primary thought that arises is that of *God*. In dogmatics this is usually treated under the heading, "The Doctrine of God." But in God-walk we do not immediately arrive at doctrine. Taking our social location into account, we need to underscore that every Christian doctrine today in the West is predominantly part of the NATO-church. We are the church in the wider context of the North Atlantic community whose branches in myriad ways are interdependent in terms of a military-industrial security system climaxing in nuclear deterrence. All the politicians are for peace. But the de facto situation is saturated with the peace lie. The prophet Jeremiah opposed the church administration of his day with its lie: "From prophet to priest everyone deals falsely. They have healed the wound of my people lightly, saying 'Peace, peace,' when there is no peace" (Jer. 6:13f.).

There are of course many church pronouncements and resolutions about peace in the North Atlantic community. But the churches have not been able as yet to set a new direction, to undo the preparation for mass murder and genocide, and to show a new way of life. It is not surprising that in the 1960s there was much talk about a death-of-God theology. Does the true God make any difference to us? Or have we already buried God? It may well be that the NATO-church is worshiping an idol, Mars rather than the God of Jesus. It is a religious crime in this situation not to take seriously the critique leveled at the idol from the perspective of black theology and feminist theology. Is it merely a "white" and "male" God we worship?

It is important for me to explain why I address the reality of God at this point. There is no ministerial student, minister, or lay person who does not at this turn of thought take an educated guess and a calculated risk in deciding on the sequencing of Christian thought. In describing the content of Christian thought in accountable teaching should one start with the church? Or with christology? Or with the Holy Spirit? Accountable teaching is propelled by the question: What is happening to us at the core of the Christian life? What takes place at the heart of Christian worship centered in the eucharist? Here we are placed outside the city wall among the outcasts and the groaning creation. There is no virtue in poverty as such. Yet God's social location is not the White House or the cathedral, but the cross, human conflict. God's own God-walk is at the center of it all. That is why we need to begin with God.

We have to see our reflection on God-walk against the foil of the Enlightenment. The North American Enlightenment was privileged to see its ideas continued from one generation to the next, in almost unbroken succession, from the eighteenth through the mid-twentieth century. It is only now that Americans are turning a critical eye on the founding fathers. The American dream of freedom, equality, and happiness has arrived at real limits, not just the limits of growth. In retrospect we realize that for almost two centuries reason ruled supreme. This has also been the case in Christian thought. Instead of laboring as co-reason, thinking together with God, it proceeded as *controlling reason*. It usurped God's place and God's power. It separated mind and heart, the cosmos and the individual, man and woman. It pulled all the strings in Christianity as well as in society and nature. It allotted Christian doctrines their proper place and function.

In these reflections I will not develop a comprehensive doctrine of God. All I intend to do is to focus on the change in understanding God that comes about when we orient ourselves in God-walk. We dare not forget: we are NATO-Christians. The dynamics of history demand the transition from the empire of man to the kingdom of God, from the expectation of the American empire to God's rule, from Manifest Destiny to human destiny.

At the core of our reflection lies the eucharistic presence of God

in Messiah Jesus on grounds of the work of the Holy Spirit embodied in the breaking of the bread and the sharing of the cup as the
eucharistic words are spoken and the eucharistic prayer is offered.
But what are we "to make of it"? There is a dynamics that antecedes our praxis. There is thought that antecedes our thought.
The whole eucharistic event is designed to liberate us from the pride
of controlling thought. Reason does not have to be humbled, but it
needs to be mellowed or tempered and made pliable to the elementary dynamics of the world process. It needs to become attuned to
the forces that shape the world from the inside.

So we start in the eucharist with the confidence that via the Bible
mediated through tradition we indwell God in Christ and share ever
anew in Jesus' life, death, and resurrection: "Set your minds on
things that are above, not things that are on earth. For you have
died, and your life is hid with Christ in God" (Col. 3:2f.). This is
not a mere *theologia crucis* (theology of the cross), and not a mere
theologia resurrectionis. It is a *theologia vitae, crucis, et resurrectionis*, accountable teaching empowered by Jesus's life, death,
and resurrection.

The reality we are pondering is obviously never as tangible as
the elements of bread and wine. We are always taking a step into
the unknown. The first dimension of that mystery is that the
eucharist unites us more fully with *God* ("O for a closer *walk* with
God!"), and helps us to attune ourselves to the divine praxis, the
theo-praxis. We try to retrace God's walk in history, to walk along
with God, and to struggle along in the divine justice struggle.
There is always in the center of the historical process a vigorous
movement we need to fall in line with and find our cues in. In this
sense reflection on God comes first in God-walk in the expectation that it leads to accountable teaching. God is the center of
what is the heart of discipleship: eucharistic worship. Here we
come to see in a metaphoric act what goes on in all of history and
nature.

The Reality of God: God the Claim vs. God the Problem

Countless people still believe that there is a God. Yet there is also
the modern "event" called the death of God. We can shrug it off
only at our own peril. Nietzsche wrote:

"Whither is God?" the madman cried. "I shall tell you. *We have killed him*, you and I. All of us are his murderers. But how have we done this? How were we able to drink up the sea? Who gave us the sponge to wipe away the entire horizon? What did we do when we unchained this earth from the sun? . . .God is dead. God remains dead. And we have killed him. . . . What was holiest and most powerful of all that the world has yet owned has bled to death under our knives. Who will wipe this blood off us?"[1]

Death of God means not just the experience of the absence of God, but the absence of any experience of God. Nietzsche does not rejoice in being a murderer. There is no celebration or jubilation. There is perhaps fright. For nearly fifteen hundred years, a millennium and a half, from the time of the early Catholic Church up to the beginning of the Enlightenment, there was an unquestioned convention of *God-talk* implying God as *theoretically necessary*, rationally cogent. It was not that God was evidencing God so as to make God reasonably cogent. Rather, in terms of logical argumentation, God *had* to be. For fifteen hundred years Western civilization took a "head-trip." It still comes out in popular phrases such as: There just has to be a Supreme Being. There has to be a God; otherwise nothing makes sense. If there is no God, all things are permitted. If there is no God, God would have to be invented.

Although there is still much religion around, the *modern* sensibility suggests that there does *not* have to be a God. The world can well be explained without God. There does not have to be a first cause as an absolute transcendent entity. A first cause may well be immanent to the world itself. There does not have to be an ontological ground of all being. Being may be able to be grounded in itself in every one of its elements. The world may be a lonelier place without God. But it does not have to be a scary place.

Western civilization had elevated God to the explanatory principle of the universe. It had put philosophy on the pedestal and made it basically a prolegomenon to any reflection on Christian doctrine. But not all human beings were living on that lofty plain. Some areas of human experience had been excluded from Christian thought— economics and politics, for example. As soon as human beings sensed that God had been kept out of human affairs in principle and made a pawn on the chessboard of philosophical thought, practical atheism sprang up and provided fertile ground for the theoretical atheism of the Feuerbachs and Nietzsches.

By the time Kant arrived on the scene (1724–1804), there were three philosophical ways of showing the necessary existence of God. It was pure reason, to use Kant's phrase, that wanted to be in control of all three of them. There was either the ontological proof, the cosmological, or the physico-theological one (argument from design). James Livingston has summed it up well:

> The ontological proof . . . was originally conceived by An-selm in the eleventh century and revived by Descartes and Leibniz in the seventeenth century. The ontological argument proceeds from the very definition of God as a perfect being. A perfect being must possess all perfections, for otherwise it would not be perfect. In the concept of a most perfect being existence must be included, for if it were not, the concept would not be that of a most perfect being. Therefore, by definition such a being must necessarily exist.[2]

The point that needs underscoring in order to understand our Enlightenment heritage in matters of God is that such a being must *necessarily* exist.

This necessary being is what "the death of God" is pointing to. The death of God is tied to the traditional philosophical arguments Kant dismantled by saying that existence is not a necessary predicate. It therefore is also not a necessary predicate of the most perfect being called God. I can postulate existence of something necessary. But that does not mean it really exists. (One thousand dollars might be necessary for me now, but do I have it?) This kind of existence, according to Kant, is derived from judgments, but not from reality itself. We can no more extend our stock of theoretical insight by mere ideas than a merchant can improve his position by adding a few zeroes to the cash account.

It is obvious that we are in the realm of philosophical argumentation. As long as philosophy was taken for granted as preface to any Christian doctrine, the orientation of the Christian mind was to that rarified air of abstract theory. But if we turn away from philosophy to the eucharist as primal orientation point of Christian thought, the scene changes completely. The core issue now takes on a different character. God may well not be theoretically necessary for philosophy. But *although God is not theoretically necessary*, God may not be dead, God may be *reasonably inevitable*. That is, our reason may not be able to escape encountering the reality we call God. But the encounter will not be mediated by philosophy and certainly does not have to be subject to what logical deduction finds *necessary*.

The proofs for God's existence appear in a social context completely different from that of the eucharist. God in Messiah Jesus does not meet us in the world of philosophy as such. For fifteen hundred years Christianity had hitched its wagon to a horse that led it down the philosophical trail. The *cosmological* argument claims: If things exist, an absolutely necessary being must also exist as their cause. Kant suggests that any cogency contained in this thought owes its logical force to the ontological argument. Much the same was true of the *physico-teleological* argument based on design. Kant argues that pure reason has no access to a transcendent being, cause, or design.

There is no point in traveling over the barren road again and again. We have to remember, however, that after Kant had reintroduced God as *postulate* of the will in what he called practical reason, Hegel (1770–1830) claimed that reason and God are identical. God was thinking the divine within reason itself. That gave Ludwig Feuerbach (1804–1872) the opportunity to turn the argument on its head. All we have in reason is human reason. Ultimately human reason is "divine" itself: "God as God is nothing but the essence of reason itself." In precise terms, Feuerbach explains the *kairos* character of this insight for the modern age: "The task of the modern era was the realization and humanization of God—the transformation and dissolution of theology into anthropology."[3]

Here we are right at the heart of what came to be called the death of God. We never dare forget that it took place in a particular social location called philosophy. But religionists in those days were totally convinced that in that very location they had to take a stand. The tremendous difficulty of black theology today to "connect" with anything that derives from the Enlightenment tradition is largely explicable within this context. James H. Cone states: "By ignoring our hopes and dreams . . . progressive theologians were saying that blacks cannot think, because they do not exist. That is why some of them could say, and still do, that there is no such thing as black theology."[4] White theology had aligned itself with a hermetically sealed-off social location of theoretical thought. The ground rules did not allow any other premise to enter. So white theology continued to feed on itself until it almost destroyed itself. It had lost touch with the reality of God.

Religionists were of course terribly dissatisfied with Kant and Hegel. Schleiermacher was the first to make a big countermove with an altogether different set of categories. The fact remains, however, that also with him (as with all who wanted to be modern Christians) *God the Problem* remained central. Theologians began spending much time correcting Kant, Hegel, and Feuerbach. God now continued to be a pro-blem (from the Greek *pro* + *blēma*, something thrown forward—in this case, at us, at our feet) to be solved and was not viewed as involved in humanity. God was an idea to be toyed with.

Here a labyrinth of emotions and a maze of thought opened up that is still with us today. Modern conventional wisdom suggests that pure reason pushing across its threshold experiences a void, a sheer nothing, rather than perfect being. Furthermore, the modern mind says, you do not need God to make things and existence explicable. The world is self-explanatory. It is easier to come to terms with the world without a creator. Not that thereby everything becomes transparent, but it eliminates one more irritant. As a consequence, however, anthropocentricity began to dominate. The human being now became the center of things. And ecology today says: Look what happened to nature with the human being at the center! Religionists might add: Look what happened to the world *without God at the center!*

At times one is inclined to think that the reasoning about God as problem was not wrong, but that the difficulty lies in the *premises.* Yet it is too easily forgotten that the *reasoning* was that of *controlling reason.* Transferred to the realm of religion, reason retained its controlling function and once more assigned religion its legitimating function, something it had done since Constantine, but which now included all the modern theories.

We cannot strongly enough stress that the whole framework in which we debate the issue is that of the Enlightenment. Jon Sobrino has explained the liberation thrust of Latin American theology

against the same foil. He makes a sharp distinction between European theology and Latin American theology. Both depend on the
liberating power of the Enlightenment for theological understanding. But in order to see the difference, Sobrino suggests we distinguish two phases of the Enlightenment, represented by Kant and
Marx. Kant heads the first phase, with the liberation of reason
from all authority. Marx heads the second phase, with liberation
from the wretched conditions of the real world. The Marx liberation brings more than freedom of the mind. European theology, on
Sobrino's terms, has been geared to the first phase of the Enlightenment, Latin American theology to the second.

The beautiful clarity of the Sobrino analysis comes through in
pithy summaries. The European Christian tie-in to the Enlightenment tries to address either the attack on the meaning of faith or its
loss:

> This restoration of meaning is liberating because the crisis in
> the real world is experienced as a crisis of meaning; the real
> threat that the real world represents for faith is subsumed
> under the crisis of meaning and then exorcised by means of a
> new interpretation.[5]

Latin American theology with its tie-in to the second phase of the
Enlightenment follows Marx in his notion of giving a new form to a
reality full of misery. It does not try to give meaning to or explain
reality. For European theology, reality is primarily an object of
thought. For Latin American theology, reality is met in its concrete
dilemmas. Sobrino also admits to the "problem of God." But he
sees Latin American theology refusing to explain the nature of God
on the level of thought. It is for him more a matter of experiencing
the reality of God as Christians try to build the kingdom of God.[6]

We learn from Sobrino and his Latin American colleagues the
seriousness of the analysis and the willingness to shoulder the
burden. It needs saying, however, that the North American Enlightenment is neither European nor Latin American. Nor is it the
third phase of the European Enlightenment, but another Enlightenment. The symbiosis of European Enlightenment ideas with the
American environment produced a very distinctive thrust of reason. The North American Enlightenment certainly does not want

to see reality mainly as an object of thought.[7] Thus the European argument about the need to postulate God, or to see God and reason identical, or the shock of the death of God were never genuinely North American issues. The death-of-God theory of the 1960s was more or less a non sequitur within the total process of North American Enlightenment influence. Its immediate impact had a lot to do with a frequently neglected practical atheism, where it struck a nerve.

In a strange way North Americans with their peculiar Enlightenment heritage want to change the world too, just the way Marx wanted to change it, only on different terms. "Give me your tired, your poor, your huddled masses yearning to breathe free. . . . " These words as motto of the Statue of Liberty make much of Marx's Enlightenment point, only not with the bent toward socialism. So there is a kind of "sibling" rivalry here. In changing the environment, North Americans also use reason as controlling reason. Controlling reason in Marxism eliminates the word "God," whereas controlling reason in the North American Enlightenment heritage makes the word "God" serve the purposes of economics and politics, so that it finally functions as legitimation of empire.

As much as North American Christians would like to be genuinely Christian, in deep commitment to Jesus Christ and the Bible, the North American Enlightenment heritage, conflated with the Constantinian mood of Christianity in the West, makes God a peculiarly American God, subject to controlling reason. Religious practices can control God for achieving our success. Robert Schuller today is one great apostle of the Good News of Success. His God of controlling reason can easily be combined with remnants of the European Enlightenment thought and be offered in North American theology as the pro-blem, literally something "thrown before" us to be tackled reasonably.

To be drawn to the God of the eucharist is an approach to the God not subject to controlling reason. To be sure, the eucharist is not celebrated in an *unthinking* world. God's embodiment takes place under bread and wine in a congregation that shares in a mindful environment. Its appeal is not to religious feeling mainly, but to a kind of reason or rationality that does not make sense merely to religious persons mystified by cults or rites, but to all persons reasonably struggling for human dignity and truth. The objection to controlling reason is not an objection to reason. In the action of the eucharist we do not need to act up, but to wake up. God is asking for a reasoned response involving heart, mind, and soul in equal measure.

The eucharist confronts all persons with their unwillingness to acknowledge their innermost "rationale." Of course they all have their excuses (Rom. 2:15). What is inexcusable is that we fail to acknowledge the source of life. The point is not to berate others. The eucharist simply says: You have no excuse for not thinking. It is an invitation for reason to discover the truth.[8] By implication it wants to say: Reviving the old ontological argument from Being to God will not lead us to God. It only encourages reason to act as controlling reason. The God of the Western head-trip is dead.

The eucharist makes God-walk appeal to conscience, co-reason—in St. Paul's sense: "By the open statement of the truth we would commend ourselves to every person's conscience in the sight of God" (2 Cor. 4:2). To a certain extent God-walk redefines reason. Truth-finding is still a matter of the head, but only in concert with the will (heart) and feeling (Schleiermacher's type). Co-reason is thus the capacity to grasp truth in the mind as an act of the heart. At the base level, each thought originates as an act of the heart. It is also a deed. Thinking is basically a doing. In God-walk, a thought without the will is an abstraction. It does not really exist. God-walk does not reject thinking, or thinking about God. However, it roots thinking not in itself, but in the heart committed to the poor.

There is no way of thinking about God apart from social location. I have developed my analysis of the eucharist in concert with God's solidarity with the poor. From this perspective, reason that is not co-reason is not very much reason at all, but is truncated reason—a mere torso. Controlling reason is truncated reason because it forgets its co-thinking character, co-thinking together with God. Controlling reason sooner or later cannot but experience the death of God. Reason as co-reason, conscience, is not a matter of mere cerebration. God deals with our whole being through conscience. Co-reason is aware of a *claim* that calls for acknowledging God's justice: "When gentiles who have not the law do by nature what the law requires, they are a law to themselves, even if they do not have the law. They show that what the law requires is written on their hearts, while their conscience also bears witness and their conflicting thoughts accuse or perhaps excuse them" (Rom. 2:14–15). If this is true for gentiles, it pertains also to Christians. There is no principal separation between the mind and the heart in the eucharistic scriptures. Though it seems that we perceive God in the heart first, the mind is immediately implicated. We cannot get away from the fact that the heart has its reasons.

In the heart, God is felt as claim addressing our apathy toward the justice struggle. Christianity offers a whole range of metaphors that try to deal with our apathy: regeneration, forgiveness, justification, sanctification, for example. Yet crucial here is the person entirely apart from any outreach of Christianity. Human beings are never without God. Underneath us ("the everlasting arms"), beside us ("God's right hand shall hold me"), behind and before ("God besets me behind and before")—wherever we turn, God is already in motion before us and ahead of us. We are expected to track God's movement through history, tune in to God's word, and fall in step with God's walk.

This means that human beings will want to embody justice, giving God what God is due, and the neighbor and the self what is their due. The claim is felt as empowerment. But we refuse the empowerment. We either usurp the divine claim on us and turn co-reason into controlling reason, which lets us become our own law and do our own thing, or we refuse empowerment by accommodating injustice out of fear and timidity, which causes our life to shrivel up. The dryness of our soul turns into dry rot. We have become wimps.

Self-sufficiency and autonomy could be wonderful qualities of human beings. But self-sufficiency is distorted in the "self-made" person. Self-sufficiency means self-made fate. Autonomy means self-made humanity, shaping itself, directing itself, empowering itself. Likewise, humility could be a good thing. And other-directedness could be a good thing. But other-directedness as submission to a usurper is just as destructive as self-centeredness. When dry rot sets in, we no longer see God and the neighbor. In both instances, God becomes in principle "invisible," and human beings are turned into invisible men and women.[9]

Within the context of the models available for Christian thought today, God's relationship to humankind is usually viewed in terms either of revelation or transformation.[10] With revelation, the notion is implied that God as God is principally hidden and has to be revealed if we are to get in touch with the divine. With transformation, the revelation is more or less presupposed and the emphasis is on the experience of the reality of God as we share in "kingdom-building."

We can begin with the premise that God does not hide the divine life. God is unconcealed in relationship to all humankind. Any concealment from God is ours. God is not interested in the hide-and-seek game of revelation. God reaches out to claim the person. Besides revelation and transformation, there is captivation. God empowers us because we are God's own.

In proud human self-arrogation or submissive self-negation—both the refusal of divine empowerment—there is no clear sense of God's justice claim on us. Without acknowledgment of the claim and of the joy in the captivation that it involves, Christians have little power to move into transformation of the world. American Indians are telling us that we are not transforming reality the right way in the first place. The elementary point is to transform reality God's way, which happens "naturally" when we participate in God's justice struggle among human beings and in all of creation. Transformation of reality is then a "by-product."

Thus, at the beginning of any teaching about God we have to stress the need to surrender controlling reason as well as diffident reason in order to turn to co-reason. Controlling reason in one way or another sets up God as a pro-blem—or denies the reality of God altogether. Diffident or passive reason avoids God as problem and hides in a feeling of dependence or powerlessness.

On the contrary, we should want to be aware that we are not alone, that we need to give an account to someone other than ourselves of what we think and do. This is not a feeling of absolute dependence. It is a *sensus communis*, a common sense, the corporate awareness of elementary accountability.[11] God is no longer the Omnipotent Puppeteer who pulls all the strings of nature and history. All we sense is the claim: "I have called you by name, you are mine" (Isa. 43:1). We cannot destroy awareness of the claim. Like light it "shines in the darkness, and the darkness has not overcome it" (John 1:5).

Where eucharist and conscience are joined, the reality of God is not felt as problem, but as claim. God's reality is realpresence in the eucharist fused with the claim of God in conscience, the "inner voice." We are owned, we belong to one who empowers us. In the Reformed tradition, the Heidelberg Catechism asks the question: "What is your only comfort in life and in death?" The answer is the plain affirmation: "That I belong not to myself, but to my faithful Savior Jesus Christ."[12] *Belongingness* is the elementary human experience. We do not need to turn it into a problem. We need to respond to its innermost claim. It puts us immediately in touch with God's involvement with all of humankind, especially the marginals, the poor, the rejected, all the wretched of the earth.

"Knowledge" of God

In God-walk we do not immediately point to a full-fledged doctrine of God. We need to sense first of all in what way the reality of God appears on the human scene. We dare not forget that in "natural theology," "philosophical theology," or "apologetic theology" the question has been raised, in what sense God is knowable. The ontological proof for God's existence is at the center: God known as Being. The death-of-God syndrome suggests the opposite: God cannot be known as Being. So there is a reasoning process that enables one to scuttle all knowledge of God today.

To know something is to share in its basic structure. If we know God in terms of concept, we know God's metaphysical structure. If we know God in terms of symbol, we know what philosophical structures the word "God" appeals to. But knowing God in terms of metaphor in God's own God-walk can empower us in new ways.[13]

I have tried to approach God in terms of God-walk, beholding in the eucharist how God is working in history through the ongoingness of Jesus' life, death, and resurrection. There are also other avenues to God that in principle differ from God-walk and yet involve knowledge of God. But what kind of knowledge?

In his helpful analysis of the relationship between faith and ideologies, Juan Luis Segundo differentiates between a basic anthropological faith common to all human beings and a particular religion as an ideology. He finds that we should not identify anthropological faith and religion. For Segundo, the former specifies the realm of values and their proper hierarchy. The latter designates a particular refusal of human beings to face up to structuring these values. Segundo scores the tendency in the United States to regard oneself as "religious" and as a consequence to assume that, in merely enunciating the noun "God," "one knows who or what one is dealing with."[14] He principally wants to avoid bringing God into the realm of anthropological reflection on faith. "God never constitutes the concrete origin of the values which dominate a human life."[15] What is more, human beings "frequently give the name 'God' precisely to . . . the personification of the values they have chosen for themselves."[16] Yet Segundo in this context also appeals to Jesus and to Jesus' attack on religion. What he does not mention is that Jesus himself presupposes that human beings make themselves a god or give the name "God" to values they have chosen for themselves, but that nevertheless the God whom Jesus represents creates in human beings a conscience to which Jesus appeals. In the rejection of the "God" of organized religion, however, Segundo certainly hits the nail on the head.

Whether in terms of informed philosophical judgment (including social analysis) it is reasonable that an *elementary* dimension of the human structure is the encounter of an Other as well as others, remains a moot question. On grounds of co-reason, appeal to conscience from the perspective of the eucharist simply takes this structure into account. It intimates that such an appeal is not unreasonable in terms of basic human reflection. Why do human beings give the name "God" to the personification of values they have chosen for themselves? Is it not because at the very point of value-making they encounter in their conscience an inner voice they need to come to terms with, but cannot, because of sin? The point of God-walk here is that *God is not rationally necessary, but reasonably inevitable*. We cannot escape God.

God is not really "known" by human beings. Otherwise sin would not be such a dilemma. God is "sensed." We are "aware" of more than ourselves. We wonder about God and do exactly what Segundo suggests: we make a God for ourselves as representation of the values we have chosen for ourselves. This is the level on which we live. It is the level on which history moves.

Consider concrete examples. A marriage is breaking up. Christians, pastors in particular, want to decide what reasonable response might be made on grounds of discipleship. At the core we always want to remember that God is working here too in terms of the losers as well as the lost. For God, no person is "born to be a loser." There are always those who give up too early—quitters. God does not give up. God is always walking the second mile. God continues in faithful relationships. The book of Hosea, for example, makes the point of God's faithfulness. Persistence in love *and justice* are divine realities. Our life is in communion with this God.

In a mill town, brown lung disease is discovered. A congregation needs to decide whether it wants to stand silently on the sidelines or stand up against injustice. The orphan, the widow, and others who cannot stand up for themselves have always been the "apple of God's eye." There is no way of escaping the equal value of others in our conscience. We can begin to judge our tasks in terms of the God of the powerless and thus "know" God.

Here a crucial step is inevitable. Segundo is to the point when he suggests that in this context faith is the issue at stake. But God-walk does not start with a general anthropological faith. Christian walk does not originate out of the human life-structure as such. It arises when a human being is confronted with the reality encompassed by the eucharist—to which belongs the Word proclaimed.[17] "So faith comes from what is heard, and what is heard comes by the Word of Christ *akoē diā rhēmatos Christou*" (Rom. 10:17). Christ is never an abstraction, but embodied eucharistic presence, which the Word is a part of. "What is heard," what *hears*, is not the outer ear alone, but co-reason, con-science, the *inner ear*, a *sensus communis*. The hearing of the outer ear is part of it. But we first "hear" with the inner ear. It is not a raising of consciousness that is primarily at stake in the Christian faith, but an awakening of conscience (in German: *Gott weckt mir das Gewissen; einem ins Gewissen reden; das Gewissen steht auf*) that issues in altering of consciousness. Guilt is not necessarily a sign of awakened conscience. Resistance is. Sensitizing a conscience is not directly connected with guilt. The point is to listen to the inner voice in our inner ear. Guilt comes in because of sin, but is not part of the divinely created conscience process. The human being is an echo-being (also an eco-being).

Reflection on God the creator is faith reflection. Faith is awakened conscience. This is "knowledge of God." Faith is an awakened *effective* conscience in which the pangs of guilt have been overcome, the anguish of a "bad" conscience. Unfaith, disbelief, is deadened conscience. We say about a person: he or she has no conscience. We all presuppose that human beings can be aware of an "inner voice."

The core of the matter here is God's own activity, theo-praxis. As God continues to struggle for justice, the inner ear cannot help being touched by it. What the inner ear hears is God struggling for everyone to find equal worth, dignity, and freedom. It so happens that it directs itself to the least and the marginals first. Others can "take care of themselves," so it seems (Luke 5:31). Conscience, at its core, is knowing together with God what counts as just. So faith in its heart is this knowledge we have together with God. It is basically justice-knowledge.

But it ought to be clear that we cannot operate with this "knowledge" as a universal dogmatic or systematic principle. We no longer have a unified image of the human being to work with. Black theology in the United States was too quickly shunted. It stressed that whites and blacks do not have the same image of the human being. A similar point has been made by feminist theology. The sensitized conscience finds a different expression in master and slave, white and black, man and woman, young and old. Yet here we are still addressing the elementary structure of conscience that is "inside" the various expressions.[18]

Faith in the "embryonic" sense of "conscience" is not belief in some specific value or religious datum. It is certainly not credulity, something usually turning into bigotry. Faith is a *conscientious* (together with God, that is) *grasping* of the dynamics of history and nature, the dynamics of reality and its goal, risking trust in the justice-peace of God's reign (Matt. 6:33). "For truly, I say to you, if you have faith as a grain of mustard seed, you will say to this mountain 'move from here to there,' and it will move; and nothing will be impossible to you" (Matt. 17:20).

Faith is not blindfolded reason, blind faith. We are not expected to believe in something because it is absurd (*credo quia absurdum*). Grasping history conscientiously, joining God's activity, is a reasonable faith. Our conscience attests to it. By this faith we are justified, not by mere "practice" of the faith in "good works." Faith is the movement of the heart in which our thought first emerges. It is part of theo-praxis.

Faith as awakened conscience is a gift. God reaches out as *Creator*, maker of heaven and earth, liberator and redeemer of conscience, *Child*, and *Holy Spirit* to make us share in history. All this is free and prevenient grace, centered in God's ultimate grace in Christ. But it can easily become a glib phrase. In God's activity as creator the fullness of God's character is not perceived or sensed. But God makes at least an impact on conscience in keeping alive the capacity for suffering together with others—as God suffers personally: the Lamb slain from the foundation of the world (Rev. 13:8). God personally bears the marks of the nails going through the hands of Jesus on the cross and God's own hands (as medieval paintings suggest). "We know that the whole creation has been groaning in travail together until now" (Rom. 8:22). And we also know that God's Spirit is involved in the misery (Rom. 8:23). God's capacity for suffering is mediated to the human creature. Justice is predicated on the empathy this capacity for suffering creates.

But there is also the blindness of reason. Conscience "functions" with most humans. But we also have to consider the deadened conscience, callous and numb. No conscience is completely clear. Human beings have long "exchanged the truth about God for a lie" (Rom. 1:25). A lie is a fiction, something that—compared with God's good creation—is unreal. It does not have created status. It is either human self-creation or self-negation, either usurpation or accommodation; in any case, more than separation or alienation. It creates dryness of the soul and finally its dry rot.

Conscience "engages" so badly in us all because in sin it deifies creatures and destroys them, idolizing creation and at the same time venting the rage of iconoclasm: one always kills the thing one loves (Oscar Wilde). A perverted conscience leads to deceptive worship, because it either wields power over creatures or submits to usurped power.

The dynamics involved here haunt us into the innermost recesses of Western thought structures. Something has happened to our minds and hearts with the transition from the Middle Ages to the Renaissance and the Enlightenment. Horst E. Richter has tried to interpret the transition as the change from protected childhood to the identification of human beings with divine omnipotence and omniscience. Psychoanalytically the pattern follows the flight from narcissistic impotence to narcissistic omnipotence. Richter here sees a cover-up. The more one usurped God's power, the more one pretended to discover God in the powers of nature in order to be more one with God.[19] The philosopher's stone expressed the wish of the human being to become omnipotent when God seemed to have disappeared. Richter also sees that the rational urge to be omnipotent implied a repression of the emotions and an oppression of women.

The ascent of reason in the Enlightenment was not merely a matter of discovering human autonomy over against God. It was reason taking the place of God and assuming omnipotence. We have not sufficiently explicated this dynamics to ourselves. We usually claim that in the Enlightenment reason abrogated all authorities. But we do not press on to show how reason became controlling, absolute reason, *the* authority. We simply assume that it was right when Schleiermacher assigned God the place of the cause of absolute dependence, or when Tillich named God the "Ground of Being." In both instances the rational individual decided on a universal principle of theology, not taking into account that for other races and classes or for women the constellation of scripture, experience, and reason brought about quite different faith configurations.

God is "known" in awakened conscience, in faith. We do not immediately have a clear concept, so that we could "visualize" God. We sense power impacting us from beyond—in the pangs of conscience and the comfort of conscience. I do not find a more adequate word than "comfort" (which in the Reformed tradition became such a key term on account of Question I of the Heidelberg Catechism: "What is your only comfort in life and in death?"). We do not know God in terms of theoretical ideas. But we know in terms of the impact on the heart—and the restlessness of the heart. When pangs of conscience and comfort of conscience fuse, we have resistance.

When we focus on the eucharist, "knowledge" of God as awakened conscience releases energy, the dynamics of the Holy Spirit that wants to make us move mountains. Christians in their faith are not the only conscientious human beings, but they are conscientious in a unique way. The priesthood of all believers is nothing but conscience trying to be God's co-worker in history.

To be conscientious cannot be something morose. It involves a healthy and affirmative attitude toward life. So it does not allow complacency. We cannot close our eyes to the vast injustice Christian nations as colonial empires have brought on other peoples and the misery they have created in their own midst. We cannot be blind to the poverty right in front of our doorstep or in our own backyard.

In God-walk, Christian teachings are not Schleiermacher's religious affections set forth in speech. They are rather word-deeds (metaphors), the *praxeis* of God, reflecting God's self-realization in history making conscience effective. Christians are meant to be conscientious human beings who understand how conscience works. They are not better persons. But they can know the power alive in conscience. They can name it, be empowered by it, share it.

Faith gives us back our conscience as "good" conscience. Here faith and reason are primordially one. Faith is *reactivated co-reason*. This is an elementary "knowledge of God." Of course, believers do not have a good conscience all the time. As Christians we are caught up in the web of human sin. But we can live with a *comforted* conscience and resist.

Such an understanding of the "knowledge of God" rejects three distortions of reason: (1) Controlling or speculative reason that universally applies what "I think" and what "I can do"—reason arrogating an omnipotence and an omniscience alien to God, for God is always working, suffering, and "knowing" together with human beings. (2) Isolated or private reason, which regards rationality an end in itself, serving the individual separated from others, disregarding especially the marginals and the outcasts of society. (3) Repressive reason, which prevents our emotions and instincts from sensing God, suppressing the "feminine" power in history and "black" power as well, oppressing persons of other color or class, and even the forces of nature.

An examination of the "knowledge of God," faith as awakened conscience, yields the understanding that in God-walk captivation goes before speculation, or obligation before ontology. Orienting ourselves in the power of conscience we can try to evoke accountable teaching. Only in activating our capacity for co-suffering—compassion or empathy—can we hope to come to relate to God and neighbor in mutual accountability and common teaching.

God the Creator

In God-walk facing the eucharist, faith in God is always first of all faith in God the creator, the maker of bread and wine. It is not a general assent that God exists, a belief in a Supreme Being. There is the instructive scripture passage about the faith of the devils: "You believe that God is one; you do well. Even the devils [Luther translated] believe—and shudder" (James 2:19). It is remarkable that the "shudder" dimension is added. Even the most theoretical assent to God creates some "soul" reaction. You believe that God exists? You might as well shudder. The devil believes it too. But in true faith the shudder is turned into active faith, faith active in love and resistance (cf. Gal. 5:6). True faith senses that God suffers along with the creation. This suffering of God is also described as love. God creates and bears what has been created, carries it on the divine shoulders. In that sense, God is the true Christo-phoros, the world-bearer and Christ-bearer. There is a painting in which Christophoros carries, besides the Christ child, also the earth globe,[20] and keeps it from drowning. That is the point Christian faith in the creator is trying to make.

Christians have nothing to say to America about God except something very simple: God resists. As God resists, God suffers. Faith in God the creator is not faith in some being among other beings, be it even the highest Being. Rather it is conscience sensing suffering—creativity in nature and in the historical struggle for justice, recalling the original creativity of God. Faith in the primordial creativity of God derives from our experience of the energizing suffering of God that conscience senses today. God submits to being broken like the bread and crushed like the fruit of the vine in order to nourish human beings who suffer and share justice in response to the divine reality in the eucharist.

Christians in the West often demote faith to the level of mere cerebral appropriation of verbal signals from transcendence. Faith thus relates to sermons coming down from a pulpit (*pulpitum*, scaffold, stage, platform; unfortunately a place where an ego can brandish itself as an imperial self). Preaching cannot be regarded highly enough. The Reformation was compelled to stress preaching in reaction to the medieval formalization and mystification of

ecclesiastical rites. But faith in the creator God based on mere
verbal transmission is misleading. In God-walk God's self-
realization in nature and history will be sensed *before* verbaliza-
tion. Too often we substitute eloquence for godliness, admiring the
smooth talker as the most prestigious preacher. We use words to
hide our thoughts. Faith in the creator God present in the eucharist
bypasses eloquence. It is based on "immanence." God is present
as creator in the suffering and sharing that unites us at the communion table.

We believe in the creativity of God because of divine-human
creativity represented in the bread and wine. In the eucharist, they
embody the body and blood of Christ for us. Much mystification
can take place over the bread and the wine, as also over the water of
baptism. But in terms of its institution it confronts us with God's
mighty self-realization in history, God's involvement in the muck
and mire of human existence. "I have trodden the wine press alone,
and from the peoples no one was with me; I trod them in my anger
and trampled them in my wrath; their lifeblood is sprinkled upon
my garments, and I have stained all my raiment" (Isa. 63:3). At the
same time, the bread and wine call attention to God's creativity in
nature, joining with human toil and sweat in tilling and nurturing
the land for the grain and the wine to come forth. God is the vine
dresser (John 15:1) and the sower (Matt. 13:3), but so are we. In
Christ the "bread of life" and the "true vine" as divine-human
creativity are eucharistically represented.

Unfortunately, the eucharist is usually celebrated in an antiseptic
sanctuary with antiseptic vessels among kind people—not a cotton
mill, shipyard, or coal mine. The proper social location for the
eucharist is a place of hard labor: "come unto me all that labor."
It celebrates the one who joined human labor and sweat, and is still
present among the losers of struggles as well as those who think
they are winners. We believe in the creator God because God has
become vulnerable by creating a world. Whoever God was "before" the creation, in making the world the Maker became vulnerable to the work. Just as parents have to suffer the weaknesses of a
child and give room to the strengths of a child, so God copes with
the weaknesses of creation while making room for the development
of its strengths. But because God is vulnerable, there is a strong
need for justice. God is injured by any human self-arrogation or

self-abasement that denies, actively or passively, God's presence in all of creation and fails to do justice to all creatures.

If in God-walk we do not join God in history, we have no right to *talk* about these things from the pulpit. Christian faith in God the creator is totally grounded in historical struggle. However, sharing in God's vulnerability and struggle for justice is only one side of the Christian story. Conscience also senses the resurrection impact in the eucharist. God's justice also prevails over the destructive dimension of vulnerability. There is re-creation of the harmed and devastated. Resurrection has its counterpart in the exodus. In God-walk, faith in creation is a reflection of our faith in re-creation.

The confessions or creeds of the church often say very little about God as creator. They usually state no more than the "fact." The Methodist Articles of Religion (1784), for example, offer a brief point: "The maker and preserver of all things, both visible and invisible."[21] This reticence about the creator God is understandable. In principle, there is no need in the struggle to know more. But we have to sense the inside at the same time—the immense creativity and fellow-suffering involved in God's "presence." What we sense is the justice the vulnerable God struggles for in the caring mode of the creator. And we sense how, through the resurrection, justice prevails over injustice as life over death.

Confession of the creator God thus for Christians is a *prayer* grounded in the justice conflict disciples are caught up in as they share in God's work as "bearer" of all things. At the core of the conflict lies conscientious witness: "We must obey God rather than human beings" (Acts 5:29). After the pristine witness of Peter, "Save yourselves from this crooked generation" (Acts 2:40), the church was formed. There is only a short time of calm, and then persecution begins. Peter and John are arrested. After they have been released, the community utters its first recorded prayer: "Sovereign Lord, who didst make heaven and the earth and the sea and everything in them. . . " (Acts 4:24). We dare not view faith in God the creator apart from the conflictual situation where disciples share in God's justice struggle. God is grasped as the creator as we see God *making justice prevail in the midst of strife.*

Thus faith in the creator is not grounded in theoretical reason reaching out to a necessary Being, but in the continuing self-realization of this God, not letting creatures play havoc with divine vulnerability. In the memory of Israel, God's prevailing over the onslaught of injustice was kept alive. Here was the God who acted decisively for a people in slavery, creating out of the slave rabble a new people. It was creative justice-activity in history that made the human being become aware of its creatureliness. It was the exodus that taught the people to ponder the creation of the world. The old theodicy question, *si deus, unde malum?*, turns faith in the creator upside down and makes God a theoretical point the theoretical mind sees as pro-blem. Faith in the creator turns the old theodicy question itself upside down, so that we now ask, *si malum, unde deus*? If this be evil, what does God do about it? So faith moves immediately into joining the vulnerable God in the justice struggle.

From the beginning in Israel, God, though not grasped as triune, was never thought of in an abstract monotheism, the divine Alone, but was grasped as the heart of the historical struggle, enabling a people to do right and to prevail. Faith in God as creator grows out of seeing God as creating new history.

For the people of the covenant, the basic creativity of God is understood in analogy with the new creation in Christ (2 Cor. 5:17) as it reflects the creation of the people of God through the exodus liberation. "Once you were no people, but now you are God's people" (1 Pet. 2:10). We believe in God as creator because God is re-creator.

The Triune God

Following Jon Sobrino, Harvey Cox stresses that "a God who loves actually and not just figuratively must be wounded and hurt just as the people in whom God dwells are hurt."[22] That is the elementary point the teaching about God as creator mediates in the eucharist as basic social location.

Yet for the Christian, God never impacts the soul as creator alone. The liberative and salvific activity of Jesus and the power of the Holy Spirit are constantly reaching into God-walk. What this triune impacting of conscience offers is the experience of a corporate self—a sharing self in which also human beings find their innermost identity.

How do we know we experience God in all this? John Macquarrie applies Rudolf Otto's notion of the Holy to the change from the experience of nothingness to the experience of Being. Otto's notion of creature-feeling serves to describe the awe in the presence of the Holy mediated by our awesome anxiety over the black holes of nothingness encompassing our existence: "This creature-feeling becomes awe in the presence of the holy."[23]

In which social location do we find Macquarrie's sense of awe? Beginning with the eucharist related to conscience, do we not become aware of awe in specific concreteness? There is a hymn that makes a different point in regard to awe:

> When the golden evening gathered on the shore of Galilee,
> When the fishing boats lay quiet by the sea,
> Long ago the people wondered, though no sign was in the sky,
> For the glory of the Lord was passing by.

> Not in robes of purple splendor, not in silken softness shod,
> But in raiment worn with travel came their God. . . .
> And the people cry with *wonder*, though no sign is in the sky,
> That the glory of the Lord is passing by.[24]

The fascinating, awesome mystery (*mysterium tremendum fascinans*) is here by no means tied to "Being." In social location with Jesus present, awe relates to God's involvement in history, God's deprivation, God's impoverishment. Instead of "Being," there is a lowly carpenter-rabbi walking the dusty roads of Galilee. There is a person struggling for justice, and there are many yearning for it.

God-walk does not begin with the lonely individual, a "lone ranger" type, approaching the Great Alone. It begins with a corporate reality that immediately involves others: migrant workers (Matt. 20:1–16) as well as the rich fool (Luke 12:16ff.), "mad" women (Mark 16:9), and criminals about to be executed (Luke 23:32). God is personally in uncomfortable company with an outcast—Jesus. How can we be surprised that God also places *us* among all kinds of persons?

We have to reconstruct what primitive Christianity can communicate to our generation. Without a reorientation in social location, there is no way of arriving at accountable teaching about God. Any so-called Christian nation that builds bombs allowing us to destroy life on earth twelve times over (or is it ten times twelve times?), does not appear to stand in awe before God. With a trillion-dollar debt and in places more than 50 percent of our black youth unemployed, do we really sense the awe God wants us to feel in the presence of others? What has to stand out in sharp profile is the shape of God's own ministry to us. *The God in Christ we worship through the Holy Spirit as triune God comes to us in lowly corporateness.* God moves in nature and history as social self that struggles with every creature. What sensitizes our conscience and turns awakened conscience into active faith is the God who appears in "raiment worn with travel."

As early as 1909 Adolf Deissmann wrote:

> Primitive Christianity, alike in its leading personalities and in the prepondering number of its adherents, was a movement of the lower classes. The water of life did not filter down from the upper level to the many and insignificant. . . . The first to drink of it were fainting stragglers from the great caravan of the unknown and forgotten.[25]

We need to examine again, very carefully, scripture and tradition in the light of our new experience in social location. Tradition may offer us an inadequate image of God in Christ for our day.

Christians do not know their God without Messiah Jesus and the Holy Spirit. God without Messiah Jesus means God without the lowly corporateness, and without the nonperson. God without the Holy Spirit means God without the realpresense of the corporate lowliness in the eucharist and in the world. Social location in the eucharist makes us attentive to the Prologue of the fourth Gospel (1:1–18) or St. Paul's reflection on the gospel and conscience (Rom. 1:16–2:16). Here the triune God is already part of the bedrock of awakened conscience. The Trinity as a doctrine obviously is no more than *a word-deed reflecting God's self-realization* as it makes conscience effective. The Trinity is developmental—in the process of becoming. We experience Trinity, as it were, in ever new ways, on grounds of how it took shape in various ages. It was not immediately present in primitive Christianity. What first appeared was faith in the creator God. And we cannot let that be absorbed by faith in Christ—or the second article of the Apostles' Creed.

Romans 1:16–2:16 reminds us of what goes on in humankind in relationship to the creator God. We are not offered a christological argument. It is a reflection on *God's reality known in conscience*, whereby conscience is basically co-reasoning about justice and injustice, right and wrong, truth and untruth. "What can be known about God" is plain to human beings, "because God has shown it to them" (Rom.1:19). What God has shown is divine vulnerability, the creator's "need" of creatures, reflected in the creatures' need of each other and of God. The godness of God can be seen in the things that are made. God has become "dependent" on creation. Yet human beings "exchange the truth about God for a lie" (Rom.1:25). That is, we create unreality, a fake world of fake values. We injure God by pretending we are not accountable to God's vulnerability and justice.

Where in conscience God could rule, we place an idol, a fake image of ourselves. We mistake the real point of God's power and try to make ourselves omnipotent or impotent. God's power rules through com-passion with creatures. We arrogate God's power unto ourselves and try to rule others or submit silently to usurped power. Instead of justice we establish or support injustice. So we do not honor the truth God creates in our conscience, and we do not give thanks (*eucharistein*) to God. Co-reason, our conscience, is no longer clear. But God's truth, God's relating to us in co-suffering, has not been ended. God ever and again creates our conscience. No human perversion, malice, or covetousness can undo it.

Thus we are without excuse (Rom. 1:20). We have no excuse for not living faithfully in keeping with God's truth. In our time, as in St. Paul's, there is a constant numbing and even deadening of conscience. The building of atomic weapons is an illustration of it. Our inability to cope with mass starvation is another.

In many respects Christianity was forced to start out among persons with notions of a distant God, distant in terms of the Holy Other, the Holy of Holies in Jerusalem; the pinnacle of an angelic hierarchy of gnostic emanations, a Platonic Supreme Good; or later yet the Aristotelean Prime Mover, recondite and removed from human desire at the end of a chain of causality. Christianity points to an interfering God, in our conscience closer to us than we are to our own breath. So St. Paul makes no apologies. God, he implies, asks you, What kind of a person are you? Do you see yourself as private self, or do you live as in a corporate self unthinkable without others? By what power principle do we "murder" (Rom. 1:29) our neighbor but ultimately God as well?

The power issue is crucial in the Trinity. The three-in-oneness of God shows that God's power is not an arbitrary absoluteness, sheer force, but the power bearing creation, interrelating its countless parts and making them interdependent. We need to redefine our terms. God's power means God bearing all things—as God bears the divine self-realization, the corporate, sharing self of God.

So the question becomes: What kind of a person are you in the light of the triune God? St. Paul put the question in his own inimitable way: "Do you not know your body is a temple of the Holy Spirit within you . . . ? You are not your own; you were bought with a price. So glorify God in your body" (1 Cor. 6:19f.). Glorifying God in the body is elementary God-walk. Or St. Paul will say: "If any person is in Christ, this person is a new creation" (2 Cor. 5:17). To be a new person is to find oneself in a different kind of walk, a walk "in company with" God and all God's creatures endowed with the same spirit.

In God-walk it is impossible merely to wrestle with the vulnerability of God as creator. What enters beyond our grasp of the creator is the reality of God in Messiah Jesus shared with us through the Holy Spirit—challenging us to discover what kind of persons we are in the light of these divine persons as corporate self. At the end of 2 Corinthians St. Paul sums it up: "The grace of the Lord Jesus Christ and the love of God and the *koinonia* of the Holy Spirit be with you all" (2 Cor. 13:14). God, in becoming more and more vulnerable as creator, in Messiah Jesus reached out to all "when the time was fulfilled" (Gal. 4:4) to establish justice and through the Holy Spirit to show that this *koinonia* is the very ground of all selfhood.

Irenaeus and Tertullian stressed what has been called the "economic Trinity," God's economy, the way God works, God's own God-walk, in three ways. There is the work of the creator (Rom. 1 and 2), the work of the liberator (2 Cor. 5), and the work of the sustainer (2 Cor. 6). The church in its first centuries was caught between two horns of a dilemma, the horn of divine pluralism (where Christ was another God) and the horn of a monism, monarchianism, or modalism (where Christ and the Holy Spirit are mere appearances of the creator, modalities or modifications). Speculative reason soon took over. Modalism involved the danger (in view of a pervasive gnosticism) that Messiah Jesus would be regarded as having an illusory body, a mere "apparition" as we might say today. The notion of the Trinity sought to guard the "integrity" of God's vulnerability to creation. It was always God's *self-realization*, whether in the creation of the Milky Way, in Bethlehem, or at Pentecost.

We are impacted from all sides: as natural, historical, and spiritual beings—by God, Messiah Jesus, and the Holy Spirit as distinct persons and yet confronting us with one question: What kind of a person are you?

Augustine claimed that in the doctrine of the Trinity we say something in order not to be silent—to make clear that we face a mystery. But the "logic" of God's faithfulness to us lies in the Trinity's threefold challenge to wake up to our own corporate selfhood. Each experience of God is distinct from the other. God's liberating/reconciling activity is not identical with God's creativity. God's sustaining/consummating activity is not absorbed by either God's creative or liberating activity. They are not even mere activities but, as Origen said, each one is a *hypostasis*. Each one is very God.

Here we face the traditional notion of the "immanent Trinity," the view that the three persons of God's self are always co-existing. In, with, and under the creativity of God there is already present and active the liberator/reconciler God and the sanctifier God. God always relates in terms of the three-in-one. Trinity means, you are not "captivated" by God from one side only, but from all sides: naturally, historically, and spiritually.

This is what the eucharist in social location transmits. It is important for us to realize that in the historical struggle God is always driving us to the most creative power source, making us come alive from the dryness of soul in new soul-force, so that we become new persons reflecting the dynamics of a threefold God. This is the very bedrock of our personhood, of historical process, and global-village life. We need to redefine the terms of the Trinity in regard to God's justice struggle. How God creates justice in nature and history is not a phantom of the imagination, the teaching of the Trinity wants to say, but the very lifeblood, the bread and wine, of human existence.

The notion of the Trinity time and again grows out of this struggle. It is a metaphor for the heart of creation—for what is at the center of our own heart. We today think of persons in terms of personality. So we get far beyond what the original teaching was trying to say in speaking of "persons." God does not help us as three distinct "personalities." God stands by us in tremendously personal ways to make us just persons, always seeking to reach us in diverse ways. The notion of the triune God grew out of the struggles to preserve our sense of the "integrity" of God as God. But Christianity was quickly caught in the gamesmanship of speculation. "One God, three manifestations." "One God, no manifestation." Even, "Three Gods, three manifestations." It makes no sense. We cannot view the doctrine of the Trinity as uninvolved spectators. It is meant to be an "extension" of our God-walk in the realm of thought.

The church did not want to say: here is a mystery; we need to find a symbol for it. It proclaimed instead: here is a claim. But it is neither simplistic nor monolithic. So we need to describe it metaphorically. There is no way that reason can control this flexible God. But co-reason can sense the dynamics.

Many Christians reduce all Christian thought to christology, or worse yet, to Jesusology: Jesus is God. But that quickly leads to new idolatry or at least unfruitful speculation. The issue is not whether Jesus is God. The point is whether God, together with Jesus, continues to be engaged in today's social and personal struggles. The Christian enterprise did not start among privileged academics. It emerged among extremely handicapped persons. There are still today the physically and economically handicapped, the nonpersons, the marginals of all kinds. But there are also the handicapped of the soul, those who have cancer of the soul or whose spiritual happiness has been destroyed. They also belong to the silent caravan of the unknown and forgotten. It is where there is no center left, no way of self-help or self-affirmation, that God can be sensed as the bedrock of our life, of body and soul, and of our social relationships. That is what the teaching of the triune God in nature, history, and the spirit is all about.

All of this makes sense only as it grows out of God-walk. In God-walk abstract language suddenly takes on some dynamics of clownish language. The person involved in God-walk is neither a hero nor a fool in the usual sense of the terms. But in this walk we all come close to being clowns. We know that God's reality does not wrest from us heroic seriousness. But we can "seriously" poke fun at the somber and funereal ways of "religious" persons the way Jesus could poke fun at his opponents (Luke 11:39–44). It is the puckish joy of making ourselves and others laugh in view of the incongruencies of human pretensions and divine grace.

We have to face the fact that the teaching of God as creator and the notion of the Trinity rooted in the creator God look equally dubious to modern science. Generally the prevailing idea in science is that of a massive explosion some ten or perhaps twenty billion years ago, or of some process continuum that does not even "know" of a beginning.[26] God-walk cannot be content simply with God as claim on the individual conscience. But God-walk senses that this claim is the power of creation that bears all things, groaning together with all creatures (Rom. 8:22). The claim intimates a suffering and sharing at the heart of the world that make things persevere in their course. Divine co-suffering urges us to live our life trustingly as handiwork of transcendent creativity (Ps. 19:1; Rom. 1:20). All things have an inherent dignity to which also science bears witness.

Tradition confronts us with peculiar needs to grasp the character of God, God's very heart. Is creation a decree of God's will or is it an emanation of God's love? To make us grasp the very character of God is the point of God's walk with us. When Adam and Eve "heard the sound of the Lord God walking in the garden" (Gen. 3:8), it was not God who was in hiding, but Adam and Eve. God walks openly among us. God is unconcealed. The whole story of God with creation and humankind in particular is the unconcealed walk of God from whom *we* hide. In this walk of God through history from creation through exodus to eschaton there is a self-realization of God offered to us that we can gratefully acknowledge as an embodiment of the heart of God as the heart of creation, the very presence of the triune God.

Jürgen Moltmann has suggested an understanding of God that combines the notion of decree and the notion of emanation.[27] The will and being of God are united in that God's life is the life of the eternal infinite love that in the creative process steps out of its trinitarian perfection.[28] In social location at the eucharist we arrive at perhaps a similar emphasis but with special awareness of God's self-limitation, deprivation, or impoverishment. God in Christ at the eucharist certainly embodies God's character as pure act (*actus purissimus*). God can be thought of here only in terms of sovereign activity, which at the same time is the elemental ground of creation. God's bringing creation into being is characteristic of the divine self-determination, not an arbitrary decree. Yet it is at the same time the wisdom of divine self-limitation that makes justice the bedrock issue of the relationship between creator and creature.

The elementary dynamics of the eucharist is holy communion-*koinonia*. God here acknowledges both nature and history: the elements of the field and the elements of a shared human life. The bread and the wine are not mere instrument, but sacrament. They are part of the mystery, the *koinonia*, as much as human beings are. This communion is the inner rationale of God's being, which does justice to every element of God's creation in the wisdom of God's self-limitation.

God creates because God finds it unjust to be alone. Can we understand it in analogy with God's saying of Adam: "It is not good that the man should be alone; I will make him a partner fit for him" (Gen. 2:18)? It is also not good for God to be alone. It is good that there be companions. Companionship is just. Creation, one might say, is a divine act to show that God as companion is just. There is no point in keeping all power for oneself. Only idols would want to. To be God means to be power-sharing, life-sharing, labor-sharing. It is "just not fair" to be God Alone. And yet God does not overpower the creature in the sharing. There is also God's self-limitation. Creatures have an integrity of their own.

God's character is ultimately defined neither by self-glorification blazing forth resplendence nor by self-offering (God's love spilling over as creation). God is justice. But God is not justice without love. So we might say, God is justice/love. But God loves because divine justice is unthinkable without love for the creature, especially the creature that suffers injustice. It is the struggle for justice that marks God's character. God created in order to bring about a just world.

Human sin interferes. But God is not "derailed" from pursuing the divine course. God's cross in Messiah Jesus shows that there never was a "moment" when God was not related to the human dilemma. There never was in eternity a situation of divine bliss not watermarked by the cross. God wants the creature to live, not to perish. Because of this justice, there is no antecedent in the divine life preceding the cross. God is involved with human limitation from the very beginning. This is love. But God loves because in justice God affirms the integrity of the creation. This is the essence of "justification." The heart of creation permeates history: "Thy justice like mountains, high soaring above. . . . "

Omnipotence, omniscience, and *omnipresence* as attributes of God in God-walk are no longer abstract notions about what we do not know. They indicate the constant turning of the creator God to the creature. The danger today is not so much that we have a false notion of omnipotence as that we try to absorb it into ourselves and play God.[29] Modern thought is an exercise in that direction. As far as *God's* omnipotence is concerned, it is God's power to share divine power, so that creatures can influence God while God cooperates with creatures. Part of the divine self-determination remains self-limitation.

God, however, does not withdraw. There is always the divine presence, the *omnipresence*. Things are held together—as are human beings. "The Lord is your keeper" (Ps. 121:5). In fact, it is a powerful keeping: "The sun shall not smite you by day, nor the moon at night" (Ps. 121:6). God stands by even the worst loser, the most devastated and utterly rejected creature. But this is not experienced as sheer almightiness, *potentia absoluta*. The self-limitation of God allows creatures to develop in their own right. Ian Barbour, reflecting process philosophy views, says that "nature has flexibility as well as structure, openness and novelty as well as regularity. . . . *Atomic indeterminacy* is a characteristic of nature, and not simply of our limited human knowledge."[30] Besides the bearing or keeping of all things (sharing the *omnipresence*), there is an opening for sharing in divine power (*omnipotence*).

But there is also the issue of the divine knowledge:

O Lord, thou hast searched me and known me! Thou knowest when I sit down and when I rise up; thou discernest my thoughts from afar. Thou searchest out my path and my lying down, and art acquainted with all my ways. Even before a word is on my tongue, lo, O Lord, thou knowest it altogether. Thou dost beset me behind and before, and layest thy hand upon me. Such knowledge is too wonderful for me; it is high, I cannot attain it [Ps. 139:1–6].

Besides the bearing of creation and the "unlocking" of creation, there is also the knowing of the heart of creation, sensed by conscience. This is where *omniscience* suggests itself.

Omnipotence, omniscience, and omnipresence in *theo-praxis* merely describe the premise for God-walk throughout humankind. We dare not see everyone locked into Messiah Jesus as *the* mode of God. We see millions of humans struggling with the *integrity* of God the creator apart from Jesus. Jews do not see Jesus as representation of God the creator and yet have a genuine encounter with God. There is a *bearing* of creation, an *opening up* of creation, and a *knowing* of creation that conscience senses *on its own terms*. The theo-praxis dynamic is not tied to the Christian church establishment. Yet conscience—of the Christian as of any other human being—is also time and again benighted by sin. No human being singlehandedly breaks through to the full grasp of the heart of creation and the heart of history. The liberation dynamic has to come into play, as it did in Israel and in the church.

In theo-praxis, the notion of God the creator grows out of the need to come to grips with our *inexcusability*. The fact that we are inexcusable (Rom. 1:20) becomes clear when we realize that omnipotence, omniscience, and omnipresence do not pertain to God as an "other," but to God sharing in and bearing creation. We have no reason not to be aware of what goes on inside history and creation, except for sin, which is inexcusable.

These reflections, in conclusion, focus on the two basic models available in tradition as to the nature of creation. The elementary puzzlement is the *relationship* of God and the created world. God-walk forces us into a hard thought process. John Macquarrie, for example, wants to combine two models, the creator model and the effulgence model, creation and emanation. The creation model can easily be grasped. There is an artisan crafting an object. Emanation, however, is a pouring-out of something. Macquarrie fears that creation models have too much of the watchmaker notion about them. So he turns to the idea of emanation, which suggests "the immanence of God in the creation."[31] What does it mean? God is involved in the stone, the tree, and the sun?

Macquarrie admits that, "an image of pure emanation probably goes too far . . . and leads us toward a pantheism in which all things are part of God."[32] So what does emanation say? God is partly one with creation, partly not?

It is unfortunate that Macquarrie does not discuss the mode and models of God's creative work before his analysis of the attributes of God. Omnipresence probably appears in the discussion because of Macquarrie's emanation model preference. It ought not to be taken "objectively to mean that God is diffused through space like some all-pervasive ether, but again that [God] is not tied to the factical situation that is a basic characteristic of our human 'being there.' "[33] Much of what we find in nature certainly reminds us of a beauty we would like to relate to God: the marvel of the sunrise and the sunset, the hue of the sky and mountains "high soaring above." Yet we also find much that is repulsive, nature red in tooth and claw, creatures preying on each other and destroying each other. If God's emanation is in creatures, it puts a lot of cruelty into God. So emanation remains an awkward model, to say the least. It reflects a theoretical approach to God.

In theo-praxis God appears not as effulgent being, but as motivation. In God-walk, we are motivated to see the world moving toward purpose. Captivation takes place here. The model is not emanation, but *concurrence*.

An unimaginably "just" claim urges the world on and accompanies it in ever-new movements of justice. We recall that faith in the creator is reawakened conscience focused on transcendent co-suffering. What concurs with our life draws us out of our isolation, egotism, privatism, and individualism, so that we become co-walkers with God through history. That is what faith in the creator as triune God offers us.

Often faith in the creator among Christians is mostly a sentimental gushing over the beauty of the earth and the glory of the skies. We are emotionally overwhelmed when we sing, "Peace I ask of thee, O river, peace, peace, peace." Faith in the creator God lifts us up in view of the grandeur of nature. Yet faith in the creator, in terms of theo-praxis, sets priorities with regard to working together with God for peace among humankind and working together with God for peace in nature. God's concurrence evokes our concurrence in justice work, which today is especially focused on peace.

It is estimated that more than half of all U.S. scientists are in one way or another involved in research connected with armaments. Exact figures are hard to come by. The likelihood is that between five and ten million Americans "now earn their livelihoods, directly or indirectly, preparing for nuclear war."[34] With SDI on the horizon, the number will increase rapidly. There are complex arguments possible on the elementary level of God-walk at this point, but the issue is very simple. Is nuclear armament the right use of nature—in view of God's concurrence with nature? Catholic Bishop Leroy T. Matthieson of Amarillo, Texas, years ago asked workers at the local Pantex plant, which assembles all the nation's nuclear weapons, to consider resigning. An ordained deacon of the diocese who had worked at the plant for ten years felt the pressure. He acknowledged that for months he had done considerable soul-searching over his job and had decided he was doing nothing wrong. He also asked to become an inactive deacon rather than give up his livelihood. Will we judge him harshly? We are all involved as citizens in the support of our government. We can only remind each other with Father Berrigan: "Americans have to hear something very simple. Thou shalt not kill." In terms of God-walk we will emphasize the positive side of this commandment in view of God as creator: God affirms life because God *is* life. We have no right to destroy the divine-human creation.

At bottom our Western attitude toward nature is at stake. The observations of an American Indian can express better than a long analysis where our attitude toward nature is wanting:

We shake down acorns and pinenuts. We don't chop down trees. We only use dead wood. But the white people plow up the ground, pull up the trees, kill everything. The tree says, "Don't. I am sore. Don't hurt me."

But they chop it down and cut it up. The spirit of the land hates them. . . . The Indians never hurt anything, but the white people destroy it all. They blast rocks and scatter them on the ground. The rock says, "Don't. You are hurting me." But the white people pay no attention. When the Indians use rocks, they take little round ones for their cooking. . . . How can the spirit of the earth like the white man? Everywhere the white man has touched it, it is sore.[35]

It is not my wish to idealize American Indians. We all are fallible humans. But they knew what course nature followed for life. They knew human limits as well as possibilities set by nature. They were aware of God's concurrence, and many of them have kept this awareness alive in spite of white oppression, deprivation, and forced assimilation. As we reflect on the triune God in God-walk, a similar awareness ought to be possible. God captivates and motivates us in *presence, power,* and *rationale* for the nurturing and sustaining of life.

There are millions who argue for the necessity of building atomic warheads. Christian arguments against it are usually drawn from the Sermon on the Mount and similar biblical sources. But faith in God the creator is the most crucial "argument." God does not appear as "God of the gaps"—an explanation of things when they cannot be explained otherwise. God is in the midst of the fray, so that justice and its peace may prevail. Where we reverse the crucial life-saving directions of the natural process we stand convicted of our criminality.

Creation, it seems, *makes us accountable to itself.* Having gone through an immensely complex development from cells and microorganisms of millions of years to the forms of human life we know today, nature asks us for our concurrence in its dynamics. But we still view ourselves as very much outside this whole process of life. Now a moment has come when we can discover ourselves as nothing else but *evolution become conscious of itself.*[36] That is, we now have the responsibility for furthering the forms that enhance life through justice because God as the inside of creation urges us on.

God-walk sensitizes us to this awareness in great intensity. There is no longer anything theoretical about God or creation behind which we could hide. A harsh truth/untruth struggle takes place even on the basic level of faith in the creator God. We are motivated by the divine processes that ceaselessly create and nurture life to become accountable to life itself. The very fabric of creation is shaping us for participation in the justice struggle of God together with Messiah Jesus.

We need to remember that throughout the centuries there has been much projection of omnipotence on God, as indicated earlier with regard to Emperor Constantine. Many of these projections have reappeared in contemporary humankind. Human beings who use controlling reason to run their technocracy in our Western society have attributed omnipotence to themselves. It is impossible to reconcile their view of themselves as god with a Christian view of God.

2

CHRISTO-PRAXIS

The Roots of Christology

John Wesley exclaims in one of his sermons: "Can anything be more absurd than for men to cry out, 'The Church! The Church!' and to pretend to be very zealous for it and violent defenders of it while they themselves have neither part nor lot therein, nor indeed know what the Church is?"[1] It is always critical for Christian thought to have part in the reality referred to. We can say of Christ what Wesley said about the church: "Can anything be more absurd than for people to cry out, 'The Christ! The Christ!' and pretend to be violent defenders of Christ while they themselves have neither part nor lot therein, nor indeed know who the Christ is?" Christian teachings, we said, are always *word-deeds* reflecting the justice-labor of God. Teachings about Christ can only reflect the effort for justice that God is engaged in together with Christ. The words we use contain the reality itself. The empowerment issuing from Messiah Jesus is always present in his word and the word of his witnesses. There is a mystery. But there is no mystification.

It is important to decide whether we shape Messiah Jesus or let Messiah Jesus shape us. We never know beforehand, not even a little, who Jesus can be. In all teaching and preaching we need to ask ourselves: Are we making Christ (Messiah Jesus) a code word for our ego? Are we preaching Christ or only mirroring ourselves? In the training for ministry we can put the same question to biblical studies, church history studies, or pastoral care. Are these studies shaping Christ? Or is Christ shaping them?

Facing this very obvious issue compels us to reflect on the very character of what we usually call christology. Today there is much debate about how to approach christology. Usually the distinction is made between a christology "from above," starting with the preexistent Logos, and a christology "from below," starting with the human Jesus. There is also the possibility of moving from the inside out instead of going from the outside in. This is the approach of the eucharistic method. We begin with the eucharist in social location. Here we are confronted with the agency of God in Christ under the bread and wine—a "stronghold in times of trouble" (Ps. 9:9).

I do not wish to bypass the difficulties of the quest of the historical Jesus. But our first task cannot be to get a minimum or maximum of fact. Jesus of Nazareth as Messiah Jesus is not mediated to us through historical study as such. If we do not begin with the very real presence of Messiah Jesus, no research as such will produce the reality of what the church is rooted in. The Christian scriptures describe the shape of Jesus' public ministry. The eucharist communicates it in worship. Whatever language is used, whatever data are mentioned, the elementary shape of Jesus' ministry wants to communicate no more than two things: (1) who God is and the human being, and (2) how the two interact.

It will be good to stay with Macquarrie's approach as a backdrop in order to discover the fork in the road we are facing today. For Macquarrie, from this fork on, the historical question is simple. On the minimal assertion about the historical Jesus (that there was indeed such a historical individual who suffered under Pontius Pilate and whose manner of life was adequately portrayed in the Gospels) depends the question whether the Christian way of life is an actual possibility and therefore to be taken seriously, or whether it is merely an idealized possibility. The true way of living human life depends on some pattern that demands *imitation*.

Jesus here becomes an example of a way of life. We get a picture that outlines the way we need to act. It would be easy to say: This is not enough, Christ is more. The issue is whether we are here looking in the right direction. The liberal approach is tempted to replace Christ as the object of worship (the Pantocrator of the medieval church) with Christ as the object of imitation (whereby we understand that imitation was also an issue in the medieval church; we are not dealing here with an absolute either/or).

In social location at the eucharist we realize that Messiah Jesus is not the object of worship or of imitation, but the subject of captivation. We are gripped by a new reality. Messiah Jesus presents us with God and in God he presents us with a new human selfhood. We receive a new energy center. It yields soul-force we have not been able to put to use before. The root of christology is a particular kind of praxis.[2] God in Christ walks us into a new selfhood that we can call christo-praxis.[3]

There is a common basis here for several christologies. One can only wish that Christians would make more use of the common basis. Macquarrie too might agree. He quotes Bultmann's view of Jesus:

> Characteristic for him are exorcisms, the breach of the Sabbath commandment, the abandonment of ritual purifications, polemic against Jewish legalism, fellowship with outcasts such as publicans and harlots, sympathy for women and children; it can also be seen that Jesus was not an ascetic like St. John the Baptist, but gladly ate, and drank a glass of wine. Perhaps we may add that he called disciples and assembled about himself a small company of followers—men and women.[4]

The issue is in which location we read these words. If we find ourselves at the eucharist in the company of the poor Christ, the core of the Bultmann reflections is the point that Jesus has fellowship *with outcasts*. There were all kinds of outcasts, not just publicans and harlots. It takes a completely different selfhood to be able to have outcasts as part of one's self. We also tend to forget that there are many who are not outwardly handicapped, and yet they are very much handicapped in their souls.

This is where the God-walk dimension stands out in bold relief. There is a social location of Jesus that is the basis of everything else said about him. This is the root of all christology. I appealed to Adolf Deissmann before:

> Primitive Christianity, alike in its leading personalities and in the prepondering number of its adherents, was a movement

of the lower classes. The water of life did not filter down from the upper level to the many and insignificant . . . The first to drink of it were fainting stragglers from the great caravan of the unknown and forgotten.[5]

We can put it even more drastically: "The scum of Palestinian society . . . constituted the majority of Jesus' followers" (Elisabeth Schüssler Fiorenza).[6] In the eucharist we so easily tend to make Jesus a cult figure, a neutral ghost who in some heavenly cloud escapes all human reality. But actually in this celebration Jesus comes to us again at the head of the great caravan of fainting stragglers.

In the eucharist of the global village we inhabit, we are sensitized to what has long been forgotten by the church as a whole. Primitive Christianity still had a holistic grasp on the eucharist, although St. Paul occasionally had to remind Christians that it was not a mere meal (1 Cor. 11:20). Each major period in the history of the church that followed brought out different aspects of Jesus: (1) The early Catholic Church issuing in the medieval church stressed the very close relationship between God and Jesus. (2) The Reformation emphasized that God was acting in this Jesus for the justification of the sinner. (3) Modern Christianity tended to stress Jesus as example—say, as "master-workman of the race" or the gentle man from Galilee. (4) Neoorthodoxy reacted to Modern Christianity by reintroducing the major emphases of the past in order to correct modern rationalizations, oversimplifications, and reductionism.

Primitive Christianity understood these points: the close relationship between God and Jesus, the way God acted in Jesus, and the impact Jesus had on the shaping of humanity. What it could not forget was that God in Jesus entered the struggle for justice among the lowly. The losers in life belonged to God as well as did the spiritually lost. God realized divinity in history by being just to the outcasts and rejects—simply by including them, whereas the religionists of Jesus' day avoided them for whatever reason. It was not they who said: "Come to me, all who labor and are heavy laden" (Matt. 11:28).

At the root of christology there is the harsh tension between religionists and disciples. Moving in Christian thought from the inside of the eucharist out toward us, Jesus' presence includes the outcasts genuinely participating in his selfhood.[7] This means, though, the losers' presence in Jesus does not primarily say something about our Christian way of life, but *about God*. The shape of Jesus' public ministry is the basic shape of God's activity. It takes account of the human predicament in sin and evil, and shows God as liberator/redeemer.

At the root of christology lies Jesus' selfhood offering us a grasp of God's selfhood and human selfhood. Liberal theology tends to view the relationship between human selfhood and Jesus' selfhood in terms of evolution. For Macquarrie, christhood is "a kind of transcendent anthropology . . . with christhood as the goal toward which created existence moves."[8] The difficulty that arises is that we get here "a parallel between selfhood and christhood."[9] The human selfhood is not viewed as having been reconstituted by Jesus. So there is a direct line of ascendency between the human self and God's self. Christhood is seen "as coming about through a process of growth."[10] But what of "sin"? What if our conscience has been so numbed and our growth so stunted that our soul-force is drying up?

What Messiah Jesus offers is a corporate self that is all-inclusive:

> For he is our peace, who has made us both one, and has broken down the dividing wall of hostility, by abolishing in his flesh the law of commandments and ordinances, that he might create in himself one new person in place of the two, so making peace, and might reconcile us both to God in one body through the cross, thereby bringing the hostility to an end [Eph. 2:14-16].

All the gentiles were "outcasts" in Jesus' "church." But now it became clear God has included all in human selfhood. God has created a new condition.

The root of christology is not only the oneness of the Child or the Logos with the Father and the inclusion of general human nature in the godhead. It is the inclusion of the heavy laden, the outcasts, the marginals, and the rejects together with everyone else in what God views as human selfhood. In Messiah Jesus it is part of God's own selfhood. So the struggle for justice is part of God's very character.

We can agree with the first two emphases of traditional christology mentioned before: (1) God and Jesus are very close. (2) God justifies the sinner in Jesus. But we cannot see Jesus merely as an example or the "pinnacle" of human growth. Modern Christianity has often forgotten that Jesus is God's presence in all of history and all of humanity (viewed eucharistically), not to speak of the cosmos as a whole. We cannot imitate this presence, but need to discover ourselves as participants in its activity.

The Core of Christology

What does christology look like from the eucharist as social location? The whole development of Chrisian thought from Nicea onward goes far beyond the datum we have been focusing on. We need to take it into account, but we also dare not let it mislead us. We are no longer permitted from a religionist perspective to add more christological metaphysics to an already mystifying cult symbol. The issue is: Which thought grows crucially out of God-walk? The teachings of the early church—though we have to view their shortcomings critically—are basically the framework within which discipleship makes sense also today. That is our premise.

It is difficult to understand the impact of christology as finally formulated at Chalcedon in 451 c.e. Of course it is a historical product. We can draw out the development of ideas that led up to this doctrinal event. The church faithfully tried to formulate its understanding of the origins of Christianity in reaction to what it viewed as aberrations. If one does not keep these aberrations in mind, one does not understand the christological reasoning. The mystery of God could not be unpacked in ideas. But in the midst of the clash between truth and untruth at least misrepresentations of Messiah Jesus could be excluded.

Ultimately, we might say that the church at Chalcedon overlooked an important aspect of the primitive christo-praxis. But we have to respect that Chalcedon helped the memory of the elementary historical configuration to survive. Christianity, in the environment in which it arose, considered the world an evil age. Jesus Christ "gave himself for our sins to deliver us from the present evil age" (Gal. 1:4). The first Christians expected the world to pass away quickly.

Yet at the same time the collective memory of the founder generation carved out, as it were, a "piece of sacred reality" from the evil age. In Messiah Jesus it had already happened. In God's deprivation—the Word becoming flesh—there was a "demarcation line" drawn around God's justice. This "piece of reality" was holy. God had set Jesus apart. Here was a unique historical configuration of personhood that humankind would never forget. However faintly, however clumsily, the christological creed of Chalcedon tried to carve out in words that same sacred spot within reality. For Christianity there is a distinct place in reality as a whole that is not a sheer metaphysical puzzle, but the space in which God works holistically on conscience in all human beings.

It is clear that the Nicene Creed (325 C.E.) and its subsequent interpretations were not written in terms of persons who were becoming "aware of their common lot with the lower classes."[11] There is not the slightest hint in the creed of God's identification with the poor. The creed offers merely an idea-framework for christo-praxis. It keeps our ideas about Messiah Jesus within a definite "demarcation" line. Today our thoughts are made to stray away from christo-praxis in countless ways. Our society is permissive in human rights as well as consumption, in civil rights as well as sex. Our social injustice is interdependent with our private injustice toward ourselves or within the nuclear family. The Christian community cannot change all that. Realism dictates that we face an immoral society and an immoral individual as well. Yet the Christian community points to a *space* in history and in reality as a whole where injustice is being overcome, where God continues to struggle against all manner of evil. There is a sanctuary where Jesus, the refugee, is our refuge. God-walk is therefore a sanctuary movement.

The Nicene Creed wants to speak of God in Messiah Jesus as real among us. But we cannot "sense" this God apart from the reality of the eucharist. We have to stop imposing the Jesus of dogmatics and the "historical Jesus" of scholarship on our worship. God-walk is informed by the Holy-Spirit-Jesus, the Jesus who meets us in the worship of the church through the sharing of the elements of creation in bread and wine as the human being truly alive. It is from this inside that we have to move out into the creed. All we get from the creed again is the invitation to look for God as real among us.

On this basis, there is no dogmatic point as an end in itself. Facing the reality of God in worship we are enlisted in a very concrete process of argument: If God is struggling for justice and faithfulness in the world, how can we not notice the downtrodden and not be faithful in our most intimate relationships?

Yet as far as the dogma itself is concerned, we had better understand what it wanted to guard and guard against lest we fall prey to similar aberrations of thought. The church from Nicea to Chalcedon developed its ideas in Greek terms basically rooted in philosophy. God's struggle in history was not the point of the debate. The church wanted to guard the "divinely carved-out" space that sets the Christian view of reality apart from other views. But it did not describe its most crucial content and dynamics.

With these caveats in mind, I proceed to comb through a few of the more subtle points of the debate. Nicea established that Christ was pre-existent. It did this in a formal way. It said nothing about how the Christ-Logos moves through history. It was difficult to nail down the pre-existence conceptually. The problem was how it related to the humanity of Jesus. The church felt compelled to reject two major aberrations, that of Nestorius (patriarch of Constantinople) causing a controversy from 428-433 about Christ as a *double being*, and that of Apollinaris of Laodicea (d. 385/95?) who contended that Christ took on only *one physis* (nature). A modified monophysite view was held by Eutyches (in a 448–451 controversy) to the effect that at least after the incarnation only one *physis* is discernible. These were aberrations of speculation against which the church held that the incarnate Logos in Jesus is not a Nestorian *double* being, as of two persons, nor a *fusion* of two beings into one nature, but one person, though divine and human. Facetiously put, the church rejected the notion of transcendent Siamese Twins as well as that of a transcendent mule, a cross between the divine and the human.

Facing a maze of weird speculation, Chalcedon tried conclusively to retain the integrity of both the divine and the human involved in Messiah Jesus:

> One and the same Christ, Son, Lord, only-begotten, to be acknowledged in two natures, inconfusedly, unchangeably, indivisibly, inseparably; the distinctions of natures being by

no means taken away by the union, but rather the property of
each nature being preserved, and concurring in one Person
and one Sub-sistence, not parted or divided into two persons,
but one and the same Son, and only-begotten, God the Word,
the Lord Jesus Christ.

The point made is fairly clear: God and humanity are not confused in Christ (Christ is not a monophysite being), but they are
also not divided (as a double being). There is one common life. God
and humanity in Jesus interact and interpenetrate similar to the
persons of the Trinity. Remaining distinct, the two "natures" constitute one personal life. It is more than a mystical union (where
fusion is intended) or a moral union (where two parties remain
basically separate).

Not very much is being said in these creeds, it seems, except that
one senses how they struggle for the integrity of God's sacred space.
What we here view conceptually, originally was grasped dynamically. If we conceptualize too much (double being or crossbreed
creature) we miss the point.[12] We want to be conceptually precise
and yet metaphorically imprecise at the same time in order to
convey the *power* of the underlying reality more adequately. The
abstract terms of Greek philosophical thought did not convey
much of the power. Nothing made the "inside" of Jesus' eucharistic presence come alive. It was hardly more than staking out the
space for a concrete encounter: these are the boundaries within
which we find the sacred. This is the way it has to be laid out so as to
enable us to inhabit it. The justice power we are offered does not
come to us "out of the blue," but is mediated through the unique
space God occupies, which the creed at best wanted to safeguard.

Under the circumstances, that was all the creeds could convey at
the time in their no-nonsense way. Whereas with modern liberalism
the dilemma is that we pretend to know *beforehand* why Messiah
Jesus can be little more than a human being, with orthodoxy we *do
not know much of the human at all*. Here the human is not only
subservient to the divine, but is practically absorbed by it. God-
walk therefore tries carefully to delimit the function of the creed
while preserving its demarcating intention. We sense that it wants to
communicate the power of God. It wants to be faithful to God as
sacred space in our lives. But for our day it often communicates

hardly more than a somewhat puzzling conceptualized cult symbol.

The bothersome drawback can best be pinpointed in reference to later interpretations of Chalcedon—for example, the so-called *enhypostasia*, which literally would mean *in*-personality of Christ, the human personhood of Christ within the divine personhood. Chalcedon, in the end, stood for the *im*personality of Christ as human being, the human person only subsisting in the divine. Philip Schaff writes:

> The meaning of this doctrine is that Christ's human nature had no independent personality of its own, besides the divine, and that the divine nature is the root and basis of his personality. There is, no doubt, a serious difficulty in the old orthodox christology. . . . We can conceive of a human nature without sin (for sin is a corruption, not an essential quality, of man), but we cannot conceive of a human nature without personality, or a self-conscious and free Ego; for this distinguishes it from the mere animal nature. . . . To an unbiased reader of the Gospel history, moreover, Christ appears as a full human personality, thinking, speaking, acting, suffering like a man (only without sin), distinguishing himself from other men and from his heavenly father.[13]

Schaff calls attention to a formidable dilemma when it comes to the humanity of Christ in the orthodox perspective based on Chalcedon. Orthodoxy was strong in clarifying the presence of God in Jesus. But the human seemed only a means to an end, a vessel for communicating the godhead, a means of revelation.[14] Liberalism tried to move into this vacuum.[15] It ended up with an exaltation of the individual human being, the human often almost controlling the divine.[16] The Jesus of the marginals was not allowed to cross the doctrinal threshold in either case.[17] It is here that a correction needs to be made.[18] The power of God that comes through in the creed, trying to define God's sacred space, needs to be joined to the new selfhood brought by Messiah Jesus—the corporate human selfhood that includes even the lowest of all.[19] In terms of the creed, Jesus assumes merely generic humanity. It is no more than an idea of humanity. It is especially troublesome, in that generic humanity was always understood in male terms only, just as the God of the *enhypostasis* was "male" in its abstraction, not granting the person of Jesus full humanity. Black theology has made the additional point that ultimately this male concept also more and more began to reflect a white view of the human. Yet the creed at least kept the church from turning Jesus into a merely human founder of another religious cult.

The Work and the Person: The Jesus Nobody Knows

As soon as we have sensed that the tradition of Chalcedon is insufficient for our day when it comes to the inclusion of suffering persons, of blacks, other minorities, and women, in the humanity of Messiah Jesus, we have committed ourselves to some hard rethinking. We need to underscore once more, though, that the strength of Chalcedon lies in the line it draws around the reality of God in Christ as "sanctuary" within reality as a whole. God-walk makes us aware of this very reality in conscience.[20] In the eucharist in social location we can also appreciate the concern of the creed to exclude idolatrous speculations. At the same time we notice that the creed itself can become a fetish. Reflection on the subject is crucial because Christianity has thoroughly been shaped by the Nicene-Chalcedonian outlook. The whole orthodox/liberal controversy can be explained on its terms.

For God-walk the major dilemma is that the formulas often seem to invite religious response, not discipleship; religious assent, not the sharing of justice. In terms of the Methodist quadrilateral, the aspect of experience is here too easily overlooked, not to speak of reason. That is why black and feminist theologies have little or no use for creeds. But we also need to point out that there is power witnessed to in the creed that could turn us in directions completely different from a straitjacketing orthodoxy.

In the eucharist we are time and again confronted with *the Jesus nobody knows*. Jesus comes to us ever anew under the bread and the wine as the one unknown—the way he first appeared to Peter, James, and Martha. Here we recognize the *shape of Jesus' public ministry*. This person reaches out to humanity as a whole, sharing himself with other "unknowns," invisible blacks, inaudible American Indians, inconspicuous women. The story of this person is important in creating faithful relationships—faithful to loved ones as well as the unloved, the unknown, the refugees. With the now inescapable cry of the poor in our midst, the poor Jesus may be introducing a *second stage* of christological formulation carrying us beyond Chalcedon.[21]

The person of Messiah Jesus cannot be seen apart from his whole work. There are the difficult problems of how much we can know about the historical Jesus.[22] But what clearly comes through to us from the eucharistic Jesus is that this person does not exist apart from faithful relationships. The personhood of Messiah Jesus is *not a metaphysical mystery*, but a *justice history*. Primarily we are not dealing here with a metaphysical anthropology (as in orthodoxy) or a transcendent anthropology (as in liberalism). We are confronted first of all with a particular praxis, the christo-praxis that coincides with theo-praxis.

Relationships are elementary here. It does not matter whether they are racial relationships, sexual relationships, or international relationships. For example, faithfulness in sexual relationships is stressed less and less by Protestantism as well as by Catholicism in North America. The fabric of many of our churches is so shot through with permissiveness that it is next to impossible to see the sacred reality witnessed to by the creed. *Time* observed as early as 1979: "In the U.S. generally, sexual pleasure has lately come to be regarded as a matter of personal gratification unconnected with social responsibility or, of course, sin. Even among U.S. Catholics the trend is toward the belief that any individual act whatever is acceptable if it can be thought to foster love or self-esteem and enrich the life of the participants."[23] The *normalcy* of unfaithfulness is all around us, almost part of "the air we breathe." The AIDS scare makes some doctors advocate monogamy and even continence at a time when pastors (and churches) are giving up on monogamy and continence. The irony of history. Christology is rarely seen to impinge on these matters. Christology without attention to christo-praxis here proves a meaningless abstraction. So it never becomes clear how Christ's humanity has much to do with faithful relationships. Justice is an all-pervasive issue.

Christo-praxis ties the work and the person of Jesus together from the beginning. What constitutes this person? His work. God's unity with the Logos incarnate is not a mechanical or automatic connection, "frozen," as it were, into the "nature" of divine being. The Jesus of the eucharistic scripture is truly human. Time and again his acts of faithfulness to God and of faithfulness toward the neighbor constitute his personhood. God enters in a peculiar way into this person as Word (Logos). The just solidarity of this person with humanity in embodying God's will for humankind is a sustained act of the whole person, of conscience and will, so that the unity of the divine and the human in Christ hinges on a *claim/response dynamic*. Unity is again and again constituted in faithful justice. This is the Jesus nobody knows.

The dilemma of our Christianity today is that Christian thought usually begins with some familiar formula or concept about Jesus in a theoretical way, mediated through divinity schools, Sunday schools, sermons, or evangelistic witness. We seldom let Jesus arise out of our walk issuing from the eucharist. I do not question the personal commitment of any Christian thinker. But it seldom is reflected upon in terms of its social location. When it comes to our teaching we have to understand that God-walk initially functions as shock treatment. It destroys some Jesus notions to which we cling. We have to steer clear of letting Jesus disappear in some "black hole" of mystery or letting him become too familiar. Not only familiarity breeds contempt, mystification does too. We do not respect what seems either too familiar or too weird. We have tried too hard to make something neat out of Jesus. A few lines by Philip Wylie about preachers nails down the problem:

> These simpering or clamorous windbags preach Christ the Redeemer, Christ the meek and mild, Christ who died for your sins . . . Christ the worker of miracles (who, since the invention of the steam engine, can work only spiritual and no physical miracles due to Ohm's law and the relation of hydrogen ions to acids) . . . Christ the physician, Christ the know-it-all, Christ the Miss Fix-it, Christ the mineral spring, Christ the autocrat of the breakfast table, and bingo on Friday night. They never preach, teach, screech, or beseech the truth, come hell or holy water.[24]

We need to learn that we dare not make Jesus over in our own image. God makes Jesus significant for us in unexpected ways. What God does together with Jesus we can discover only in being "co-workers" ourselves (1 Cor. 3:9).

This sounds as though we assume we have *the* answer. The opposite is true. We have the question. Any christology today has to be christology after Auschwitz.[25] The German people had a highly sophisticated church. Christology was "on the books" everywhere. And yet it did not bring the Jews and the Germans closer together. It certainly did not keep the state from persecuting the Jews. It had been forgotten that Messiah Jesus was tied inextricably to his Jewish people. What he had done, he had done first of all as a Jew. He had brought God very close. He had brought God's end-time activity into the present: "If it is by the finger of God that I cast out demons, then the kingdom of God has come upon you" (Luke 11:20). God's kingdom had not come in the governing Roman empire, but in a conquered country with the Romans as occupiers. God was very near in a Jew, a member of an occupied people. Here was embodied eschatology.

Jesus became Messiah exactly by bringing God's justice, promised to Israel, to bear on all human beings, even the most despised and rejected, until he had become one of the rejected himself. We can have Jesus apart from the Nicene/Chalcedonian *homoousios* (same with God). But we cannot have Jesus without the Jews. That is why the Hebrew scriptures always stayed with the church. The church of the "German Christians" wanted to have an Aryan God without the Jewish people. Earlier, Schleiermacher had wanted a God without the Jewish people.[26]

In God-walk we realize that *Messiah Jesus* means: we become part of the Jewish people, God's promises and God's keeping of the promises. We saw the significance of Chalcedon in the sacred space, the sanctuary it keeps open for God. Now we can say that it is this space of the God of Israel that we enter in God-walk, of the God of justice and love. As far as the humanity of Messiah Jesus is concerned, it is first of all Jewish humanity in terms of a caring justice, the inclusion of the widow and orphan, the oppressed and the outcast. It is this humanity that finally does not stop to include all rejected and lost, also among the gentiles.[27] In this sense, there is a *radical difference* between the Messiah-Jesus-humanity and our humanity. We do not constitute our selfhood the way Jesus does.

We cannot grasp the Messiah Jesus person apart from the work. A Messiah-Jesus-humanity presents an all-inclusive corporate self. Schubert Ogden wrote a book on *Christ Without Myth* (1961). In his finely honed view Jesus is defined entirely in terms of universal human selfhood. "Christian faith is to be interpreted as man's original possibility of authentic existence as this is clarified and conceptualized by an appropriate philosophical analysis." Some general anthropology is the base. Its core is authentic existence. According to Ogden, "the doctrine of revelation must be formulated rather differently from the ways in which it has traditionally been presented. [It is] . . . necessary to affirm that authentic human existence, or faith in Christ, can be realized apart from faith in Jesus or in the specific proclamation of the church."[28] The person of Jesus is defined as an authentic expression of universal human existence. We first know authentic existence as such. Jesus is then made to fit in.

Dare a christology in our Lenten age proceed this way? Ogden's Christ realizes the selfhood that is the potential reality of every person's life. Christ realizes Adam, as it were. Jesus is "nothing less than the God-man relationship that is the essential reality of every human life."[29] Or, "Jesus is the decisive re-presentation of the truth of man's existence."[30] Humans, according to Ogden, already have a measure of self-understanding in a divine-human relationship. We all know the possibilities of our existence. Jesus is clearly a fine manifestation of it. In this approach, reason is very much *controlling reason*. Christology here at best is some transcendent anthropology. Jesus expressed the basic human selfhood.

In God-walk, we are not first of all attuned to authentic existence or universal human selfhood, but to the Jewish selfhood of Messiah Jesus. It is a selfhood not disconnected from human self-understanding. But it is a new selfhood because it goes beyond the imperial self that seeks its own legitimation. Here is a corporate self of justice/love that is *other* than our individual self.

The Jesus nobody knows: never was this Jesus more needed than after Auschwitz. Messiah Jesus is not the familiar buddy of every Westerner. We do not find in him what we already know of our innermost self. Schweitzer was right, Messiah Jesus comes to us as "one unknown." Adam is only a *typos tou mellontos* (Rom. 5:14), a foreshadowing of who was to come, a type of the coming, the truly human being. There is an analogy between Adam and Messiah Jesus, but not ultimate identity. In Messiah Jesus we are confronted with what St. Paul calls a *kainē ktisis*, a new creation

(2 Cor. 5:17). In God-walk we cannot even say that essential or original human nature is found in Christ, not in Adam (as Barth put it in *Christ and Adam*).[31] In Messiah Jesus we are dealing with a radically new selfhood.

Christology after Auschwitz had better remember that the new selfhood of Messiah Jesus is a corporate selfhood: "When I am lifted up from the earth, I will draw everyone to myself" (John 12:32). The Jesus nobody knows wrests from controlling reason the definition of who we are and who others are. Who we are is the mystery of God in justice history, not our self-definition rooted in transcendent anthropology. Chalcedon understood one thing besides the "sacred space" of God carved out of reality as sanctuary: the personhood of Messiah Jesus is not defined by our normal identities. Jesus is a new identity center. But Chalcedon defined it individualistically, whereas Messiah Jesus of the gospel has been portrayed corporately. In consequence the Logos-Christ, no longer tied to the Jewish people, soared into ever more distant mystification, and—Germans killed Jews by the millions.

If we try to visualize how a "christo-praxis christology" differs from the modern position we can think of two circles. In the modern view they are concentric, the smaller one designating the Adam/Eve selfhood of humankind, the larger one the christhood self. The latter is here merely an expansion of the Adam/Eve self. In the christo-praxis position the two circles are not concentric, but separate from each other, though with comparable centers on the same level. The small circle again is the Adam/Eve self. The larger circle this time is the corporate selfhood of the Jesus nobody knows. There is a radical break between the two, yet, in terms of the circle shape, there is analogy in humanness. In con-science, the creativity on the side of Adam/Eve selfhood meets the new creativity coming from the side of corporate selfhood. Because of sin (the radical break between the two circles), con-science cannot be predicated on the elementary identity of the two circles. There is a "mutation" in humankind because of Messiah Jesus.

In moving from christo-praxis to christology we want to be aware of the difference between an intellectual game and an accountable teaching. Any christology that builds on familiarity between Jesus and us breeds contempt. Christo-praxis wants to guard against developing a christology that allows us to do with

Jesus whatever strikes our fancy. Do we face God? Or do we face merely ourselves refracted through rationalism or hedonism? Tradition offers us an emphasis on the uniqueness of the historical configuration that is Messiah Jesus. But in terms of the humanity of Messiah Jesus, Chalcedon formulated a paradigm insufficient for us today. In God-walk we realize that it takes Holy Spirit reality in full communion of the people gathered as congregation to make us see the significance of Messiah Jesus. Without corporate conversion there is no access to understanding: "You have died [in your old selfhood] and your life [your new selfhood] is hid with Christ in God" (Col. 3:3).

Christo-praxis is shaped around four basic notions. (1) It grows out of encounter with the shape of Jesus' public ministry in God-walk. (2) In God-walk we do not meet a metaphysical mystery, but a justice history. (3) The justice history confronts us with the "multipersonality" of Messiah Jesus, but now in terms of a claim/response dynamics. (4) There remains a radical difference between the corporate Messiah-Jesus-humanity and our individualistic humanity. Even so, Messiah Jesus is as truly human as he is truly divine.

As con-science is sensitized to the christo-praxis dynamics, we see God-walk developing in us around the triune encounter with God, the christo-praxis falling in line with the theo-praxis. Keeping in mind that we are never bereft of the Holy Spirit presence, there is also spirit-praxis involved. So in con-science encountering God, Messiah Jesus, and Holy Spirit we are aware of (1) the caring impulse (creation), (2) the sharing impulse (liberation), and (3) the daring impulse (re-creation).

Liberation-Atonement

As we focus on christology after Auschwitz, everything in tradition takes a new turn. It grows out of God-walk. For example, the eucharist in social location reminds us of the Suffering Servant Israel. We no longer view reality from mountaintop experiences, but only from Calvary. Here we do not encounter a neat religious formula, but a very corporate human event of fellow suffering. It immediately inserts us very deeply into the vast range of human suffering today, some of it self-inflicted, some of it simply happening and completely beyond our control, but much of it inflicted by others. Almost any encounter with our sisters and brothers from the Third World, including the Third World in our own midst, confronts us with an inescapable question: What do we do about abysmal poverty and want?

Christo-praxis takes us right into its center. As soon as we understand the poverty dynamics, it is impossible to go on with christology in terms of "business as usual." The church cannot do everything, but it can keep from blindfolding its eyes to human misery. In the face of so much pain there is the danger of shrugging our shoulders and saying: "We cannot help anyway. It's *their* problem." Then there is also the bleeding-heart syndrome that makes us assume we can bring about a new world in the nick of time if only we turn our mind to it.

What do we turn our mind to in God-walk? This is a very crucial issue with regard to understanding the implications of the person and work of Messiah Jesus. Edward Huenemann has written about the church:

> It is the emerging community of those not bound by the necessity of the status quo, not made powerless by idle dreaming, nor enervated by compromise and surrender to "realism," but those engaged in the struggle with the oppressed who can see through the self-deception of the powerful who know no power but their own and the defense of it—even and especially when that power is baptized in the name of Christ.[32]

The challenge is to find a new sense of fellow suffering. We do understand limits and limitations. But our inability to change *all* misery does not force us to resign ourselves to the way things are. And because at times we cannot change anything at all, we do not have to lose heart. To a large extent, human beings have made the world the way it is. We can try not to add insult to injury. There are three temptations we need to steer clear of. (1) The head-trip. Liberal theology rightly reminds us that we have to use reason, but it dare not become the be-all or catch-all, the "man in charge." (2) The guilt-trip. Those who ponder Third World publications might get sucked into a mire of guilt that has nothing to do with christo-praxis. (3) The bleeding heart–trip. There is often the idea that we somehow need to compensate for the sins of the fathers and mothers, and our own, by going about doing good, which can easily turn into condescension.

We have to approach the world as it is. Awakened con-science instantly might make us realize how each one of us is contributing to the misery—in gluttony, overconsumption, and in ignorance of "small is beautiful." It is crucial that we understand this wide world with all its poverty in sharing in the eucharist as our _social location_—the place where God has put us. In one of the great hymns of the church we sing over and over again: "This is my Father's world, and to my listening ears, All nature sings, and round me rings The music of the spheres. . . .This is my Father's world: He shines in all that's fair. In the rustling grass I hear him pass, He speaks to me everywhere." The world of humankind, the human family, is as much our Mother's world as our Father's. If we glorify the natural world of a "father" creator, we had better not forget that part of our social location includes the suffering mothers of the world and of God's history. We dare not get bogged down in nature mysticism or nature romance. As the God of Israel could "cry out like a woman in travail" (Isa. 42:14), so Jesus could compare himself to a mother hen (Matt. 23:37), offering justice and comfort.

All I am saying is, give justice a chance. The church bears its share of responsibility for the direction of history. Christians have a task. There is the task of the care of souls, and there is also the need of the poor. We no longer can meet this need through almsgiving-benevolence. We have to turn away from symptoms of poverty to causes. Poverty is first of all a systemic problem. Through the person and work of Christ—that is, the person in the light of the work—the systemic nature of human misery is being addressed as much as is individual misery. In discipleship we know that christology is for sharing the Good News through care for souls as well as for sick, hungry, or tortured bodies. Christology for our time can grow only out of christo-praxis.

It is within this context of christo-praxis that we realize how much we are dependent on Messiah Jesus' own praxis. Macquarrie has summarized the teaching of the church:

Christ the king, who wins his victory over the enslaving forces, is also Christ the prophet who gives us the "example" of obedience, but still more he is the priest who utterly gives himself as sacrificial victim and thereby brings right into human history the reconciling activity of God in a new and decisive manner.[33]

Understanding the work of Messiah Jesus is part of understanding his person. But we cannot construct the work from concepts as such. We behold Messiah Jesus in the eucharist at the center of the church. Here his work as an ongoing work of God in the church through the Holy Spirit confronts us time and again with a *new reality* between God and humankind, person and person, the individual and the neighbor. The history of the church has complicated in doctrine what at the center is very plain and direct as *new reality*, the "new wine" of God's inclusive justice (Matt. 9:17), and the new bread that is Messiah Jesus himself (John 6:35).

In the eucharist there is Messiah Jesus together with the gathered community, and there is Messiah Jesus *as* community (the body of Christ)—the corporate selfhood of God and humankind. It is full communion, communion in every aspect of Christian life. The crucial dilemma is that God's just order in relating to the creature has been usurped either by controlling reason or diffidence. There is a "falling out" between God and us, and among ourselves. We have exchanged the truth for a lie (Rom. 1:25). We do not live according to the justice of God. The exchange of truth for a lie is also the exchange of the corporate structure of selfhood for all kinds of privatisms, religious as well as secular.

In the eucharist we meet Messiah Jesus as the truth about our life, the one who does not usurp God through controlling, dominating reason or diffident, submissive reason. We are at odds, at variance, with God, either in terms of superiority or inferiority complexes. Our soul-force has dried up. We might also speak of disobedience. But the word "obedience" often gives the wrong impression, as though God wanted to "lord it over us." We misunderstand obedience as a false submissiveness. The point is, Messiah Jesus freely is not at variance with God, nor out of tune with God. It is exactly in the eucharist that we celebrate the at-oneness between Jesus and God. Jesus is the one person, in response to the claim of God, who embodies faithful listening (Latin, *obedire*) to God's word. This is the primal dynamics of the at-onement in the eucharist. In this sense the church speaks of Messiah Jesus as the prophet.

The reality of the unique person of Messiah Jesus in life, death, and resurrection is also real for us as he overcomes the evil in which we are caught up with each other as human beings. Jesus identifies with us in our destructive antagonisms, Jew and Samaritan, Jew and Roman, Jew and Gentile, elect and reject, rich and poor, man and woman, black and white. At the cross there were Jews as well as Roman soldiers. In the global village today we do not have to do anything but recognize Jesus' social location *as our very own*. In overcoming the dividing wall between human beings and all evil forces, the great victory over evil was won. God "disarmed the principalities and powers and made a public example of them, triumphing over them in him" (Col. 2:15). In terms of Ephesians 2:14ff., Christ as our peace is all that humankind is not. It is this reality of justice/peace we behold in the eucharist that accounts for the second great dynamics of the at-onement. The evil that has beset humankind as a dividing wall has been done away with. Here are assembled *in one* all human beings, poor and rich, reject and elect, black and white, women and men, and no one is just by herself or himself, not one—*except* the one Messiah Jesus. Here the church speaks of Messiah Jesus as king.

There is finally a third dimension we need to take into account. Sin as usurpation, whether as controlling reason or different reason, is an injury to God. Our God can be hurt. The injury has to be undone. Justice has to be reestablished. In that sense, Jesus has to heal the divine wound caused by our sins. It is not that a big divine ego would constantly have to be satisfied. Rather, the injury inflicted upon God needs to be stayed, straightened out. The wounded God needs to be made whole by a priestly healer. In this regard, the church speaks of Jesus as priest.

If one takes these three dimensions together in the encounter with the eucharistic Jesus, at-onement involves *liberation*. It frees us in the state of creation, in the structure of our individual life and interpersonally.[34] But at-onement also involves *salvation*. It offers each person eternal life, oneness with God. At no point is the issue a question of the social vs. the private as such, but of reality vs. illusion, of truth vs. make-believe, of corporateness vs. egocentricity.

Here we need to clarify the historical background of the atonement doctrine. It came to a head some six hundred years after Chalcedon in the work of Anselm of Canterbury (1033–1109). St. Anselm's approach is the most ripened fruit of Augustinian thought in the Middle Ages. One has to understand that Anselm's great goal was to discover the rationality of faith. He was concerned with "faith seeking understanding," searching for the logic of the atonement, wanting to demonstrate its rational necessity.

God created the human being as the rational being, Anselm argues. Human reason is able "to discern justice and injustice, good and evil, and between the greater and lesser good."[35] In one respect it means that human beings somehow can discern the mind of God. In another respect, and more importantly so for our purposes here, it means that rational existence is extremely valuable in the sight of God. "Now if it be understood that God has made nothing more valuable than rational existence capable of enjoying him; it is altogether foreign from his character to suppose that he will suffer that rational existence utterly to perish."[36] On account of sin, though, human beings have been dooming themselves to eternal death. So God had to find a way out for the most valuable creature. And more yet. God's *honor* was at stake in sustaining the life of this most valuable creature.

From this follows an important logical step: "Therefore it is necessary for [God] to perfect in human nature what he has begun. But this, as we have already said, cannot be accomplished save by a complete expiation of sin, which no sinner can effect for himself."[37] All this is, as it were, rooted in eternity. God is not taken by surprise (in the process) as the history of humanity unfolds. "For what man was about to do was not hidden from God at his creation; and yet by freely creating man, God as it were bound himself to complete the good which he had begun."[38] Yet though the omniscient God was not surprised, what the creature was going to do dishonored God.

Within this overall rationale a rather complex argument develops:

When we say that God does anything to avoid dishonor, which he certainly does not fear, we must mean that God does this from the necessity of maintaining his honor; which necessity is after all no more than this, viz., the immutability of his honor, which belongs to him in himself, and is not derived from another; and therefore it is not properly called necessity. Yet we may say, although the whole work which God does for man is of grace, that it is necessary for God, on account of his unchangeable goodness, to complete the work which he has begun.[39]

Anselm thought it logical for faith to assume that God does not will the death of the most valuable creature. But because God's honor has been tampered with by the sin of this creature, something has to be done about it. This leads to a blow-by-blow account of why God had to become a human being: "If it be necessary, therefore, as it appears, that the heavenly kingdom be made up of men, and this cannot be affected unless the aforesaid satisfaction be made, which none but God can make and none but man ought to make, it is necessary for the God-man to make it." As one reflects on the "great discovery,"[40] the notion of satisfaction reminds one of a duel. Not long ago, men who felt their honor had been tampered with challenged the insulting person to a duel. The medieval "theo-logic" apparently implied a similar notion of honor. Anselm's *social location* cannot be disregarded. He does not argue here with biblical categories. Hence, with the notion of making satisfaction to God, Anselm moves more in terms of his own logic.

Still there is a kernel of truth in the argument. Sin does injure God. The usurpation of God's power is a threat to God, whether by taking human control—the "male" temptation—or by submitting to a usurper—the "female" temptation. But that God's honor should be at stake is another matter. God is not like a medieval knight bowled over when honor has been tampered with. The notion of *doing satisfaction* to God's *honor* is misleading. Yet it is scriptural—and understandable for our day—that Messiah Jesus steps into the breach to create a new reality where God is not injured. Jesus stops the injuring, the interference, with God's activity.

Anselm's view is comparable to that of Chalcedon. He also "carves out" a piece of reality, God's sacred space, a sanctuary.

There is something happening above and beyond us in God personally when sin occurs. The universal structure of reality is being tampered with. In God-walk we cannot do without elementary orientation in God's "space," God's social location.

What is this space filled with? The labor of Messiah Jesus concurs with God's labor. Jesus' work is liberation-atonement. Jesus opens the space to show where God struggles for justice among all humankind. Jesus makes us not only one with God and neighbor, but liberates from sin by atoning for it, keeping sin from interfering with God's work. Messiah Jesus steps into the breach between God and humanity exactly at the point where we ought to be laboring together with God for a just world.

Jews and Christians

These liberation-atonement reflections dare not become part of sheer Christian monologues. The injury inflicted on God expresses itself in manifold ways. Today it is experienced especially in the relationship between Christian and Jew. The inroad on God's corporateness is felt as infraction of human corporateness. It is moving that members of the Jewish community now see Jewish thought and Christian thought intersecting exactly at the point of liberation theology. Dan Cohn-Sherbok thinks positive dialogue possible, because liberation theologians have returned to their Jewish roots in the Bible. They have stressed that they will not theorize abstractly about christological doctrines, but regard the earthly Jesus as starting point. Truth emerges as one follows Jesus' life. Liberation theology is not interested in analyzing Jesus' dual nature as God-man.

> For Jews, liberation theology thus offers a new orientation to Jesus. . . . In the past Jews and Christians have been unable to find common theological ground. Instead of attempting to build a bridge with Christianity, Jews have repudiated Christian claims about Jesus' divinity and Christians have denounced Jews for their unwillingness to accept Christ as their Savior.[41]

At heart the gospel is subversive in stressing the Israelite hope that domination of one human being—or one group—over another will end. It involves the elimination of poverty and oppression as a sign of the coming of God's kingdom, which is not something otherworldly. "Of central importance for Christian-Jewish encounter is the liberationist's insistence that the coming of the kingdom involves individual participation in the creation of a new world."[42] The kingdom becomes manifest in a moral order on earth. The human being is understood as a co-worker with God in the creation of the new world.

This is the crucial point of intersection between Jewish thought and liberation theology. An otherworldly conception of God's work is denied by both. The exodus is especially paradigmatic. God guides the outcast and the slave. God leads the people into freedom. Both Passover and Sabbath are reminders of the exodus. What is at stake is always human liberty and the ethical task. In this context faith is understood as response to God's will—participation in God's act of liberation:

> For Jews the emphasis on the concrete dimension of faith is vital. The Jewish hope lies in God's rule on earth. This is the goal of the history of the world in which the Jewish people have a central role. . . . As in liberation theology, the Jewish religion focuses on orthopraxis rather than theological orthodoxy. Theological speculation is not seen as authoritative; instead moral praxis is at the core of faith.[43]

From this basis Cohn-Sherbok sees the possibility of Jews and Christians working together as never before in areas of social concern. As God's suffering servant throughout the ages, the Jewish people are especially ready for social concern in solidarity with the poor. This has to be spelled out, however, with regard to the implications of liberation thought. For example, the reasons for a rejection of a developmental approach that does not get at the root of structural evil among classes and nations have to be articulated. The special needs of the black community, of other ethnic groups, and of women, call for attention. There is the decided advantage that a number of Jewish feminists have already worked on restructuring the role of women in traditional Judaism. In many respects it is widely understood, according to Cohn-Sherbok, that the hope for bliss in a future life is not the crucial point, but a better life on this earth for all oppressed, afflicted, and persecuted creatures.

The whole argument is a great step forward. Yet the question arises whether or not there is a tension between liberation-atonement and the moral emphasis of Cohn-Sherbok. Crucial is the notion that in the exodus God is leading the people. Christians struggle over how God leads *through Jesus* in history. Practically all we "know" from tradition in this regard comes from our Jewish heritage. For us today it is not Moses who is the prophet. Jesus is seen as prophet of a new exodus. He is also regarded as king and priest. God's leading is seen here as yet more complex than in Israel's history up to that point. Messiah Jesus as a particular configuration of history injected a new dynamics in Israel's history that those who continued his work as his disciples had to think through in terms of Israel's imagery. But it was not a theory that was first developed and afterward tested in moral praxis. It was a new orientation of the heart and the whole of life within the Jewish context. Reflection on this point cannot be an attempt to invite Jews "to accept Christ as their Savior."[44] We are compelled to give an account to ourselves of what happened in Jesus within Judaism that still impacts us today. Elisabeth Schüssler Fiorenza sums it up: "The Jesus movement articulates a quite different understanding of God because it had experienced in the praxis of Jesus a God who called not Israel's righteous and pious but its religiously deficient and its social underdogs."[45]

The point of Schüssler Fiorenza's argument is the observation that the Jesus movement had experienced God in the praxis of Jesus. Several Jewish understandings of God were now coinciding. At the center may lie an experience of God as sophia-God, wisdom-God. Says Schüssler Fiorenza:

> The earliest Jesus traditions perceive this God of gracious goodness in a woman's *Gestalt* as divine *Sophia* (wisdom). The very old saying, "Sophia is justified [or vindicated] by all her children" (Luke 7:35 [Q]) probably had its setting in Jesus' table community with tax collectors, prostitutes, and sinners, as well. The Sophia-God of Jesus recognizes all Israelites as her children and she is proven "right" by all of them.[46]

We cannot come to terms with the sophia-praxis if we understand it merely as moral praxis of human beings. The yield of the argument is a different understanding of God. God's self-realization involves a divine self-limitation. There is the self-limitation of God to the broken bodies of the poor, represented by the broken body of Jesus and the bread Jesus offers at the eucharist. In a very definite way, the sophia-God is the self-limited God—limited to the elements of a suffering creation.

Schüssler Fiorenza rejects the notion of atonement: "The Sophia-God of Jesus does not need atonement or sacrifices. Jesus' death is not willed by God but is the result of his all-inclusive praxis as Sophia's prophet."[47] The question of course is what one means by atonement. The goodness of this sophia-God can be hurt. Sin creates havoc with this goodness. Sophia itself can be hurt. Sin injects anarchy into sophia. In his suffering, Jesus alleviates the hurt of the sophia-God by sharing in the divine suffering, and thus he atones. Jesus stands up against the evil of noninvolvement and the notion of omnipotence that threatens the sophia-God as well as the human being.

Whether the notions of prophet, priest, and king are the most helpful to characterize Jesus' praxis in communion with sophia is a moot question. The point is, Jesus not only communicates the word of wisdom, he also suffers for wisdom's sake and struggles together with wisdom against the evil that attacks it. What we learn is the self-limitation of God. Wisdom requires the self-limitation of human reason as response. Cohn-Sherbok writes: In the past "Jesus has been understood as the risen Christ who sits at the right hand of the Father."[48] Looking at Jesus' praxis under the aegis of the wisdom-God, there has been a complete bouleversement of Jesus' role. From the Jesus sitting at the right hand of God we have come to the Jesus *struggling as the right hand* of God in history.

Cohn-Sherbok always speaks of the Jesus standing in the prophetic tradition. Would it also be possible for Jews to see Jesus standing in the priestly and kingly tradition? These are not superimposed notions. They grow out of experiencing Jesus in praxis as sharing this kind of God. Christians can only say to Jews: This is the way we experience the God of the Jews. There is no superiority connected with it. But one would need to stress that it is this God that leads Christians through the wilderness of contemporary class struggle and other conflicts. We are co-workers with this God. We are in partnership with this God. What this sophia-God requires is "obedient participation in the act of emancipation" (Cohn-Sherbok).

In a praxis of wisdom-sharing, hurt-bearing, and evil-daring, Jesus struggles as the right hand of God ahead of us, but also on our side in the justice struggle. According to Ephesians 2:11ff., Jew and gentile in Jesus are already one, the dividing wall of hostility having been broken down. We can take this to mean that in praxis we are both experiencing the same God—but in different ways.

Besides the Judaism/Christianity split—the breach that Jesus steps into as the right hand of God—there is also the Christianity/ world religions split and, within Christianity, the clergy/laity split. I shall return to them later. Meanwhile suffice it to say that atonement in each case is an important liberation dynamic that underlies all Christian praxis. Without the empowerment of God leading the way and being involved in the fray, no liberation takes place from the conflicts represented by these splits.

Justification

In walking together with this God it becomes obvious that we human beings do not find it easy to overcome splits and other conflicts. Jesus as the right hand of God is in the struggle, prevailing. We falter. With regard to the praxis that raises the question of the *person* of Christ, I appealed to the Greek church tradition, especially to Chalcedon. As to the question of the *work* of Christ, I turned to the view of the medieval church, especially to Anselm's *Cur Deus Homo?* As soon as our human faltering becomes an issue in Christian praxis, we need to turn to the Reformation. There was progression in Christian thought through christo-praxis. The church first learned the in-depth dynamics of the mystery of God's *deprivation* in the so-called incarnation. It next had to grasp the resulting *reconciliation*. Finally praxis penetrated the hard skull of the church with the notion that both God's deprivation and reconciliation involve *justification*.

When we think of the Reformation with its justification struggle, we remember also the Reformation emphasis on the *priesthood of all believers*. From this perspective there are a few caveats with regard to the doctrines we reviewed. The Chalcedonian point actually is a hierarchical point, the view of bishops in partnership with their empire. It is orthodox. Anselm's product is a scholarly, priestly argument. It is medieval-scholastic and basically monastic. The Reformation, however, is more a movement of the laity, a breakaway from hierarchy and priests. It tends toward the communion of saints, the priesthood of all believers, full communion. A Christian is a free agent ruling all things and subject to none (Luther). Justification is the core of this freedom, the direct encounter between God and the person, without human mediation, without emperor, bishop, or priest. And yet there is still a lot of chaff left in Reformation dogmatics, and it needs winnowing out. Whatever justice power we can derive from the Reformation traditions we want to honor. But we also want to be as self-critical as the Reformation itself, remembering that popes, councils, and bishops—Reformers as well—can err.

In christo-praxis we re-produce tradition. But that means we need to know the dynamics of christo-praxis in the past with its light *and* its shadow side. We cannot relive from a theoretical perspective the road from the deprivation (incarnation) doctrine through the atonement-substitution notion to that of self-discovery on grounds of justification, and hope to make sense of God's world as it suffers and struggles. It is the other way around. As we suffer and struggle together with God in christo-praxis we discover similar configurations of thought that call for our very own expressions of deprivation, atonement, and justification.[49] We have to go through the same process of God-discovery as did the primitive church. Along with God-discovery comes self-discovery. Today, in the praxis of liberation, we discover the corporate God and the corporate self.

Christo-praxis gives rise to a number of key thoughts: (1) We are truly confronted with God as mystery, a "sacred space" in reality (Chalcedon). (2) God acts in our behalf and becomes our stand-in (Anselm). (3) Even in our failures God stands up for us justifying us the way we are (Reformation). (4) God comes to us as corporate self, so we can discover our own corporate self (liberation).[50] These are four thoughts that grow out of christo-praxis in which finally primitive Christianity comes to full fruition. Primitive Christianity is here not just naive and pristine beginnings.

"Primitive" here means "genuine"—that which counts as the real thing.

The Reformation justification dynamics is summarized in Article IX of the *Methodist Articles*: "We are accounted righteous before God only for the merit of our Lord and Savior Jesus Christ, by faith, and not for our own works or deservings. Wherefore, that we are justified by faith, only, is a most wholesome doctrine, and very full of comfort."[51] The doctrine of justification has become so much a part of our mental equipment as Protestants that reference to it often triggers no more than a yawn. On Reformation Sunday nostalgia overwhelms us; only a semblance of historical truth filters through to us.

Does justification by faith arise from christo-praxis today? In social location at the eucharist we encounter the eucharistic Jesus. The dynamics of scripture, tradition, experience, and reason merging in the eucharist immediately translates itself into the struggle of God for justice, with Messiah Jesus as God's right hand, impacting our lives for participation. As we join God's activity, we are thrust into the class struggle and other personal and social conflicts. All the while we cannot escape failing God time and again. We are beings with vast limitations. Our souls wince at our failures, which cover the whole range from the socio-political to the very personal.

Justification is tied into God's justice struggle. Justification by faith acknowledges us as just: we are declared right in God's sight in spite of our failures. God looks at us with an eye to Messiah Jesus. In him, God sees us as just. "Since we are justified by faith, we have peace with God through our Lord Jesus Christ" (Rom. 5:1). Or, in the formulation of the *Methodist Articles* quoted above: "Wherefore, that we are justified by faith, only, is a most wholesome doctrine, and very full of comfort."[52] Justification by faith is justification by awakened conscience. In conscience God can reach us and can claim us. In awakened conscience *the basic human condition* is acknowledged: we live not by "doing" anything, but by what is happening to us through God's presence in our doing. That presence is what counts, not our successes or failures in the struggle. Lightened of the burden of guilt, we continue joyously in our walk with God.

In recent North American theology, justification often becomes, as it were, a subheading of *salvation*. Paul Tillich's *System-*

atic Theology is a good case in point. Much of contemporary theology in the United States has stressed salvation as *healing*. The premise is that we human beings are estranged from God. I indicated earlier that estrangement plays a role. But I focused mainly on the usurpation of God's power and place, either in wresting power from God or in passively letting it go to waste by yielding to false authority, drying up in the process. In any case, it is continually "exchanging the truth of God for a lie" (Rom. 1:25). It is replacing the real human condition with an illusory "reality."

What happens through *justification* in the liberation-atonement is an awakening, a waking up to reality in God's sight. It is a *disenchantment* from the spell we have cast on ourselves, a sobering up from our intoxication with usurped power or our lack of trust in God's power. As human beings in sin we deceive ourselves about reality. We dream up a state of affairs that does not exist. Justification makes us sober. Now we see things as they are—in God's sight. So justification by faith does not offer a "high" of religious theory. On the contrary, it makes us live "justly" in the midst of falsehood. Only on grounds of justification can we fully appreciate 1 Peter 5:8f.: "Be sober, be watchful. Your adversary the devil prowls around like a roaring lion, seeking someone to devour. Resist him, firm in your faith"—*firm* in justification faith.

Contemporary theology occasionally has beclouded the issue. Paul Tillich offers the following rationale:

> Regeneration can also be defined as in this system, namely, as participation in the New Being, in its objective power, however fragmentary this may be. If defined in this way, Regeneration precedes Justification; for Justification presupposes faith, the state of being grasped by the divine presence. Faith, justifying faith, is not a human act, although it happens in man; faith is the work of the divine Spirit, the power which creates the New Being, in the Christ, in individuals, in the church. It was a pitfall in Protestant theology when Melanchton placed the reception of the divine Spirit after the act of faith. In this moment faith became an intellectual work of man, made possible without participation in the New Being. For these reasons, one should put regeneration, defined

in the sense of participation in the New Being, before Justification.[53]

A little later, Tillich claims: "As a divine act, Regeneration and Justification are one."[54] Tillich complicates matters. Again we need to begin with the scriptures in social location among the poor of the world. Our turning to God is never a step of success, but an admission of failure, insufficiency, or incompleteness. Either we have not as yet struggled together with God for justice and are moving only toward a "sacred space," or we are inside Christianity and have failed as co-workers of God. God *always* needs to act by making us just—that is, drawing us out of our enchantment with the private self. God breaks the spell in which we drive ourselves to succeed. So we need not put regeneration before justification, as Tillich suggests. He is of course right in rejecting the notion of placing the act of faith after the reception of the divine Spirit. We can also agree that the idea of a "forensic" justification, a sheer declaration of all and everyone being just, is pointless. But Tillich overreacts in placing regeneration before justification.

"Whom God called, God also justified, and those God justified God also glorified" (Rom. 8:30). In that God justifies, God also renews. The process of regeneration begins with the justifying act of God time and again. Faith as awakened conscience comes about through God's justifying action. As God justifies us, we join Messiah Jesus as right hand of God in the justice struggle. Tillich proposes that besides the objective side of justification (whether forensic or not), the subjective side also needs to be considered. This involves especially acceptance. In this regard Tillich develops his famous formulation of justification: "There is nothing in man which enables God to accept him. But man must accept this. He must accept that he is accepted; he must accept acceptance."[55]

Acceptance is here a psychological category. It should not be excluded. Yet with Tillich it is directly tied to the notion that regeneration precedes justification "as the actual reunion"[56] between God and humankind. In social location at the eucharist, faith as awakened conscience immediately is aware of being enlisted and thus accepted. God enlists the oppressed and the misfits of the world. No wonder we, too, feel accepted. But we have "no time" to reflect on our acceptance or on any reunion. Reunion makes sense for alumni at a homecoming. At the core of the justification event, however, lies the hard reality of God's presence in conscience. Because God is present in con-science, nothing needs to be reunited. God does not let the sinner go—ever: "O love that wilt not let me go. . . ."

The notion of reunion makes it abundantly clear that Tillich thinks of the Christian faith as a religious transaction and not as justice action. There is a peculiar kind of emotionality and bliss involved, a feeling level characterized by the notion of reunion. From God's side there is no estrangement and therefore no reunion involved. God's right hand is indwelling our con-science all along. We need only wake up to it. As God through Messiah Jesus as right hand of God justifies us—that is, makes us just—our con-science awakens and faith emerges. The problem is that on our own— without the justifying activity of God's right hand—we do not acknowledge the reality in which we breathe and move and have our being. Justification is the act in which God does everything for us through standing by us—in spite of ourselves. "While we were yet sinners Christ died for us" (Rom. 5:8). This is a metaphorical expression of God's right hand activity being ahead of us all the time. God undoes the injury our sin inflicts on the divine life. Justification is the moment when—in spite of ourselves—we feel right and good about ourselves. Our human condition is set right. God is straightening out things we have done wrong. We only have to act upon our enlistment. That is faith working in justice.

We dare not lose sight of the elementary dynamics of christopraxis. The presence of God is never in question. What is doubtful is our attention to the struggle of God in which we stand. God is not removed from human beings. Yet God in being present to us is constantly "hurt." This provokes the act of God's nonviolent "self-defense" in atonement with its consequent justification. The usurpers of God's power are "righted"—in spite of themselves, for God shares in their vulnerability. No act of reunion needs to precede our God-walk. God's power is life-energy, moist and verdant like grass in the spring. Usurping it we dry up. Living by it we involve ourselves in justice-making.

Thus in social location at the eucharist we do not practice acceptance of acceptance on grounds of reunion, but we experience enlistment on grounds of justice—the basic condition in which we exist. It is not an emotive process, but a facing of reality. God *rights* the human condition justly. God's rights on us are reaffirmed in justification. Faith as awakened conscience is our *enlistment* in God's justice-sharing with all creatures. There is obviously a dimension of personal renewal or regeneration involved. But the new factor is that the private usurpation or timidity of sin has been turned into an awareness of our corporate strength as persons of God who deal justly with each other. Submissive usurption or usurping submissiveness has been stayed.

Justification does not mystify us by placing us in an unfamiliar, different human condition. There is nothing religious about it that we would need to add to our humanity. "It is no longer I who live, but Christ who lives in me" (Gal. 2:20). St. Paul links justification to radical transformation. But Messiah Jesus does not translate us into another world—a never-never land of religious bliss. We are transformed for new life in this world. God is interested in "making disciples of all nations" (Matt. 28:19). That practically means for all nations to acknowledge God as justice-love and to accept God's peace with thanksgiving (*eucharistein*).

It is in this sense that justification "is the immediate consequence of the doctrine of atonement."[57] Tillich offers us several *principles* of the atonement.[58] For God-walk, only the *dynamics* of liberation-atonement will do. For what does the at-onement bring about? Tillich's principles move us into the separate realm of religion over and above the human condition. We can agree to the *first* principle: "The first and all-decisive principle is that the atoning processes are created by God and God alone."[59] But the difficulty arises with the second principle: "There are no conflicts in God between his reconciling love and his retributive justice."[60] Although this sounds all right, the explanation turns out to be more religious speculation than acknowledgment of God's rights: "The justice of God is the act through which he lets the self-destructive consequences of existential estrangement go their way. He cannot remove them because they belong to the structure of being itself and God would cease to be God—the only thing which is impossible for him—if he removed these consequences."[61]

God never lets the self-destructive consequences of sin go their merry old way to the end. God counteracts them. Yet it is in the very nature of sin to oppose God in that activity too. All we are asked to do is to acknowledge God's reality and work. Consider how God works in history. Recall my earlier point that the reality of God is perceived through the works of God. It is crucial to remember: "As I live, says the Lord God, I have no pleasure in the death of the wicked, but that the wicked turn from their way and live" (Ezek. 33:11). "For I have no pleasure in the death of anyone, says the Lord God; so turn and live" (Ezek. 18:32). In the Christian scriptures the same note is sounded: "This is good and acceptable in the sight of God our Savior, who desires all human beings to be saved and to come to the knowledge of the truth" (I Tim. 2:3f.). God wants all human beings to be liberated and saved. The awesomeness of sin lies in our building up a dreamworld and denying the very activity of God, even though it is unconcealed. From God's side there is the offer of liberation and salvation for all. But from the human side there is often destruction.

We can skip the third of Tillich's atonement principles, which is a repetition of the first two from another angle. But the fourth principle calls for critical assessment:

> God's atoning activity must be understood as his participation in existential estrangement and its self-destructive consequences. He cannot remove these consequences; they are implied in his justice. But he can take them upon himself by participating in them and transforming them *for those who participate in his participation. Here we are at the very heart of the doctrine of atonement.*[62]

What does this amount to in the social location of the poor Christ and the poor at the eucharist? God atones—that is the point of justification. God atones even when we human beings refuse to participate in God's participation in our dilemmas. So God time and again *overrides* our sin and brings about justice in the human condition in spite of ourselves. Does this equate justification with the historical occurrence of justice in the world? To the extent that divine justice happens among us in history, justification is real. But divine justice is not our human achievement. It is what God does in spite of our injustice. It goes on all along, whether we notice it or not.

God is at work in the world regardless of what we Christians are doing or not doing. God may have long ago rejected parts of the church for carrying out the divine purpose. We tend to tie God down to our Christian faith expressions and our Christian religious thing, the four walls of the sanctuary. Christianity as religion would like to control God—as much as any individual would.

At the most crucial point here in Tillich we get an inactive God. The justification doctrine is the most intensive word-deed of God and is independent of any religious cooperation of human beings. Tillich, as it were, reins God in among the ontological structures of his system.[63] But God is working out the divine purposes in history and does not need ontological structures invented by Christians. "Do not presume to say to yourselves, 'We have Abraham as our Father'; for I tell you, God is able from these stones to raise up children to Abraham" (Matt. 3:9).

God's justice work, the righting of the human condition, is going on in the world unceasingly, far beyond the vision of us wise religious experts. That is the core of liberation-atonement. God is not boxed in by us. The earth moves around the sun. We cannot do anything about it. We can, and we need to, acknowledge its truth. We attune our bodies to its rising and setting. But we cannot change the work of the sun. It happens. So also with God's justice work in the atonement.

Does this mean that there is no special atoning through Messiah Jesus? What Messiah Jesus does as atoner is God's very own work: "That they may all be one; even as thou, Father, art in me, and I in thee. . . .The glory which thou hast given me I have given them that they may be one even as we are one" (John 17:21f.). The special dimension of atonement in Messiah Jesus lies in his doing nothing without God. That exactly is the deepest truth of his atoning work. The justification word-deed shapes it into conscience.

Liberation-atonement yielding justification is a Christian thought growing out of christo-praxis. It does not intend to mystify. But it has to be clearly focused. A lay person commented: "God's gift to you is to stamp you O.K. and if you believe that it's true, it will be true."[64] It is not just a stamping, however. It is also a placing. In God's sight we are now viewed "in Christ." That has to be clearly understood. As already indicated, Article IX of the *Methodist Articles* on justification underscores that justification is "a most wholesome doctrine, and very full of comfort."[65] The

Reformation had wondered, though: "Does not this teaching make people careless and sinful?" It answered its own question: "No, for it is impossible for those who are ingrafted into Christ by true faith not to bring forth the fruit of gratitude."[66] The *Methodist Articles* two hundred years later retain the same movement of thought. Article X claims that by good works "a lively faith may be evidently known as a tree is discerned by its fruit."[67]

The awakened conscience is active in justice. It is faith truly active also in love. It is joining in God's ongoing activity in the world, in history, and in nature. The emerging global village experience is very much part of it. We have to see the liberation-atonement on the horizon of global discipleship.

From the Laity/Clergy Split to the Layhood of All Ministers

Global thinking easily turns into "universalizing" while right under our nose in our own churches christo-praxis is put on hold. Discipleship is not meant to be a killjoy. A student pastor wondered out loud: "My people are happy. Should I go and make them unhappy?" The elementary question is whether we want to promote a "religious Christianity" or get involved in christo-praxis. Expanding our horizon in christo-praxis is not an "unhappy" development. But it will mean for all the laity to get drawn into the liberation-atonement. Often it seems that only the pastor mediates God's truth—a perversion of the divine reality we stand in.

The question is whether laity and clergy as a people's church will work on *accountable teaching*. It is most often the laity that is asking the right questions today. The whole point of God-walk is for the clergy to see itself among the laity together with the suffering of the world at the eucharist. What shapes up in this understanding?

1. A goodly number of lay persons understand quite well the elementary principle of christo-praxis. So William E. Diehl, a Lutheran layman, says: "The preacher starts with theology and then works it into examples of real-life situations."[68] It is the other way around. Christian thought needs to grow out of real life. Ministers as well as lay persons need to reflect on real-life situations as they focus sharply on social location. It is never a matter of just single-issue dilemmas. We have to start where we are located in

terms of the total situation. That may be a cotton mill. But the
challenge expands right away from the difficulties of the cotton
mill to world peace, for example. The point is the *awakening* to the
fundamental dilemma of the laity/clergy split. Religion in the
churches has often pitted clergy and laity more against each other
instead of standing with each other in the justice struggle of God.
William E. Diehl writes:

> The most common delusion in this area is the conviction of
> ministers that what they preach on Sunday has a direct influ-
> ence on what their listeners do on Monday. This conviction,
> because it is so important for the self-image of the minister, is
> adhered to despite mountains of evidence to the contrary.[69]

There is no at-onement to speak of between clergy and laity here,
and certainly no liberation-atonement. Diehl gives many examples
of the dilemma. The church is often basically patterned according
to the clergy/laity dualism rather than justice engagement. All the
dynamics of a local congregation tend to center around the minister, his or her whims and needs. The first illustration Diehl brings
describes a minister starting a sermon with a good biblical rationale:

> He was good, very good. Having developed a strong case on
> the basis of. . . theology, he turned to the real-life applica-
> tion. Looking out across the congregation, with great passion
> he threw out this challenge: "Next time someone asks you
> why you are a Christian, what will you say?" My heart sank. I
> sighed in keen disappointment. That was not the right ques-
> tion. In all the years of work and travel in my career as a
> businessman, in all those conferences, at all those business
> meals, on all those plane trips, not once did anyone ever ask
> me why I was a Christian. Associates of mine who were aware
> of some of the things we were doing in our lives may have
> asked why we were doing them, and thereby may have of-
> fered an opportunity for discussion of faith, but I've never
> heard the direct question asked the way the preacher seemed
> to think is perfectly commonplace. The real question is,

"How does a layperson initiate a discussion relating to his faith without immediately turning off the other person?" I thought about the letdown of the sermon for several days. Was the minister so removed from the reality of lay experience that he didn't realize the inappropriateness of his question?[70]

The difficulties of our theory-oriented ministerial education are obvious. In the congregations, we often lack the eucharistic praxis that saves the minister from taking off into head-trip religion. Our worship services "function" in spite of ourselves. Yet much of what we do around pulpit and altar does not make possible a holistic grasp of the activity of God by pastor and congregation. As a consequence, pastor and congregation, as in Diehl's example, are more like runners on different tracks than co-workers together with God. Lay persons are pressing more and more for a new method that allows Christian thought to emerge from the concerted discipleship of pastor and laity. What does it mean to be disciples together in the global village?

2. We also need to mention the "nerve center" of congregational life: the budget. In a majority of cases, in the average-size church, the minister's salary is the largest single item in the church budget. A large portion of the local church budget is used for institutional maintenance focused in the minister. Although many ministers do not receive adequate compensation, we cannot overlook the fact that in many churches hardly any money is set aside for *lay ministry*—for example, in factory situations, public housing, or nursing homes. The church budget is not geared to an empowerment of the laity for ministry in the world. Church building or building improvements often rank very high in the church budget. This again shows the priorities by which a local church lives. We do put our money where our *mouth* is. We do not put it where our *praxis* needs to be.

3. The third point follows from the second. Our major problem as congregations is that we rarely have an idea of the power of worship when focused on the eucharist. Atonement is grasped by us as the people of God gather in worship. That is where the budget needs to be anchored. That is where *all* expressions of our Christian

life are anchored. But we do not live holistically within worship. We do not worship in terms of a rehearsal of our Christian life. For many it still is a strange cult act with its own dynamics apart from our lives. Says William Diehl:

> It is time that the professionals in our national denominations begin spending less time tinkering with the *forms* of worship and begin dealing more with the *nature* of worship. When surveys continually reveal that laypeople find great difficulty relating the Sunday worship experience to the weekday life, perhaps the liturgical elitists in our denominations had better start listening to the laity talk about their struggles in that weekday life. Gibbs and Morton say it well: "Worship still seems to depend on the work of scholars; it still needs to be explained by the clergy. Worship thus becomes something at second hand for the laity." An action which has to be explained to people quite obviously does not arise out of their daily lives.[71]

Christian thought in divinity schools often proceeds as though almost every lay person would understand what worship is about—plainly a false assumption. Why is there such a split between a clergy that seems to know and a laity that seems ignorant? Liberation praxis suggests: we simply do not gather around the atonement presence of God in the congregation. We do not even make the attempt to relive it. We have especially built a wall between sermon and eucharist, so that the atonement offered is truncated. How can we begin to root the sermon in the concrete expression of the atonement in the eucharist? We can begin listening to the laity reflect on its struggles in its everyday life. We can so reflect on our own praxis that the eucharist does not become something second hand for the laity. It makes no sense to address the liberation-atonement base apart from a common praxis base. It is because there is so little of this base that we have the pastor/laity split. No theoretical discussion is ever going to overcome it. We have to begin together in christo-praxis. Beyond exercising the priesthood of all believers (Luther), lies the new work for the layhood of all ministers.[72]

The Eucharist

To date, dogmatics or systematic theology has not brought christology and the teaching of the sacraments together, the doctrine of Messiah Jesus and the eucharist. Yet in terms of atonement-liberation we cannot understand christology apart from Messiah Jesus' own praxis in the eucharist.

1. There were sacraments before there was christology. There certainly were sacraments before there was a church. In definite ways, the sacraments even constitute the church. Or, Messiah Jesus constitutes the church through them. First there was Jesus' baptism, the origin of our baptism. The first eucharist took place in the upper room, consummated on the cross and in the resurrection. Both took place *before* the church—in our usual sense of the term—existed. So both sacraments are much more intimately tied to Messiah Jesus than to the church. And yet they often appear in our doctrinal textbooks under the heading of the church. Obviously we cannot have the head of the church without the church as his body. Yet first of all we cannot have the head of the church without the sacraments. Important about them is what God is doing in *atonement yielding justification*. God acts in the body-language of the sacramental act, however unworthy the administrator might be.

2. The act of the sacrament makes no sense if one simply assumes that the sacrament is effective on grounds of proper technical performance, by reason simply of the work performed (*ex opere operato*). There needs to be the understanding of the people gathered around the sacrament. As regards infant baptism or the frequency of the eucharist, the laity has to think hard, together with ministers, why we have so many truncated or largely formal sacramental occasions.

Many of us consider the sacrament a cult act. What is more, some feel that perhaps we ought to help God along in the sacrament. We bring the water. We bring the bread and the wine, or our faith, or our repentance. Therefore God does something. But it is just the opposite. "Nothing in my hand I bring." The sacraments say: God acts. God is at work in our lives, as already in the vast universe, without our help. The sacraments embody this sovereign activity of God in such a way that we can "taste and see" it (Ps. 34:8).

We need to remind ourselves of something most of us know, but often do not usefully apply:

> Scientists can now envision a still expanding universe that began almost 20 billion years ago, extends for 20 billion light years and contains 10 billion galaxies—each one an island of hundreds of billions of stars. Looking into the star-filled firmament, astronomers actually perceive a four-dimensional universe, one that has the added measure of time. Travelling at 186,000 miles per second, the light that long ago left distant stars and galaxies is only now reaching the earth. Thus we see the nearby sun as it was little more than eight minutes ago, the nearest star to the sun, Proxima Centauri, as it was about four years ago, and some farther galaxies as they looked billions of years ago.[73]

Faith in the creator God believes that God is at work in all this vastness of space and time without our help. God was understood since the days of ancient Israel as the one responsible for all this glory of light: God "who made the Pleiades and Orion, and turns deep darkness into the morning, and darkens the day into night, who calls for the waters of the sea, and pours them out upon the surface of the earth, is called the Lord" (Amos 5:8). If we view God in social location at the eucharist, we rejoice that the one who guides the farthest star does what needs doing for justice/love on earth, whether among aborigines of Australia, Hindus, Muslims, or us noisy Christians. We think this thought on grounds of the life, death, and resurrection of Messiah Jesus as we are confronted by his realpresence in history. The mystery is that God wants us to be co-workers in this great work. God tries to activate the unspoken word in conscience, its silent voice, not just among us, but among all peoples everywhere. In baptism in Jesus' name we seek to acknowledge it as antecedent to thought and action. In the eucharist we acknowledge it as continuing gift. In concrete historical action we find confidence that we can see the mystery of God's action "through a glass darkly" (1 Cor. 13:12). In baptism, we acknowledge God's action in all humankind as impacting the individual. In the eucharist, we celebrate this same action as creating the corporate person.

Any eucharistic action makes us face the radical immersion of

God in a person's life and the immersion of this person in the life of God—yet now in the corporate form of many persons—that is, in "holy communion." In essence, it does not add anything new beyond baptism. Both sacraments confront us with the need to participate bodily as well as spiritually in what God is doing in Messiah Jesus in the world (Rom. 6). We are baptized with Messiah Jesus into his death. We rise with him to newness of life. We fully share in the reality of this unique person. His corporate selfhood becomes our corporate selfhood. This is also the core of the eucharist, but it underscores death as reconciliation, as liberation-atonement, creating the corporate body, the corporate person from the two (Eph. 2:14ff.). In sharing death and resurrection, however, we share the whole person and work of the crucified Messiah. The eucharist relates the whole fabric of life as Messiah Jesus ties into it. He was not specializing in anything, whether counseling, pulpiteering, or visitation. He put his life on the line whenever necessary. He was with the lepers. He counseled the mentally disturbed. He preached to the rabble. The state sanctioned his cruel death outside the city wall on a hill set aside for criminals. Dying and rising with Messiah Jesus means to share wholly in the shape of this life and what it stands for. Jesus' justice struggle is our struggle. We share in it in spite of ourselves. We are put into the midst of the whole fabric of life, the weal and woe of humankind, especially that of marginal persons and peoples.

The crucified and risen one did not create a magic spell in the sacrament, something spooky that would turn its administrators into pseudo shamans. He also did not offer a rite effective in its merely mechanical performance, something that would work like a prayer wheel, with clergy in rationalistic control. What we have in the eucharist is a community gathering at God's behest to embody the character of God. In this community Messiah Jesus as the host personifies the mystery of God righting our human condition at its deepest level. God is profoundly involved in all of humanity. We behold this presence in the eucharist concretely through the Holy Spirit.

Monika K. Hellwig points out that one of the key issues of the eucharist is hunger—hunger of the body and hunger of the soul. Without sharing in the hunger of the body we cannot understand the hunger of the soul. Here christo-praxis has its deepest roots in the eucharist:

As a child I was given an explanation of the eucharist somewhat as follows. People need to eat food regularly to sustain the life of their bodies. In the eucharist, Jesus provides us with the real food for the soul (which he is himself), therefore we should receive it often and be very grateful for it. This explanation is certainly not incorrect, but it is too facile a formulation which quickly covers over the depth dimensions of human experience—precisely all those dimensions that must be explored in order to find the way into the fullest possible personal participation. First of all, the explanation described the action as coming to eat, not as coming to share food. It portrayed the participant as a passive and isolated individual, not as an interacting member of a community. Secondly, it did not invite reflection on what is hunger, what kinds of hunger there are, and what food for the soul might possibly mean.[74]

The first thing the eucharist in social location with the poor makes clear is that in coming to the altar the community needs to understand that Jesus *shared* food. Chapter six of the fourth Gospel underscores what is at stake. There is first of all Jesus feeding the five thousand. With the disciples participating, Jesus speaks of himself as the food of the world: "I am the living bread which came down from heaven; if anyone eats of this bread, this person will live forever; and the bread which I shall give for the life of the world is my flesh" (John 6:51). Willingness to share food with the hungry is "the other side" of Jesus' eucharistic self-offering. Coming to the eucharist in the community means willingness to share food—as in the feeding of the five thousand. God wants justice/love through Messiah Jesus to spread to all hungry persons in the concrete form of bread-sharing.

Part of what is happening in the eucharist is also the stilling of the hunger of the soul. In communion we acknowledge our imperfection, our failure. When we think of all the misery under the roof of a local congregation or a divinity school from one celebration of the eucharist to another, we might be close to despair: envy, callousness, broken promises, gossip, foundered marriages, sloth, dishonesty—you name it, it is found among us—because we are human beings, sinners. But we cannot leave the matter within the ambience of the generality of sin, if we focus on the eucharist within the ambience of liberation-atonement.

Sin has expressed itself structurally as well as personally. There is a network of injury we inflict upon God, other human beings, and ourselves. Often it is not at all at our personal initiative that we inflict injury. It is within the structures of sin that we cannot help being racist, sexist, and classist. What initially was programed for us by society, gradually turns into our own sin. Gender struggle, race struggle, and class struggle continually permeate our social and psychological structures. As in our relationship toward God, we either agressively or passively injure others or ourselves in these structures. We always tamper with the rightful place the other person holds in relationship to us. We cannot stand the justice involved in the presence of a God granting equal rights to all humans, persons of another color, sex, or class. So we start dividing our world in terms of poor/rich, worker/manager, slave/master. As a consequence, the eucharist is also not a place where all meet in equal dignity, but where many are still excluded.

As far as sexism is concerned, consider the churches where women are not permitted to administer the Lord's Supper, though at home they are not only allowed, but expected to prepare their husband's supper. Racism has often enough been excoriated with regard to the eucharist. And yet we need to be reminded of it time and again lest we be satisfied with present conditions. We might congratulate ourselves that our church or seminary has an "integrated" communion altar. But there are still more churches in the United States than one cares to admit where not everybody is welcome at the communion table. Social stratification or the difference between classes and generations usually brings members of one group to the table. Youth groups often like to share communion their own way, without grown-ups. There are relatively few situations where managers and workers commune together. And there are even fewer situations where labor/management issues are part of the communion dynamics. The eucharist is not supposed to make us "feel good" within our own group. It invites us to see Messiah Jesus in the "enemy" and the outsider.

There is the hunger of the soul. Soul-force wants to break through. Our hearts are restless until they find rest in God and a world not divided. Deep down in our conscience we know that the injury we inflict within the social structures of sin needs righting. So we understand why judgment in the household of God (1 Pet. 4:17) begins especially at the eucharist. "For those who eat and drink without discerning the body, eat and drink judgment upon themselves" (1 Cor. 11:29). We have nothing to congratulate ourselves for. Our missionary task is first among us Christians and our Christian nation so-called. We need to convert ourselves, pre- or post-Christians, to the gospel, even within the majority of our churches.

"Because there is one bread, we who are many are one body, for we all partake of the one bread" (1 Cor. 10:17). Where there is a change of mind, repentance, as also with regard to "structural sin," there *forgiveness* satisfies the hunger of the soul. The eucharist is often truncated because we use it *only* as a means to satisfy the hunger of the soul. We close our eyes to God's sharing the bread also for the bodily needs of humankind. We see the eucharist as an event of individual co-union with God, but not radically as co-union with all of humankind, the hungry bodies of human beings in whom we also "discern" the body of Christ.

Much of Christian ministry today is viewed as a fairly manageable thing to be taken care of by good professionals. The notion of the professional skews the issue. Ministers, above all else, are eucharist servants. They are not above the congregation, which, as a whole, celebrates the meal as a community of corporate selfhood. Ministers serve at table together with members of the congregation. The communing people in the eucharist face the *mystery* of the eucharistic Jesus, the kind of life God embodies in Messiah Jesus and shares with all types of persons, whether they think of life as mystery, joy ride, or rat race. At the eucharist life becomes utterly valuable, for all beings share in the corporateness of God, which gives value to every element of life. Present in the meal is the whole Jesus, the reality in which God changes history and nature. This is not a mystification shutting down our reasoning faculties and paralyzing action. The mystical presence of God in Messiah Jesus evokes soul-force and communal power.

The eucharist is the corporate sharing of humanity through Messiah Jesus as we share food (bread and wine) for satisfying bodily hunger throughout the world and stilling the hunger of the soul. In the midst of life it sensitizes or awakens the conscience, which God "makes" in every human being, to the unspoken Word in us all. It reflects time and again the whole mystery of God's impoverishment (incarnation) in Jesus. He said to the Twelve: "To you has been given [to know] the mystery of the kingdom of God" (Mark 4:11). St. Paul speaks of it as "the mystery which was kept hidden for long ages" (Rom. 16:25; cf. 1 Cor. 2:7). In Ephesians there is stress on the "mystery" of God's will (Eph. 1:9). The *mysterion* (Mark 4:11), the real sacrament, is that *in the unspoken Word in every conscience* God is struggling to evoke justice/love—a divine voice in human affairs.[75] God wants to have a say, and the eucharist "midwives" the birth of God's power in us.

In his body-language offering the bread, Jesus says to the disciples at the supper: "This is my body broken for you" (1 Cor. 11:24). In body-language offering up the cup, Jesus adds: "This cup is the new covenant in my blood" (v.25). Likewise, St. Paul is asking: "The cup of blessing we bless, is it not a participation in the blood of Christ? The bread we break, is it not a participation in the body of Christ?" (1 Cor.10:16). There can be no doubt, in terms of body-language, that Jesus sees himself fully involved in the bread and the wine. Realpresence of Messiah Jesus is intended.

We see in the meal what God's presence in the world as a whole is all about. Yet in the world as such we do not understand the full meaning of the breaking of the bread or the gift of the wine: Messiah Jesus is laboring together with God in nature as well as in history.

The historical question of what is happening in the sacrament cannot be bypassed. The *Methodist Articles* (Article XVI) say: "Sacraments ordained of Christ are not only badges or tokens of Christian men's [sic] profession, but rather they are certain signs of grace, and God's good will toward us, by which he doth work invisibly in us, and doth not only quicken, but also strengthen and confirm, our faith in him."[76] In many respects it is a wise statement. The sacraments are not primarily what human beings do by "profession" of faith, but they are acts of God. We have to add, though, that the body of Christ is already present in the gathered community—the church being the body of Christ. The strengthening of an individual's faith can happen only in this body.[77]

We need to remember throughout that in the gathering of the community Messiah Jesus as host is really present through the Holy Spirit. To think of the eucharist as a *memorial* alone makes no sense. It is deeply rationalistic. On the other end of the scale of historical options we find the notion of *transubstantiation*. In some ways, it is even more rationalistic than the memorial view. Priestly traditions developed the notion that the power of the sacrament was absolutely in the hands of the priest. The consecration of the elements, as it were, brought about the change of bread and wine into the body and blood of Christ.

Yet "this is my body" (1 Cor. 11:24) means in body-language the entire action of the meal and is a metaphor of the committed life. With the giving of the bread Jesus gives himself. With the wine he gives himself again. If it were not such a mystifying term, one might say, *consubstantiation* happens here. The realpresence of the host is a reality in the Spirit. Messiah Jesus as the host of this meal, *with* the bread and the wine—that is, with the elements of nature—is offering his body and his very blood. We have here the whole Jesus present, life, death, and resurrection, not just his death. But the kind of death Jesus died throws light on the power of his life on earth and his life in the Spirit today. As we eat the bread and drink the wine, we share in the whole embodied deprivation history of God in Jesus. What is told in the Gospels and in Paul's first letter to the Corinthians in words, is here offered in concrete reality. In this sense the scriptures are truly the eucharistic scriptures.

Once again I have to stress: this is not a mystifying cult meal. It is in our participation in the mystery that God *can and will* have a voice in human affairs. The mystery is embodied in God-walk, in the human flesh and blood of the disciples. The sacrament does not demand "virtuosos" of spirituality and giants of conscience, but fully human persons alive in God's image. On these terms we can say: *we are what we eat*. At the same time we remember: we are what we celebrate!

The joy of the eucharist consists in sharing in the mystery of this body-language. It evokes in us the inner voice, a "new song" (Ps. 33:3), making us aware of what is going on in history from God's side, the healing of the nations, of nature, and of the soul. The challenge of the sacrament is to draw out the creativity of the realpresence of God in Messiah Jesus in human beings, to evoke their creativity by awakening their very senses, and to make them whole. In "trusting" and seeing God's body, we are able to embody community ourselves. Baptism points to the *individual* in terms of this corporate selfhood. The eucharist celebrates the *corporateness* of the individual members. When one member suffers, all suffer (1 Cor. 12:26). As the *Methodist Articles* say, it is God who here works in us, strengthening and confirming our faith. To know what God is doing for humankind in this meal makes us celebrate holy communion in joy and thanksgiving,[78] so that we truly receive empowerment for the justice struggle.

The eucharist is the contemporary liberation-atonement. The divisive structures of race, gender, and class are tackled and broken down time and again by the one who works as the right hand of God. A piece of reality is again carved out where God's work is beheld by human eyes. There is a vast consensus emerging ecumenically in this regard.[79] God brings persons together to form the human family. Sharing the substance of life is crucial. "The essence of Christianity is eating together."[80] In primitive Christianity the meal was the center of the new reality Messiah Jesus had brought. Whoever sat down at the table of Messiah Jesus took a long step. Primitive Christianity tore down walls that had separated human beings from each other for centuries. Tabus were destroyed. Such action was subversive. "If merely the pro and con of a new doctrine had been at stake, one might have more easily come to an understanding. But the disagreement pertained together with the doctrine also to a way of life."[81] This is the crucial point of the interdependence between liberation-atonement and eucharist. We are dealing here first of all with a new way of life, praxis.

Some of the insights of the German Kirchentag at Nuremberg in 1979 and Hamburg in 1981 have made a wide impact along these lines. Rolf Christiansen reports that this awakening pertains less to the relationship between faith and programmatic action than to faith and "life together."[82] The eucharist rehearses the whole life of the Christian community. What is encountered in the celebration does not remain confined to the table of Messiah Jesus, but influences life. There is a eucharistic way of life emerging, shaped by gratitude for the gift received and making it relevant in the praxis of life. The only drawback here is the continuing notion of praxis as *applica-*

tion of previously attained insight or knowledge, in this case the grasp of gratitude. On grounds of a social location perspective, the eucharist itself would be part of the praxis—in fact, the core of the praxis. God-walk could never be understood as second step. And yet the intention of the German project overlaps with the view of the eucharist I have presented. Praise of God and responsibility for the world go hand in hand. In trying to hold the two together a new eucharistic spirituality is emerging. Christiansen details it in four steps.

1. The eucharistic way of life is concerned with the stewardship of creation. Bread and wine on the altar are God's good creation gift. Present in the elements is what we all need for staying alive. One cannot take bread and wine on Sunday at the Lord's supper as God's good gift and on Monday poison the soil. Where bread and wine are no longer produced responsibly, celebrating the Lord's supper does not make sense.

2. The eucharistic way of life is communion at table with the poor and hungry. One cannot fill oneself with the "bread of life" and keep bread, the stuff of life, from the hungry. For those who receive the bread of life it represents a challenge because there are still countless persons who go hungry every day. So the dire need of the world dare not be kept from the eucharistic celebration. Otherwise we in fact have really "closed communion."

3. The eucharistic way of life is committed to reconciliation and peace. Jesus reconciled the world to God on the cross. One cannot receive the gift of peace from God and at the same time continue in strife with one's neighbor. In German Protestantism there is often a division between *eucharistia* and *diakonia*, faith and social engagement. It can be healed only at the Table. In primitive Christianity the eucharist was the place where conflicts were struggled through in table community. It is difficult to imagine that something similar might happen today. But in a world that no longer knows places of reconciliation, it is all the more important not to circumvent the issue.

4. Finally the eucharistic way of life is ecumenical. It overcomes barriers of race (Jew and gentile), sex (man and woman), and class (slave and slaveowner). The struggle against racism, sexism, and class oppression is part of an ecumenical way of life. At the same time there is the need to overcome ecclesiastical divisions.

The point of this summary lies in indicating how widely the same tendencies of eucharistic orientation are today clearly perceived. A difference in assessing the importance of the eucharist I find, for example, in Christiansen's notion of the meal as "symbolic confirmation" of faith: "In the Lord's Supper believers are reassured of the ground of their faith."[83] In terms of God-walk, the eucharist constitutes the Christian life, placing us into the midst of God's justice struggle. The eucharist certainly also confirms "faith." Yet we first of all need to have an understanding of what faith is. There is at least as much misunderstanding of what faith is as misunderstanding of the eucharist.

It is difficult to grasp the justice function of the eucharist apart from the struggle of the primitive Christian community. The first Christians wanted to draw a sharp line between what was happening in society and their encounter with God in Messiah Jesus. So St. Paul would say: "Shun the worship of idols" (1 Cor. 10:14). Do not eat food offered to idols (v. 19). You cannot drink God's cup and the cup of demons (v. 21). The basic drive was to insist on the realpresence of Messiah Jesus in the Meal, meeting human need and offering the strength of resistance to injustice.[84]

In terms of God-walk, there are "particulars" of the eucharist that are "nonnegotiable." (1) The realpresence. There is God's direct involvement in the common life of those participating. We experience it through the Holy Spirit. (2) The embodiment of the mystery of the realpresence in the sharing of food. The essence of Christianity is eating together as we partake in the mystery of God's gift of life through the elements of nature. (3) The embodiment of the realpresence in judgment and forgiveness. God's realpresence in Jesus enables us to discern the body for the sake of satisfying the hunger of the soul. (4) The corporate implications of the realpresence. The corporate selfhood of God is shared for human corporateness, the healing of the race, sex, and class divisions, the divisions between generations, and the healing of the nations.

No bleeding heart pity is involved in the eucharist, but the good news of what things are really like in God's sight. This is who God is, sharing divine reality. The eucharist engages the whole person, body as well as soul—corporately, not just privately. The eucharist ultimately is the paradigmatic thanksgiving meal. The essence of Christianity is eating together—giving thanks in caring, sharing, and daring. Eating together makes it the justice meal.[85]

Baptism

In contrast, baptism stresses a sudden change in "heredity" (sin being "inherited"). Christians are "mutants."[86] Accountable teaching tries to come to terms with the Christian as a mutant individual. Much of this is already happening in our churches in a new understanding of the sacrament that designates entry into Christianity. Baptism, just like the eucharist, embodies God's activity in history. The mystery of God's activity is the same. Also here is *indirectness*. Our physical eyes do not see God's activity on display in history. Baptism enables us in faith to enter into the new humanity God is laboring for in history. The eucharist, then, time and again reactivates the new humanity in Messiah Jesus.

We dare not see the mutation happening here as activating a mere activism. It is a holistic renewal. In baptism (similar to the eucharist), the reality of death is crucial: "We are buried therefore with Messiah Jesus by baptism into death" (Rom. 6:4). In the eucharist, "As often as you eat this bread and drink this cup, you proclaim the Lord's death until he comes" (1 Cor. 11:26). The metaphorical language of the Christian scriptures speaks of death in terms of the result of sin: "The wages of sin is death" (Rom. 6:23). Death is here absolute separation of human life from eternal life, ultimately from God. What is overcome in sin has world-historical implications. *Usurpation* is overcome, both as reach for power and as yielding to power. The obfuscation, disorientation, and dislocation are gone. The obstruction of God's justice is removed. In baptism, God struggling together with Messiah Jesus in history inserts us into the divine work for justice.

Baptism does not say anything else than what the eucharist says, except that it directs God's justice struggle particularly to one person, enlisting this person. Just as the eucharist includes the marginals and all those who belong to the corporate selfhood of Jesus, so baptism reaches out to them, inviting all without any condition. God's struggle for a new humankind *cannot* be viewed as a new humanism based on sheer ethical imperatives. Just as the eucharist is the immediate expression of the person and work of Christ, of corporate selfhood and liberation-atonement, so is baptism. It belongs to christo-praxis. But baptism can be understood adequately only in the light of the eucharist. It is a one-time event directed toward the individual person, but integrated into the meaning-fabric of the ever-repeated eucharist. In this regard baptism introduces *a whole new structure of experience*, a different way of being human. The one baptized is offered the eucharistic life as her or his real home. The individual person is made participant of Messiah Jesus' life, death, and resurrection, dying and rising to newness of life in the history of this world.

Four points need to be highlighted in this regard. (1) In baptism Messiah Jesus inserts us into the new world of God's justice/love and enables us to struggle for peace. (2) The struggle is so fierce that Messiah Jesus gets "killed in action." We need to experience death too. "Repent, for the Kingdom of God is at hand" (Mark 1:15). Repentance is an uncomfortable word. It means that our old identity in private egotism has to go. (3) We share in Jesus' death as the destruction of our usurpation or resignation. This is forgiveness of sin, a part of the dying and rising. (4) We are made participants of the one "killed in action" by sharing in his resurrection. We are provided with a new identity. In baptism (as in the eucharist) *the whole story of God's self-realization in history* is made our very own.

There are two elementary ways in which we can shape Christian thought. According to the one, everything is basically decided abstractly, either in terms of absolute Being or in terms of eternity. According to the other, things are worked out in partnership or process between God and humankind, in God-walk. Baptism figures differently in the two elementary views. The first approach can be put as follows:

> The creation decision was the first stage of the unique decree of God that willed the Incarnation. The God-Man . . . was willed and foreordained in all and through all, and we (together with this all) were elected and blessed in him. . . .The Incarnation here is essentially a means of salvation against sin. Nothing tells us it would have taken place without sin, for in that case there would not have been so much reason to display God's mercy as to celebrate his love. But, at the same time, the Incarnation was willed for its own sake.[87]

Rationally trying to figure out *what God wills* from all eternity amounts to the idea of incarnation plus universal salvation. In this view our eternal history or the eternal being antecedes whatever we think, will, or do as humans. It has all been decided for us beforehand in eternity. What does this imply for baptism? Here the individual enters a closed society in which rational necessity predetermines the outcome. This view posits a rational eternity-mind of God where all things have to fall into line with what has been decreed. Baptism is here an insertion into the eternal status quo.

In the second approach to Christian thought we enter an open society in which our accountability is appealed to. There is an open outcome envisioned in the partnership between God (the mystery) and human beings. It is God's outcome, in the end, but human beings are co-workers with God who brings it about.

In the God-walk perspective, baptism represents the social location of the church as open society. God is actively involved in establishing justice. It is not "blind justice" based on the efforts and merits of those we usually associate with. It is "seeing" justice that has an eye for the losers as well as the lost whom *we* usually overlook. We are baptized into the activity of the creator, reconciler, and re-creator. It is a justice/love affirmation. This is the good news of baptism: God, through forgiveness of sins, the elimination of our usurpation or resignation in Messiah Jesus, places us into the open society of the family of God exactly at the point of the justice struggle.

God in creating the world imposes a self-limitation on the godhead, especially in creating the human being. The freedom of the human being in turn imposes on humankind either salvation or damnation, liberation or bondage. Whoever is baptized into Godwalk is free to be part of God's struggle for a just life and eternal life. Those who deny God's offer condemn themselves to isolation. God's justice/love here is felt as wrath because in isolation from God human beings suffer in wielding usurped power or in yielding to such pseudopower.

In baptism *God joins persons to working out the divine purpose of justice/love.* Nothing is absolutely decided beforehand. God acts and continues to act in response to human action. God can "repent" and "relent" (Jer. 18:8; Ps. 106:45; Luke 11:8). Obviously justification comes *first*, the divine initiative. But that evokes divine/human cooperation. In church language cooperation is sanctification, which is not, however, some new religious super-structure above history, but plain participation in God's historical struggle, re-creation, forgetting the little bailiwicks of meaning we have "created" in absenting ourselves from history. Baptism is dying to religiousness for its own sake, religion as personal security. The sacrament of baptism focuses on the mystery of God's pres-ence in each individual life. That is what *sacramentum* means: mystery.

Perhaps some would wish to abandon the notion of sacrament al-together. Melanchthon (1497–1560) already moved forward calling them *signi,* signs. Over the years I occasionally lapsed into talking about the sacraments as *visual aids*. But we dare not give the impression that the sacraments are symbols of an event in the past that make sense apart from the congregation, the corporate assem-bly of the people of God. The *sacraments* are the *thing itself*, albeit not directly for our physical eyes. *This is it. Hoc est.* God in Messiah Jesus made present by the Holy Spirit is here concrete in water as in bread and wine. This is not transubstantiation. But it is even less a sheer memorial act. All sacramental acts have some memorial character, but that is not their essence. In the baptismal water we verily share in the reality of God's death in Messiah Jesus on the cross, as in the bread and wine we share in the body and blood.

Much could be added about the water. It is basically the same thrust as with the bread and the wine. The elements share in God's creator/liberator/re-creator activity. Water is an essential life-giving and life-sustaining element not only in a hot country like Palestine. Fifty to ninety percent of every living thing consists of water. Rain and rivers, dew and springs are archetypal images for a continually creative life force. Hebrew believers saw God's guid-ance in the image of being led to "still waters" (Ps. 23:2). They compared their "thirst for God" to a hart longing for "flowing streams" (Ps. 42:1–2). In John 4:10 Jesus offers God's "living water," and the book of Revelation speaks of the fountain and the river of life (Rev. 21:6; 22:1). Water, in addition to making life possible, revitalizes and cleanses. Abbess Hildegard of Bingen (1098–1179) compared the life of the Spirit to a "verdancy" or even "juiciness," and sin to a "drying up." Says Hildegard: "It is through the water that the Holy Spirit overcomes all injustice, bringing to fulfillment all the Spirit's gifts. . . . With these gifts humankind might thrive in the moisture of justice and stream to spiritual things in the current of truth."[88]

Just as in the eucharist bread and wine invite us to be stewards of the creation, which brings forth grain and fruit, and to share its resources with the hungry, so baptismal water invites us to preserve the waters of the earth as life-givers and to give the "cup of cold water" to those who are thirsty (Matt. 10:42).

There is a motif in medieval German art that shows Christ treading the winepress of God's wrath (see Isa. 63:3; Rev. 19:15) while blood is flowing from his body, indicating the suffering that brings healing. The image merges baptismal and eucharistic imagery—the body-language of dying and giving life.

What we basically need to pay attention to in baptism—as in the eucharist—is *body-language*. Before our eyes we see as well as feel the real thing. It has an outer voice and an inner voice. In baptism not just the body of the minister speaks, but the body of the people assembled, and with them the body of history and the body of the universe. Baptism is a world-historical event, in fact, a cosmic event.[89]

Inner Voice

Sacrament is always body and Word, water and Word, bread/wine and Word. As baptism takes place, the body event in "tapping" water seeks to tap the unspoken word as much as the spoken or preached word. Underlying all our communication, verbal or nonverbal, is the *unspoken word*. God makes every human being a conscience. "What the law requires is written on their hearts, while their conscience also bears witness and their conflicting thoughts accuse or perhaps excuse them" (Rom. 2:15). So we speak of the *voice of conscience*. This is the unspoken word, unspoken by humans. It is to this voice that the water and the spoken word appeal. Here the dying of the sinful self, of usurpation and resignation, domination and accommodation, takes place. The acknowledgment of God's openness to all human beings in Messiah Jesus is understood as reactivating conscience for justice/love to prevail. This is faith as awakened conscience engendered through baptism. God's very nature as justice makes an inroad on conscience. It seeks out the unspoken word of conscience to make itself heard in baptism. Through baptism we begin to act together with God. The whole of history is in suspense here. Nothing has been finally decided as yet. But baptism makes a beginning toward finality.

Outer Voice

In the event of baptism we can see and hear the truth of God's historical drama. Christian tradition uses the words: "I baptize you in the name of the Father, the Son, and the Holy Spirit." But these words make primary sense only for the community in which this happens—*of which the person baptized becomes a part*. The dying to sin, the awakening of conscience, is the crucial element in the rising to new life.

What baptism does time and again is to add another human to the awakened state, the great awakening of the human race. We through baptism enter a different sphere or state of being human, a "noosphere"—to use Teilhard de Chardin's phrase, a sphere or state of purposive consciousness-altering. The repressed powers of consciousness and unconsciousness are being tapped. We get down to the very taproot of our life. We become different human beings—mutants. We relate to history and the universe in new ways. That is why the newly baptized in many Christian communities throughout the history of the church received a new garment, an image used in the book of Revelation (for example, 3:5; 6:11).

Though baptism is directed to one person, it cannot be understood *individualistically*. It does not set us apart as an "elite." It joins us to a *community* whose consciousness is being altered corporately. Externally the drama of baptism and the community have always belonged together. No person is baptized for herself or himself only, but into a concrete community. That is also the way baptism was first recorded:

So those who received his word were baptized, and there were added that day about three thousand souls. And they devoted themselves to the apostles' teaching and fellowship, to the breaking of bread and the prayers. And fear came upon every soul; and many wonders and signs were done through the apostles. And all who believed were together and had all things in common; and they sold their possessions and goods and distributed them to all, as any had need [Acts 2:41-45].

A state of new corporate consciousness obtains. It is not something that is being added to the human race. But those baptized are *enabled to get in touch with a dimension of reality that sin as usurpation and resignation had covered up.* That state cannot be attained without *corporate accountability.* The accountability from the very beginning is part of the event. There is no such thing as baptism apart from a community in which human beings are accountable to each other. The people of God as sharing in the new consciousness through awakened conscience shares the water of life: this is the body-language of baptism. It implies that baptism in homes, private baptisms around the living room table and TV set are not "for real." Nor are baptisms in empty churches. Of course, in case of sickness or other need, exceptions will be made. But the congregation ought not to begin with the premise that a dying child needs baptism to be saved. It is a magical premise. Emergency baptisms usually misconstrue the whole network of meaning in baptism.

All along we need to remember that Jesus himself was baptized. He took upon himself in the Jordan the sins of the world, anticipating his death and his rising to newness of life. What we principally do in baptism is nothing but immerse the person into the baptism of Christ as the right hand of God in the justice struggle.

Infant Baptism

From the perspective of christo-praxis infant baptism obviously raises serious issues. The small child cannot develop the thought of entering a community sharing in God's justice struggle. Infant baptism will function as a *dedication ceremony*, a worship act of placement (into the church). But it was fundamentally an afterthought of the institutional church. The primal way of celebrating baptism had not included infants. The covenant between Christians and God was not based on ties of flesh and blood. Children are not automatically members of the *new* covenant of God just because their parents are. God's promise is also to children, but not because of blood ties.

There was, however, the right intuition of the church that the renewal of humanity is not something that demands a developed intellect, mature reason. One does not have to be a grown-up to be part of what is happening in baptism. What is crucial in infant baptism is that here also the unspoken word can be trusted to activate conscience—especially in the context of the Christian community. It does not happen apart from the external spoken word, as is also the case in adult baptism. Yet for conscience to speak and become "hearing" (active), we do not depend on the right baptismal understanding evoked by the external words.

The work of God is going on all the time. It reaches every human being. God's creative influence, God's reconciling, renewing, and re-creating impact is at the center of every heart. Sin makes it ineffective. Baptism is the seal that God's work has reached the hearing of the human being. The infant cannot express its participation in that work in a confession of awakened conscience. That God comes to us before we can respond does not have to be expressed through *infant* baptism, just as we would not express it through insertion or infusion of the eucharistic elements into the mouth of an infant. Each sacrament as such expresses God's initiative. Therefore, a church policy where adult baptism besides infant baptism is optional is a step ahead in the liberation process.

In God's liberation process, infant baptism (once performed) is not "invalid." The affirmation of the activity of God also toward a child, conveyed in the body-language of baptism, is not ineffectual in the Christian community. What is more, God comes to all of us primarily, as it were, against our willing, whether we are adult or child, baptized or unbaptized. As sinners we are inclined toward injustice and do not will participation in God's justice work in history of our own volition. And yet each child mirrors the fact that Jesus was baptized as the child of God. This is not a rationale for infant baptism, however. It merely affirms our elementary human condition before God.

Yet infant baptism can hardly escape abuse. The baby in its natural innocence and beauty becomes a crowd-teaser or a crowd-pleaser. We all can vote for the natural sentiment. Everyone is moved by the presence of a child at the font. But then there have been baptismal fonts with rose petals swimming on the water. Notice also that some pastors are tempted to take the baby in their arms and to kiss it (no biblical warrant for that gesture). One is inclined to think that a "kiss of death" *before* the use of the water and a mouth-to-mouth resuscitation afterward would be more appropriate, especially because "sprinkling" instead of the "dipping" is already obscuring the seriousness of the "dying to sin." We tend to make the overcoming of death, the result of usurpation or resignation, a pretty thing, spiritual beauty culture. So we at baptism through our misleading body-language express the opposite of what it stands for. God is struggling for justice and "enlists" each individual. Some join in the struggle. They hear the external word resonate in the inner word.

The sacrament of baptism dare not be scary or unctuously solemn. But we ought not to hide the reality of God in Messiah Jesus suffering and dying in history for the least of human beings and all of creation. Participation in the liberation/reconciliation process needs to be expressed also in baptism. It is difficult to see how the average infant baptism will embody this elementary reality. Infant baptism can be viewed as dedication ceremony. The community dedicates the child to God. What God does at this juncture in a human life is not ineffectual. It points to the liberating activity of God. But that is exactly what has to be made visible in the communal body-language of the event. Our dedication ceremonies ought at least to help us understand infant baptism in social location among the "invisible human beings," the wretched of the earth. Every child baptized into the Christian community ought to remind us of hungry and abandoned children around the globe who also need our real "dedication."

As the struggle for accountable teaching continues, infant baptism will become less and less acceptable. Many of its dilemmas need to be addressed in significant pastoral care. Briefly, it needs to consider at least three points concerning children and the sacraments. (1) Early baptismal counseling of the parents. In most churches it is not being done thoroughly enough or not done at all. (2) The issues of infant baptism need to be very carefully related to the eucharist. (3) In case children in some churches are invited to share in Holy Communion, they need to be prepared for it in a careful catechumenate.

The Eucharistic Word

It is difficult to see proclamation within the new God-walk context, for it has been so much shaped by the lecture-type talk in the average sanctuary. Preaching always has a great fascination for laity and clergy alike, especially in Protestantism. But how does it grow out of christo-praxis? There is no way of avoiding proclamation in the eucharist. Here it offers as external voice what God ceaselessy offers to the inner voice in the justice struggle. If one compares the elementary insight of christo-praxis with the de facto present-day function of preaching, one might be perplexed.

Preaching, we discover again, is (1) significant if it opens our eyes to the eucharistic presence of Jesus, the radical immersion of God in history. Eucharistic preaching is a word-deed that changes minds and hearts—and the world. (2) The one who preaches is not an orator standing on some elevated pulpit pedestal. The sharing of the word makes the proclaimer a vicar of Christ in the world, a stand-in for Christ shaping the world together with God standing among the people. (3) We talk too much when we preach. If preaching is a deed-word changing the world, it will distinguish itself less by its eloquent sounds than by creative pauses. Eucharistic preaching is marked by silences: the pause that refreshes. There are moments when God's suffering and acting alone have to speak.

The World Alone Dare Not Set the Agenda

Since the 1960s there has been the notion that we need to be where the action is. It kept us from eucharistic preaching. Theology occasionally has been compared to a floating crap game. Church and world were not seen as coinciding, but as principally apart. Encounter with a dimension of the world was not encounter with an aspect of the church, or vice versa. An editorial in a professional theological journal offers an instance of how even theologians still see the world setting the agenda for the church:

> The crisis marking 1980 may well mark the end of a historical period. Many thoughtful analysts suggest that the turbulent period we are living through is best interpreted as a transition to a postmodern period. . . . As the modern world was radically different from the preceding period of the Renaissance,

so the postmodern world still invokes radical shifts not only in technology but in ways we think about ourselves and the world and in the institutions we will fashion to serve our societies. As a result, the role of theology again becomes significant.[90]

These words are typical of how, in a wide range of opinion, theology is still looked upon as a function of the times, of the world, and of the contemporary situation. The world is still setting the agenda: "As a result, the role of theology again becomes significant."

For the church, God first of all sets the agenda. We look to God to find the divine agenda in the world. Contemporary analysis is important. But it is not *so* important that one could say: "As a result. . . ." Theology does not become significant again because of a changed scene. Christian thought is always significant as the idea-framework that grows out of praxis. The church as the structure-framework for these ideas is significant in itself at the point where God's presence in the world coincides with God's christo-praxis among Christians. We had too many theologies legitimating some facet of the contemporary scene, a death-of-God theology, a social change theology, a theology of play—even a theology of UFOs. The whole point of God's work is not to make us concentrate on some facet of the world, but to see the world in all its facets as gripped by the God who is struggling for justice.

Eucharistic preaching today pays attention to God's indwelling the world—not only the church. The sacrament is the elementary social location of preaching. What we need to sense in all preaching is God in Messiah Jesus taking sides with the poor as mediated to us through the biblical word. It is not a humanistic crusade of good people. The poor are no more "good" than we are. God who stands by them is good. That is why we, too, are called to take sides. So the world alone cannot set the agenda for Christians. The truth of the agenda-setting Word is that the world is the place where God is at work.

Mary, Mother of Jesus, Witness to God's Agenda

How can we best offer a model for the church coinciding with the world? I was using Ernesto Cardenal's *Gospel in Solentiname* a while back with a class on prayer and contemplation. It was amazing to notice the "dialogue sermons" that grew out of the book among the students. It was not a "back to the Bible" trend, but a "forward with the Bible" thrust. The book contains dialogue sermons from Nicaragua before the fall of the Somoza regime. Early in the book appears a conversation on Mary's Magnificat:"My soul magnifies the Lord, and my spirit rejoices in God my Savior," etc. The peasants, fishermen and fisherwomen in Nicaragua amazingly take up the thrust of the Magnificat. One woman exclaims:

> She says that people will call her happy. . . . She feels happy because she is the mother of Jesus the Liberator, and because she also is a liberator like her son, because she understood her son and did not oppose his mission . . . unlike other mothers of young people who are . . . liberators of their communities. That was her great merit.[91]

The poor peasants and fisherfolk sense what we often overlook. Mary is a model of eucharistic presence in the world. The major point of the Magnificat is that God works in the world as God works in the church. As God scatters the proud "in the imagination of their hearts," puts down the mighty from their thrones, God also exalts those of low degree, filling the hungry with good things, and exactly *in this work* God helps Israel and "remembers" the divine mercy (Luke 1:51-54). Israel and world, church and world, liberation history and world history, coincide where God sets the agenda. They are different, but they are not completely separate. Mary offers us a good model of eucharistic preaching. It is a woman's approach, a realistic assessment of the human condition. Women, among the disadvantaged, have insights that are lost among rulers, high society, and the established church.

God Makes Church and World Coincide

It is because of the God-work or God-walk in history as a whole that world and church, though different, coincide. Preaching is sharing God's activity in the world, God's justice struggle for a more human life in the global village. The word of preaching embodies it as it unpacks the treasures of the eucharist. It is thus an efficacious word.

Words in preaching are not mere words, empty words. Even in our daily use of words there is often much efficacy contained in a word. Take the negotiating talks concerning the American embassy hostages in Iran in the fall of 1980. We all realized that on Warren Christopher's words (and those of his team), hung, as it were, *actions* with tremendous consequences. It is much the same with the eucharistic word, though with its own spirituality dynamics. Arising from the power of the eucharist, God's own justice struggle, the eucharistic word is intent upon creating change in the world. There is utter seriousness in what happens in the world through eucharistic preaching certainly as much as in the freeing of hostages through words of negotiation. What is at stake is also a freeing, a liberating event. We need to be utterly clear about the terms. God's justice always remains God's. Preaching does not transport God's justice into our scheming minds so that it would translate into social and psychological programs. Yet it puts us under pressure, it "prods" us and challenges us to wake up to our human justice capacity. We need to learn to live gently and justly with "justice under pressure."[92] We can show justice under pressure, just as we can show "grace under pressure" (Hemingway), for "my yoke is easy" (Matt. 11:30).

Where is Christian thought going in the 1980s and 90s? It is going to church. It is going to the eucharist. It is put through the tough test of praxis. So it is going to the world at the same time. For God makes both world and church coincide in the eucharist. Dogmatics as an esoteric, elitist, or academic affair disappears, and accountable teaching takes its place. Eucharistic preaching makes it come to fruition.

Preaching the Church in the Global Village

In listening to the proclamation, Christians want to keep in mind the nature of the church—both Messiah Jesus as head and the church as his body immersed in the world. This does not mean developing accountable teaching apart from published dogmatics. But the realization is growing that beyond what theologians have produced thus far in books, a more faithful struggling with the worldly immersion of the church embodied in eucharist and sermon is called for. Metaphoric visibility and orality have to be added to the literacy of the printed page.

God in Jesus becomes flesh, takes on a human body and soul. After Jesus' life, death, and resurrection, God's self-realization in one person happens time and again through a new body, which is the church (1 Cor. 12:27: "Now you are the body of Christ and individually members of it"). As we preach God in Jesus, we always participate in a new realpresence of God in the world, a new involvement of God in the affairs of global humanity. In the church, there is no *imitatio Christi*, no imitation of Christ, called for. The church is not the extension of the incarnation either. The point is the *innovatio Christi*, a kind of clowning, holy laughter. Human beings in human frailty try to manifest a measure of the divine reality in new ways. It often appears funny. Not many persons really try it. But the "clowns of God" are taking the risk.

In this regard the sacraments make a crucial point. They summarize the mystery of God's present activity in the global village as justice activity. As one of the peasants in Solentiname suggests of Mary: "She says that God is holy, and that means, just. The just person does not offend anybody, the one who doesn't commit any injustices. God is like this." The sacrament embodies the just God. Preaching tries to evoke an understanding of this embodiment.

We do not see God directly on display. There is only indirectness and incognito. Yet for discipleship God becomes accessible in baptism and eucharist in worldly form. In baptism God effects our "immersion" in the new corporate humanity of the world. In the eucharist as the justice meal God time and again effects the new humanity to be shared in the natural form of bread and wine. Through the sacraments God compels the church, as it were, to be faithful to the world in the justice struggle for all humankind. Yet we need to keep in mind carefully that God's work always is twofold: reconciliation and liberation. There is the gift of the forgiveness of sins and through it enlistment in the struggle. Preaching needs to take the twofold dynamics into account.

Preaching as Eucharistic Word in the Global Village

Through baptism and eucharist we are always part of the world-liness of God in the church of the global village. That is a mystery we need to discern. "For those who eat and drink without discern-ing the body, eat and drink judgment upon themselves" (1 Cor. 11:29). We are always part of Christ's global village body. It is that reality we have to discern time and again, the gift and the enlist-ment. Through "grace under pressure" and "justice under pres-sure" God aids us in this discernment through the *deed-word* of preaching, compelling us to work together with God, reshaping humankind in the global village of which we are a part. Obviously it is never a matter of our molding humankind on our own. The point is that God is already shaping the human core. All we can do is share in this process of dramatic formation of the human sub-stance.

Preaching: A Sacrament. Proclaiming God's justice/love is holy reality faithful to the world in the midst of the global village scene. It is not that we have merely sacrament *and* Word. In the Word itself there is sacrament, mystery. The work of God's justice in the global village is what we "eat" (take into our body as gift in the sacrament). But it is never without the Word—the inner unspoken word of conscience, and the external word of the sacramental rite. "When we are 'discerned' by the Lord, we are chastened, so that we may not be condemned" (1 Cor. 11:32). This "being discerned" by God's faithfulness to the world is never perceived apart from the Word, external and internal.

Preaching is an "effecting" of Christ's body for the global village. It creates for the world who we are in Messiah Jesus. What we term preaching is effecting the realpresence of Mary's God in the minds and hearts of others as a wordpresence the same way baptism and eucharist effect it as a *body-presence*, reality repre-sented in natural elements.

The reason why baptism and eucharist in dogmatic reflection need to be clearly interwoven with preaching is that the church has strangely split up Jesus time and again into *two* forms of self-representation: sacrament *and* Word. In Catholicism today the Word often is still seen as appendix to the sacrament. In Protestantism things frequently appear the other way around: the sacraments turn into an appendix of the Word. Preaching in many Protestant churches is the supersacrament. It functions as substitute for the eucharist.

Yet Word and sacrament are part of one historical activity, God's justice struggle among humankind. They are of one piece as the expression of God's faithfulness. They are of equal concern. We cannot do more to be faithful to the world than to be faithful to this activity of God expressed in Word and sacrament. In this way Mary was faithful: "Behold, I am the handmaid of the Lord" (Luke 1:38). This "handmaid" was not submissively serving God, but "co-creating" Messiah Jesus, and in the Magnificat she proclaimed God's justice even before his birth.

Preaching is faithful to the world when it delves into the sacrament and emerges from its body-language, even when the eucharist is not celebrated in the same service. There is no reason, however, for eucharist and preaching to be kept apart. It is an abuse and not a proper use of the eucharist. Faithful preaching is essentially faithfulness to the worldly elements of bread and wine, to the natural substance of this world. Preaching is the eucharistic or baptismal event all over again as *word-deed* empowered by Messiah Jesus, broken on the cross for the healing of the global village. Jesus' commitment of his own body in life and death sacramentally affirms our preaching.

Preaching: Standing in the Midst of God's Justice Struggle. We often do not achieve what we intend in preaching. We let it well up too much from our experience, our religious feelings, or our doctrinal preferences. Often preaching is more "delivering a message" than lifting up a whole congregation before God in a eucharistic thanksgiving for God's faithfulness. Even the "best" sermons often leave the impression that preaching is a professional performance. God's own impoverishment activity in our preaching, however, is not a professional performance. What happened in Messiah Jesus reaches out in God's faithfulness to the world everywhere. God, through the Word of Messiah Jesus, evokes not only personal creativity in individuals, so that each discovers their true selfhood, but also communal interaction that impels communities toward greater justice: "Seek first the kingdom of God and its justice, and all other things shall be added unto you" (Matt. 6:33).

We are entering the age of the *laity*. Ministers might have to play an "underprivileged" role in the future. The minister in the pulpit vividly and intensely enacts and represents the task that all lay persons have to perform day in and day out. There is indeed a sacred space of God, but it is in the midst of the world's turmoil. What Jesus presented as God's faithfulness to the world in a small community of what is now the Middle East, God does all the time among all peoples. It happened "once for all times," which means, in a unique, eternal as well as historical way. And yet the reign of God is at hand in Messiah Jesus time and again. As the right hand of God, Messiah Jesus is ceaselessly activating the reign of God "at hand." Preaching seeks to let that faithfulness of God to the world break through on Sundays, so that the congregation will be more aware of its breaking through everywhere during the week.

This immediately raises issues about "sermon preparation." Preaching today cannot ignore careful focus on social analysis and moral analysis.

1. As to *social analysis*, Mary, Mother of Jesus, for her time pointed to the clash between the rich and the poor. She derived her insight from scripture as well as experience: the Magnificat interweaves various images from the Hebrew Bible. Taking the Bible seriously, we have to do much the same for our time. As regards our own experience—initially at least—the challenge appears to be a North/South issue. We in the North in the First and Second Worlds are the "haves," whereas those in the South are largely the "have-nots." We cannot leave out class analysis. We therefore also cannot leave out a study of Karl Marx. The destitute of the world are estimated today by the World Bank to have reached 800 million; there were "only" 700 million at the beginning of the 1970s. Nearly 40 percent of those who live in the South survive in a poverty that does not allow the basic necessities of life. Millions die every year of malnutrition. These harsh data are very much part of the texture of preaching. But we need to probe the terror in terms of its basic principles.

We often encounter the notion that liberation theology pertains only to the Third World. The fact is that the power of the First World can be maintained only by empire. Schleiermacher spoke of the feeling of absolute dependence, a dependence on God.[93] In our situation all of us who live in the First World live in absolute dependence on empire. The welfare of the free world depends largely on the economic and political power of the United States. There is a definite gulf between dependence on God and dependence on empire.

2. As to *moral analysis*, Mary also pointed to the stray imaginations of the proud. We dare not leave the analysis here to newspaper columnists. For example, we need to be as deeply concerned as they about what is being presented on our TV screens, the forces that daily shape our minds. In social location at the eucharist we cannot help asking ourselves: How can we watch all this TV obscenity when millions in the world are starving? And when at the same time there are countless people fighting for freedom? Early in the decade the *Washington Post* commented on the new CBS program *That's My Line:*

> The CBS entry in the amazingly incredible, real-people, variety freak-show genre . . . lurches impishly from a feature about a man who teaches other men "how to pick up girls" for quick sex to a fey hunk of sleazery about a Topeka, Kansas, clothing store where men strip down to their underpants while women ogle and shriek at them. . . . Basically it's another monomaniacal titillation derby.

Put that type of thing next to a face marked by hunger!

Television has shaped our minds to expect nearly everything to be entertainment, whether news or religious programs. What is upon us here is not Orwell's *1984*, but Huxley's *Brave New World*. Guards, prisons, and truth ministries are not necessary. The public is simply sidetracked by trivialities and fails to discern the life-and-death issues. The world is turned into a mammoth circus. Citizens become mere spectators. Public affairs turn into variety shows.[94] In this atmosphere, moral analysis of the threat of nuclear war or of world hunger has a hard time making an impact. A while back, the Chinese seriously expected the world to be engaged in nuclear conflict by the end of the 1980s. Nuclear threat and moral collapse are closely related. Eucharistic preaching needs to take into account the impact of empire on the social situation and its moral issues. In fact, our absolute dependence on empire is the framework in which we need to grapple with the moral issues.

Mary was a wise woman. She preached a model sermon faithful to the world, bearing the truly human one coming into the world to reach the "least" of its people. Any sermon today needs to be "conceived" as faithfully giving birth to thought from praxis. The dependency framework of empire with its attendent moral chaos has to be uncovered. This means that the sacredness of life is grasped only as we ourselves stand in the midst of God's justice struggle.

Preaching: Sounding Forth What the Sacrament Bodies Forth. The preacher thus becomes the vicar of Christ. If we have done our social analysis and moral analysis, and move to the actual texture of the sermon, we realize that we stand in Jesus' place in sharing God's truth. The pope is often considered the one vicar of Christ— a wrong perception. Preaching sounds forth the faithfulness of God in the justice struggle that the sacrament embodies. The heralding, the announcing, is not a mere noising of sound. It is an evocation of God's presence in the world. The Word here is very much the performative Word.

Thus the one who speaks the Word in the sermon becomes the vicar of Christ. Preaching is shaping worldly words to share in the historical work of God embodied in the sacrament. It evokes mutual accountability among Christians on grounds of forgiveness of sin and reconciliation, justification and liberation. Here is the good news that God takes our place as we "taste" it and "see" it in the sacrament. Thus, as we preach, in the sacrament God begins to liberate us from empire and to save us in spite of our failure to live justly. A woman here is as much a vicar of Christ as a man.

The preached word *bodies forth* Messiah Jesus in worldly form no less than the body-language of the sacrament. The difference here is that the concrete elements of sound shape new reality of Spirit in our minds and hearts, almost as in Mary the words were helping to shape God's Messiah already in the womb. This bodying forth, letting words give birth to new reality, makes the preacher unique: the vicar of Christ. Nothing magic. It is simply the realpresence of God taking on living form once more in the Word.

Preaching thus understood is certainly not lecturing— communicating religious or moral ideas. It is also not commanding a platoon—trying to get "Christian soldiers" to march. It is not self-communication of the preacher—sharing the depths of a beautiful soul. It is the creative and re-creative act of the Spirit in which Jesus again takes bodily shape among the people. It expresses God's continuing faithfulness to the world, the healing of the nations, in the global village.

Inasmuch as Jesus is evoked in us in the *deed-word* of preaching, preaching is basically *evocation* and *creation*. The one who speaks the Word shares in the creative deed of God's faithfulness to the world. "So we are ambassadors for Christ [vicars of Christ], God making appeal through us. We beseech you on behalf of Christ, be reconciled to God" (2 Cor. 5:20). It is crucial to remember that the liberation-atonement functions centrally in preaching. God straightens things out time and again in Messiah Jesus. Human beings are invited to share in this reconciliation between humankind and God.

Licensure, ordination, installation—all these somewhat awkward ordinances accompanying the pastoral office try to come to grips with the mystery of being the "vicaress" or vicar of God's struggle with the world. The church never lost sight of it completely. We can of course develop an elaborate doctrine of *ordination*. It can never accomplish more than state the transparent truth: the minister does not have some special indelible character (*character indelibilis*). She or he is not the super-Christian. The minister-preacher is the human being, graced by God's gentle justice pressure on persons-in-community, who is set aside by the church to embody in Word and sacrament the sacramental presence of God in history, and thus God's faithfulness to the global village, our habitat. Mary can well serve as model. We can be "pregnant" by God's power with the truly Human One.

This does not mean that the minister-preacher is "something special." All this person does is embody the layhood of all ministers as well as of all believers. All of us are God's children. All Christians are vicars and "vicaresses" of Christ. But to make sure that the power of this truth does not get lost, the church sets aside individuals to remind us of it again and again by their very walk.

The minister-preacher evokes Messiah Jesus once more in the midst of humanity. To become a Christ to one another (Luther) has its special cutting edge right here. Preaching concretizes what being human in God's justice struggle with the world is all about. As it ties in with eucharist and baptism, it is an utterly responsible task.

I stress the minister as vicar of Christ especially because ministers share in Christ's power. Messiah Jesus embodied God's power among persons, not so much *meditating* on the mystery of God as *realizing* it in history in faithfulness to the world, the poor, the sinners. The preacher is not a little Jesus. Preaching shares in the mystery of God's power present in Jesus on this earth: "As Jesus finished these sayings, the crowds were astonished at his teaching, for he taught them as one who had authority, and not as their scribes" (Matt. 7:28f.). Although the power here is that of God and God alone, our preaching shares in the faithfulness of God to the world. God again wants divine faithfulness to the world to take on human form.

No Eucharistic Preaching without Primal Authority of the Eucharistic Bible. Not *sola scriptura*, but *scriptura prima* is the hermeneutic principle for our day. The *sola* was crucial for the Reformation. The *prima* is important today. The body of Christ cannot avoid or circumvent encounter with the primacy of the biblical Word that places us among the losers of the world, the countless people who suffer in body and soul. The preached Word shares in the biblical Word. The authority of the Bible is ultimately God's justice—vulnerability in impoverishment.

I am pointing here to the sacraments not as rites, but as justice events. The Bible is the book where God's justice was first unfolded in a great variety of experience and language over a long period of time. Here God's justice struggle was first discerned:

> Take away from me the noise of your songs,
>   to the melody of your harps I will not listen.
> But let justice roll down like waters,
>   and righteousness like an ever-flowing stream
> [Amos 5:23f.].

The Bible has been abused many times—for example, as a book of magic, or ethical precepts, or exciting history, or beautiful literature. "Take the Book off the pulpit, shelve it," a young minister told me several years ago. "We do not need the Book anymore. We ought to preach from contemporary events." What he forgot was that effective preaching is evocation and creation of God's faithfulness because of the justice power shared by this book.

The Bible is never merely the text for the sermon: "My text (this Sunday) is. . . . " It is certainly also text. But what we have in the text is first of all *text*-ure, something in context composed of closely interwoven justice elements. With the biblical Word, tied to the sacrament, we have a justice texture in a justice context, reflecting God's faithfulness to the world as justice (some texts having been written in prison or exile, for example). A texture we can indwell like a garment or home. Crucial for God-walk is that we can indwell the scriptures, that they are not merely a book on an academic shelf or the pulpit.

Preaching in this context is the unfolding of the very texture of God's faithful justice struggle, not merely expounding a text. We share in a re-creative justice act that authorizes our action. Preaching in this regard is re-creating God's justice struggle with its past (Israel's covenants) and its future (God's coming reign), the way it happens in Mary's Magnificat. Faithful or accountable preaching helps the assembled people of God experience the justice presence of God in Christ in the world through the Word as verily as that people bodily tastes and sees bread and wine in the eucharist.

It makes no difference whether the sermon is eloquent or filled with stories, whether it is designed to make its hearers rock with laughter or quietly to share an experience. Accountable preaching certainly will not be dull, monotonous, lifeless, spineless, or humorless. But at its center it will "publicly portray" (Gal. 3:1) God's justice struggle in Christ, as though God were again in Messiah Jesus walking among the lilies of the field, liberating the poor, and healing sinners by the roadside in Galilee. "Not in robes of purple splendor, Not in silken softness shod, But in raiment worn with travel came their God; And the people knew His presence, By the heart that ceased to sigh, When the glory of the Lord was passing by." It is exactly this glory as glory of God's justice passing by that distinguishes accountable preaching as eucharistic Word. Here the people stand in wonder, though no sign is in the sky. Here is the place for silence, for pauses. We talk too much when we preach.

Accountability to the global village means letting the world quiet down in the hearts and minds of hearers as the Word is embodied also in silences—giving God a chance to step forth in the world. It implies that part of the sacrament of preaching is *prayer*. How many of us are praying when we preach? No preaching remains accountable without prayer built into it, just as there is no eucharist without eucharistic prayer. Here are the openings where even silences have their place in sermons, creative pauses. We have to be able to hear God walking through the world. In order to sense it, we have to become silent—to listen with the inner ear.

"We do not know to pray as we ought, but the Spirit personally intercedes with us with sighs too deep for words" (Rom. 8:26). Sighs too deep for words! This is the character of creative silence in preaching where we hear God walk through history. I do not mean to suggest that we ought to be dumbstruck in preaching. But because God's faithful justice has to break through, there need to be pauses where God can get a foot in the door. "Let go and let God"—also in the sermon. That is the prayer moment in preaching. We can learn from the silence of Quaker worship.

Preaching thus becomes a thanksgiving for the reality we celebrate in the sacrament. Yet it is also a petition that on *grounds* of this faithful justice, God will assist us in embodying the divine justice in our own struggles. Thy will be done! That will is to be prayed through not *merely* in the closet, but in walking together with God in the midst of the historical struggle, on the frontline of the ghetto as well as in the comforting and healing work of pulpit and visitation, in the warfare against powers and principalities as well as in binding wounds inflicted in the struggle.

What distinguishes us most as human beings is our accountability to God. We can also say: to be human is to pray, especially to pray *together*. The human being is the *animal orans*, the praying animal. *We are what we pray* (as we are what we eat, and as we are what we celebrate). We pray as Christians as we weave our words sacramentally around the texture of the Bible and experience the interdependence of God-presence and poor-presence in the global village.

It is exactly at this point that preaching needs to take note of the counterpoint of this interdependence—the tragic dependence on empire. We are prisoners of a socio-political system that usually determines even what we believe. We need to break the iron bars of this prison, as God has done it for us and is still doing it. Without an awareness of this tension between interdependence and dependence, preaching becomes glib—smooth religious talk.

In the midst of the tension between the interdependence of God-presence and poor-presence and our tragic absolute dependence on empire, our minds and hearts need to be content with the concrete embodiment of God's justice struggle in the sacrament and the sacramental Word, the faithful deed-word. We do not get to know more of God. We certainly do not know all things divine. We know a few important things. But we know in part and prophesy (preach) in part (1 Cor. 13:12).

Even when we do not fully know, we are being fully known (1 Cor. 13:12). In the unspoken word of conscience God knows who we really are. So the ministry of prayerful preaching, accountable preaching, is always caught up in the inner space of God's justice/love in faithfulness to the world. In this regard, preaching is always in keeping with 1 Thessalonians 5:17: "Pray always," and 1 Thessalonians 5:18, *en panti eucharisteite*, in everything "preach" eucharistically—that is, with thanksgiving, sacramentally.

In more "technical" terms, we might say that in the Word (Logos) God knows us, makes us aware of who God is, and gives us meaning in the unspoken word of conscience. Through our preaching, the Word mediates Messiah Jesus as justification of all human beings. But only together with the Spirit, in Word with Spirit, does God fully labor over changing us. The Spirit brings to bear in us the *heart-changing* activity of God in Messiah Jesus. One might say, in God's walk through history the Spirit is God's change agent.

We ultimately can do no more than place ourselves within the texture of God's faithfulness to the world, as reflected in the justice Word of the Bible. In preaching, ministers face themselves and the people before this truly accountable God—which is an attitude of prayer. In such a stance God makes all of us a conscience, sensitizing us to our sin, but also offering us—through liberation-atonement—the power to overcome it. Thus we can truly "let go and let God"—let God's justice take over.

Embodying the church in preaching means "walking" the Word in many situations. We stand close to the parents of a newborn child trying to be faithful to God's gift to them. We share in a couple's struggle to find faithful relationships. We share the joys and tears of the kindergarten where children learn the first steps of being faithful to the immediate environment. We stand by families torn in strife, parents worried to death over their drug-captive sons and daughters, children hatefully lashing out at their parents—or vice versa; inmates in prison, hostages in captivity, and families in shacks; the shut-ins, the lonely, the sick. God's struggle with the world is at the well-known crossroads of life as well as the unknown ghetto, in the hospital room as well as the sanctuary, in the hostage cell as well as in the plane that returns the hostages, and in El Salvador in the death of five North American women and their assassins. The world's needs to which God is faithful are endless. We are not called to serve these needs as pseudoshamans, trusting our own healing powers. In the divine struggle against the demonic structures of injustice, as well as in the binding of wounds and forgiving of sins, we discover God's faithfulness to the whole world and share it in preaching.

How eucharistic preaching is deeply steeped in meditation of God's eucharistic reality becomes clear, for example, in Hildegard of Bingen's work.[95] In her illuminations, no isolated picture of Jesus' crucifixion can be found, as was popular in later medieval iconography. In one of her four crucifixion pictures, in the upper half Jesus is shown on the cross with the mother church standing next to him holding a vessel into which flows blood from his side mixed with water. The lower half depicts an altar with the communion cup and the bread. There is a golden stream flowing from the cross toward the cup and the bread. Pictures reflecting scenes from Jesus' life surround the stream: birth, death, resurrection, and ascension. The mother church seems to have placed the chalice on the altar. Now she stands with outstretched hands praying for more power to flow from the cross.

Seeing this thorough interdependence of cross and eucharist is a first step in realizing how Jesus' suffering continues as inroad on history. It is present reality, not mere memory. It also brings resurrection and ascension into the midst of historical conflict. They are part of the eucharistic event: Messiah Jesus as right hand of God is in the midst of the historical struggle. Here is the ultimate reality that interweaves nature and history, and makes us co-responsible for moving them on.

Preaching will want to depend on a meditation that reaches far beyond the immediate eucharistic context, just as Hildegard von Bingen could span the whole cosmos with her thought centered in the eucharist. Matthew Fox describes her illumination:

> The altar is carefully lined up with the axis of the cross: it represents the new center of the universe. The Jews believed that the Temple was the center of the universe, and Native Americans still believe that the center of their worshipping circle represents the center of the universe. For Hildegard too, worship is a cosmic event. Power emanates to and from the center of the universe. Hildegard tells us how Christ, when he "killed death and shattered hell," actually "turned the circle of the earth in a different and better and newer way."[96]

At the eucharist compassion is poured out on the church, causing the sharing of bread and wine to become celebration as much as justice making.[97] It is always God's justice itself that is breaking through, shattering every injustice.[98] Human beings need to learn that it is not rational—not true to the rationale of the universe—to be unjust. Creation itself is not silent in the face of injustice. As Hildegard envisioned it: "I heard a loud cry rise up from the elements of the world and they said: We cannot follow the natural course assigned to us by our Creator because human beings have thrown us into confusion with their evil works, just as though they were millstones around our necks."[99] Deeply steeped in the wisdom of God, Hildegard sensed the significance of God's eucharistic presence for the rational grasp of God's justice-making throughout the cosmos. Preaching for our day has to make it more explicit yet, for we see the connection of the crucified one not only with mother church and mother nature, but also with humankind as a whole, especially the wretched of the earth.

Apart from the eucharistically centered activity of God, the mentally retarded would not receive their due, but neither would the rich recluse. Because God is faithful in justice-making, preaching is a deed-word and we cannot be "ashamed of the Gospel: It is the power of God for salvation to everyone who has faith, to the Jew first and also to the Greek. For in it the justice of God is revealed through faith for faith, as it is written: 'the person who through faith is just shall live' " (Rom 1:16-17). Only through the con-science, awakened by God, is a person made just. True life exists only in this "alien" justice, the justice God gives us. Here we are ultimately grounded in the joy of God and the angels: "My soul magnifies the Lord, and my Spirit rejoices in God, my Savior. For behold from henceforth all generations will call me blessed" (Luke 1:46-48).

It is hardly by chance that this joyful discovery of God's justice is attributed to the woman Mary—and in a patriarchal time. It is also hardly by chance that Hildegard of Bingen "illuminated" her visions in a time of very masculine scholasticism. Both women were powerful preachers.[100]

3

SPIRIT-PRAXIS

All the thought developed up to this point is basically Spirit-thought. God-walk yields a "theology of the Holy Spirit." It derives from God as Holy Spirit shaping our thought. Yet nothing is gained by inverting the traditional sequence of dogmatics and beginning with the Spirit instead of God the creator. God-walk evolves from the presence of the Holy Spirit toward ideas that do not make more sense if one starts changing around their traditional sequence. There also have been suggestions that thought arising from praxis ought to begin with ecclesiology.

But this game of musical chairs is played out rather abstractly, with little reflection on de facto praxis. What emerges in praxis is not necessarily right away "church-thought." We have to cope with a constant rumbling of God in our souls. There is also our encounter with the same God in Jesus. Each notion of faith emerges independently as well as interdependently. If one presses it too much into logical sequence, one is back in the groove of systematic theology, the system that straitjackets thought in terms of a previously developed theoretical principle.[1] Under the aegis of the Spirit, the eucharist makes Christian thought evolve surprisingly new ever and again. The movement of thought is here neither linear (as in male-dominated Western thought) nor circular (as in more "feminine" Eastern thought), but a "spiral" propelled forward by the Spirit toward God's just rule. It might also be seen in the image of a tapestry in which the Spirit interweaves the threads of nature and history, of male and female, consummating God's design.

Stressing the corporate and personal appropriation of God's presence in eucharist and baptism means appealing to the work of the Spirit. Reference to dying with Jesus or rising with Jesus is ultimately a reference to the dynamics of the Spirit. Being transformed while not being conformed to the world basically happens through the work of the Spirit. Human beings long to be transformed by the Spirit.[2] They do not really want to be soothed by spiritual lullabies, but desparately seek to be confronted by the truth. So they do not like to be preached *at*. But they do want to preach *along*, expounding the eucharistic realpresence of the crucified God, to use Moltmann's term.

Accountable teaching grows out of discipleship, God-walk. This amounts to a teaching of the Holy Spirit that takes seriously God's presence in the church.[3] It begins with the eucharist in that here God's work in the world and the church is most concretely experienced as the work of the Holy Spirit.

God's creativity is peculiarly at work as Holy Spirit in terms of liberation outside the church.[4] The work of the eternal God is not limited to the historical deprivation of God (incarnation).[5] This does not mean that reconciliation and re-creation, besides liberation, would get a hearing from all peoples. But God certainly has always had an impact on Israel: "Create in me a clean heart, O God, and put a new and right spirit within me. Cast me not away from thy presence, and take not thy Holy Spirit from me" (Ps. 51:10f.). Israel experiences God's Spirit in countless ways.[6] What happens in Israel is the prototype of what happens in humankind everywhere. The Christian church is not the only place where God's Spirit is at work and often not the most crucial place.

For each human being God's Spirit-activity is "at work" in conscience. The Holy Spirit proceeds from the creator and activates the inner Word, the Logos, in us. It is not an *inarticulate* rumbling of some soul tissue. God "makes sense" to everyone who listens.[7] In this activity there are foreshadowings or mirror images of what God embodies in Messiah Jesus. But because of usurpation or self-negation human beings do not always "connect" with God, instead turning deaf ears to the voice of the Logos.

The Western church saw a kernel of truth when the *filioque* was added in the Nicene-Constantinopolitan Creed (beginning in the sixth century C.E. in Spain and culminating in the eleventh century in Rome). It is important to see that the Holy Spirit also proceeds from the Child: God's liberation of the human being is always accompanied by a measure of reconciliation. And because it is the Holy Spirit who carries the reconciling activity to every person, there is also a measure of re-creation.[8]

In the church, the Holy Spirit proceeding from the Child is continuously making present the person and work of Messiah Jesus—as Paul was able to do in person for the Galatians "before whose eyes [Jesus] was publicly portrayed as crucified" (Gal. 3:1). This is nowhere done more concretely than in the eucharist, which, with the eucharistic Word, brings about a public portrayal of what happens at the heart of creation and the history of humankind.[9]

Lest I seem to be moving off the point of praxis, let it be understood that spirit-praxis is that activity of God through which, in a "networking" of spirit, God draws all human beings together in the corporate self of Messiah Jesus and expresses special solidarity with all those who are suffering and oppressed. As creator, God is working on the liberation of all, especially those under the heel of tyranny. *Freedom* is the birthright of every human person created. The Holy Spirit, in creation activity, draws all human beings to God for freedom. At the same time, human beings often reject freedom. They misunderstand the nature of freedom. They want to be in control as "navigators" of the cosmos, or they fear freedom and readily submit to control.[10] All of this happens because God's place is not rightly acknowledged. But *justice*, a right relationship between God and humankind and among persons, is the birthright of every human being. Through the liberation-atonement, things are righted between God and humankind and among humans, and reconciliation takes place. The Holy Spirit makes human beings aware of the reconciling action of God.

It is impossible to develop a fully adequate concept of God's mystery. Holy Spirit reminds us of what was said earlier about the function of Christian words. "We realize God's reign does not consist in talk but in power" (1 Cor. 4:20). The issue is ultimately the new life energy these words generate. Created freedom is a gift that makes justice possible. At the same time, justice bestowed on us by liberation-atonement creates new freedom.[11] It it not the neat logic of words that counts here, but the energy effect the Spirit engenders, the "closer walk with God," which at the same time involves the closer walk with other humans, especially rejects and outcasts, the bereaved and the hungry.

It is in this sense that we can call the dynamic appropriation of the eucharistic presence of God in the Christian life *sanctification*, an activity of God setting us apart, a unique re-creation. Yet in setting apart God at the same time "sets together." In sanctification, Christians find themselves set in motion as corporate selves— joined with one another and with neglected others and neglected creation.[12] United with God in the justice struggle, they are the body of Christ.

The inner dynamics of sanctification is often referred to as election, justification, conviction of sin, and repentance. We appropriate sanctification through the realpresence of God in the eucharist—that is, the divine involvement in history and the attendant Wordpresence of God. The clear grasp of the Holy Spirit reality comes through the eucharistic Word. "If I do not go away, the Resistance Spirit will not come to you; but if I go, I will send the Spirit to you. And when the Spirit comes, this Spirit will convict the world concerning sin and righteousness and judgment" (John 16:7,8). It is in the context of the promise of the *Paraclete*, the Resistance Spirit who is also comfort and counsel, that Jesus affirms our "election": "You did not choose me, but I chose you and appointed you that you should go and bear fruit and that your fruit should abide" (John 15:16).

1. *Election* is primally this compelling "setting together" in solidarity with the losers and the lost of this world. Messiah Jesus has entered the scene and put us in a different "place" of selfhood. Humanity is certainly not separated into two cities, the city of destruction and the city of life; or into two camps, that of the winners and that of the rejects. Election means we are chosen to embody humanity as a corporate self. But we are chosen under the aegis of the Resistance Spirit. We are chosen to resist injustice and the self-destruction of body and soul.[13] We might not be able to transform the world, but the Spirit can help us to keep from being changed by the world.

2. Along with election comes *justification*. The justification of liberation-atonement is not a mere verbal assertion, but gets into our hearts through God's activity as Holy Spirit. We do not have to

legitimate our God-walk. We discover that what makes us just is God's reality (in which we are made to participate), which is in itself just, whether we fail or not.[14] Justification makes sense today only where justice is at stake— corporately as well as personally. In its dynamics God's setting apart takes on momentum: justification happens through Holy Spirit as Resistance Spirit, enabling us to take a stand against the self-righteousness and self-legitimation that pervade our life.

3. *Conviction of sin* is involved in election and justification because human beings set apart for joining God's justice struggle and therefore "set together" with the poor are convicted of usurpation of God's power or of self-negation, submission to pseudo power. We are convicted of not awakening in conscience to God's rights on us and to human rights grounded on God's rights.[15] We realize that we do not justly acknowledge God and the neighbor. The Resistance Spirit makes us aware of the sin of injustice.

4. Election, justification, and conviction of sin amount to a process of *repentance—metanoia*, conversion. We are turned around entirely, our consciousness is altered, and we begin anew. The Resistance Spirit aids us against inroads of the former spirit.

Standing apart, having been "set together," not legitimating ourselves, realizing that we move from sleeping to waking conscience, from blindness to sight: this is the way Holy Spirit is received and experienced.[16] Messiah Jesus is the center of the Holy Spirit shaping us into corporate selfhood. In God-walk all this arises from resistance on grounds of the realpresence of Messiah Jesus and his Wordpresence.

Holy Spirit finally comes down to two things: (1) Human "verification" of God (we are not left to our own devices in knowing God) and (2) Divine-human cooperation. God ceaselessly involves us in the divine struggle as partners.

As to human "verification" of God, how do we know that we are not harboring illusions? How does reason judge the truth of Christian claims? Verification cannot be absolutely foolproof. Yet we are offered some verification that is viable for lay person, pastor, and theologian alike. For much of Christian liberalism in the church, *religion* functioned as a kind of elementary category of verification, religion as a general "equipment" of humankind. We meet it everywhere. Christianity is viewed as true because it is a religion among others. Religion is viewed as true because it is an anthropological fact. Christianity is true because religion is true, not the other way around. The God-relationship is considered as something common to humankind everywhere—beyond which we cannot probe. So Christianity appears as a mere modification of what is generally regarded as true—for example, that human beings can be in tune with Being and Holy Being. As a case in point, we again can mention Macquarrie who tries to show "through description and interpretation, the conditions of the possibility of any religious faith whatsoever."[17]

The great value of wrestling with Macquarrie lies basically at the point where for our day he offers a solution in keeping with the way most of us have been trained. We judge the truth of Christianity on grounds of our general grasp of religion. What verifies Christianity is the religious capacity of the human being. We can all produce the God-thought and make God-talk.

But God-walk compels us to find verification in conscience as the checkpoint of truth as justice/love. The justified person stands in the full light of truth within reality as a whole. The affirmation of the Holy Spirit, however, turns into a question at this point: Does history, do human relationships, shape up more creatively on grounds of the Spirit's justice than otherwise? "The Holy Spirit will realize (glorify) me in history. For the Holy Spirit will take my very life (what is mine) and embody it for you" (John 16:14). God in history through Messiah Jesus as God's right hand is struggling for justice to prevail among humankind.[18] The Holy Spirit makes the work of this right hand efficacious:

> When the Holy Spirit comes, this Spirit will convict the world concerning sin (usurpation and self-negation), and justice (righteousness), and the administration of justice (judgment): concerning usurpation and self-negation because [the ungodly] do not trust me in their conscience ("do not believe in me"); concerning justice, because I continue working with the Mother/Father, although you will no longer see me directly (as historical person in Galilee and Judea); and concerning the administration of justice because the ruler of the world (the devil, the ruler of injustice) has been cast out (receives his just deserts) [John 16:8–11].

By now, after two thousand years, there is a tremendous religious ballast that goes along with Christianity. But at its center is a plain fact: the just person Jesus who invites us in the Holy Spirit to the just life as *eternal* life. It is (as indicated all along) not the sheer this-world "equity," but the fusion of God's worldly justice with "kingdom justice," a justice at the center of which lies God's work as Holy Spirit.

The religious dimension is not eradicated or covered up. But it is certainly not religious feeling as such or some spiritual awe that Christianity ought to appeal to as verification. It asks us to sense the new reality of God's justice, and to move from there to acknowledge the reality of God—of which we all are aware in conscience.[19]

Here we encounter *the divine in itself*, "the thing in itself," so that no vague feeling arises that it might all in the end be entirely different. Wherever this justice/love is not acknowledged in some relation to conscience and in a verification praxis, it makes no sense to claim a universal truth to have been found in the Christian religion. We do not have a verification principle in God-walk. *We have merely a verification praxis*: spirit-praxis. Justice/love is not mere fancy, but ultimate truth. Cognitive co-reason can understand itself as accountable to it—without necessarily understanding itself as subject to it (as though we were slaves or vassals of God). All of humankind has to live by this truth. God's truth is not found in becoming or Being (or some such abstraction), but in acknowledging the other as true Justice. Reason can understand itself at least as *accountable reason*, the reason of wisdom that is communion of Spirit.

"Verification" usually means a method of deciding the truth or falsehood of a judgment by predetermined criteria. Without such a method, judgments are viewed as expressions of the subjective state of a person and not acts of cognitive reason.[20] Yet under the aegis of God's Spirit we today are first thrust into praxis to discover what is true. So there is a great change in the area of Christian thought at this point. We are thrust back upon Jesus himself and his praxis.

No one comes to the Mother/Father but by Jesus' praxis. Jesus makes it clear that the way to God is the God-walk embodied by him that acknowledges the just God.[21] God does what needs to be done in history regardless of our religious aspirations. In terms of history God as justice/love makes sense to the person struggling for justice. Ultimately the *praxis test* is decisive: "If any person wills to do God's will, this person shall know whether the teaching is from God" (John 7:17).

The question whether we can verify divine-human cooperation arises from another angle as well. In what sense is *God* acting as Holy Spirit and in what sense are *we* acting? Are we not confusing our own motives and activities with those of God? Perhaps the only ones acting here in the first place are human beings.

Macquarrie has stated the problem (historically it arose between Augustinianism and Pelagianism) in very clear terms—with regard to his own position:

> We must . . . try to conceive of the action of the Holy Spirit in such a way that while indeed we recognize his initiative, we do not destroy that measure of freedom and responsibility that is indispensable to the conception of personal existence in man. If we fail to do this, then Christianity offers not the salvation (making whole) of human existence, but really an escape from existence, whereby we shed its responsibility and become marionettes, to be arbitrarily and externally operated by this mysterious Spirit of God.[22]

We have to understand two things. (1) Our angle of vision is at times distorted. We do not necessarily "see" things the way they "are." Here is a glass of water. We place a straight stick into it. The stick appears bent. The point is, our vision as finite beings in many ways is skewed. This is especially true because of sin. It skews our spiritual vision. (2) Biblical words pertaining to God's initiative and our response do not invite picturing them in an exact geometrical diagram. I have repeatedly stressed that, "filtered" through the eucharist, these words are meant to be energizers for us to live a life of discipleship. The very words that tell us about grace and human response in faith resist the diagrams, where we could measure, as it were, 51 percent God, 49 percent human.

Spirit-praxis makes radically clear that God's justice struggle is not *our* invention.[23] There is much going on in history and nature that is for us a *given*. We cannot add a cubit or an ounce to it. This is especially true of God's liberating and salvific activity. Obviously we are also not marionettes or robots whom God pulls on strings or directs "electronically" by remote control. *All* the willing is ours. But we will on grounds of a "divinely given." "Geometrically" pictured or "mechanically" viewed, there is no real solution to the problem of human freedom—that is, the agency of the will. But we have an "angle." Our thought and action can turn on spirit-praxis. We need to be leary of "theological mechanics." God and human persons do not work together like parts of an engine. The cooperation is lodged in a different environment.[24]

We always act in terms of an environment, taking off the jacket when it is too warm in a room or bundling up when it is cold outside. Similarly, with regard to social behavior we notice environmentally determined differences. For example, it is unlikely that someone will get drunk in church. Yet someone we have met in church might get drunk in another environment, a bar or a homecoming game.

Spirit-praxis empowerment begins with the divine initiative. It means, God creates for us a new environment. Conscience can orient itself in a new justice context. The sinful environment is eliminated: "If a person is in Christ, this person is a new creature" (2 Cor. 5:17).

For faith as awakened conscience, this is like the straight stick put in a glass of water appearing crooked and yet known to be straight. It is quite clear what God does, and we respond to it. So we have no choice. We obviously think we can choose. But not heeding God's environment is like walking without an overcoat in subfreezing temperatures. The spiritual environment God creates through the Holy Spirit as countermeasure to sin does not invite a nonsense response, unreasonable behavior. The choice God pre-pares for humanity is quite clear. The *given* of God's liberation-atonement, God's justice struggle, is inescapable. Yet we often see God's reality as the broken stick in a glass of water or not at all. Every so often we seem blind.

Who works salvation, God or the human person? "I sought the Lord, but afterward I knew, God made my soul to seek God seeking me. It was not I who found, O Savior true, no, I was found of Thee." Grace means that God takes the initiative. Justification means that God continues to take the initiative. In spite of all our waywardness, absentmindedness, and God-forgetfulness, God creates the new environment in which we are able to engage fully in the struggle for justice/love issuing in a world in which we acknowledge one another as members of one human family. That is why in the Apostles' Creed Spirit and church are set side by side: "I believe in the Holy Spirit, the one, holy, catholic church." We would not turn to God in our conscience, had not the church provided the Spirit-environment that enables us to respond.[25]

Faith knows that change of will happens because of this new environment. We know "the stick in the water is not bent." But we bend our will so as not to admit it. God definitely overrides our willing, just as the sun overrides our willing. In reaction to the sun we do not "bundle up," but yield our bodies to its rays. Obviously it is *our* will that responds to the divine will. Philippians 2:12–13 makes a fundamental point: "Therefore, my beloved . . . work out your own salvation in fear and trembling; for God is at work in you [creating a new environment ever again], both to will and to do—according to God's good purpose." There is no "freedom of the will" the way we usually understand it, a kind of independent self-triggering mechanism of the human spirit. Free will is always experienced as "grace under pressure"—God's pressure, prevenient grace (John Wesley). Holy Spirit here means: God is always ahead of us creating the justice/love environment, not only in the church, but also on the inside of history and creation. The church itself is never a merely external environment apart from the Spirit dimensions of the human being. Our will reacts to the Spirit because it is acted upon first. Baptism and eucharist communicate the eucharistic Word that the cooperation between divine and human "factors" is the transformation of the human will.

The experience of the Holy Spirit in this respect recalls the exodus experience. God is going ahead of us still: "The Lord went before them by day in a pillar of cloud to lead them along the way, and by night in a pillar of fire to give them light" (Exod. 13:21). However, in Messiah Jesus, spirit-praxis makes us encounter the Spirit not as cloud or fire, but as person. Because of Jesus, God is ahead of us time and again not as impersonal force, but as the power of a corporate person, the divine empowering the nonpersons and all creation. The end of all of God's ways is shared personhood and—in the wide-ranging Creator activity of God—

shared creaturehood. Spirit-praxis makes us aware of it. It is from the praxis of God's justice-love that we form the thought of the person as divinely shaped part of the cosmos.

How closely divine Spirit, justice, and sharing personhood are related becomes clear from the Hebrew image of wisdom. "By me kings reign, and rulers decree what is just" (Prov. 8:15). And more yet in the direction of sharing personhood as part of the natural world: "When God established the heavens, I was there; . . . when God made firm the skies above, when God established the foundations of the deep . . . then I was beside God, a superb worker, and I was daily God's delight, rejoicing before God always, rejoicing in God's inhabited world and delighting in human beings" (Prov. 8:27–31). The Hebrews see Sophia as a person sharing in the divine Spirit and in the order, justice, and joy of all creation. She is the "feminine" dimension of God overlooked by centuries of patriarchal rule, even though Messiah Jesus "probably understood himself as the prophet and child of Sophia."[26] One of the oldest Jesus-words declares that "wisdom is justified by all her children" (Luke 7:35).

Sophia is "identified with the spirit of God and subsequently with the Torah."[27] The Spirit aspect of Sophia involves concreteness and even earthiness. Only in Philo's day she becomes separated from her earthly aspects and is seen as mother of the Logos who in turn assumes Sophia's divine role on earth.[28] Her more ancient character, representing the "gentle yoke" of law, is expressed in Sirach 6:24–31 and is directly reflected in Jesus' words: "Come to me all who labor and are heavy laden. . . . Take my yoke upon you" (Matt. 11:28–29). A Sophia view of Messiah Jesus that takes the feminine side of God seriously will see Holy Spirit as sharing both the power of creation and the power of justice. We might also say, the power of justice is contained in the power of creation.

Christian Anthropology in Accountable Teaching

The way things shape up in the flow of thought that grows out of God-walk, we can discern an almost direct transition from the doctrine of the Holy Spirit to Christian anthropology. The creeds do not contain anthropology. The human being is not mentioned as a specific theme. What thematizes the human being is our mode of being partners of God in the eucharist—addressees of the eucharistic Word, and co-workers with God in the justice struggle. Where in spirit-praxis the question of the freedom of the will arises, Christian thought has been compelled to shape thoughts that articulate who the human being is in God's sight.

For the Christian disciple, in God-walk there is no "freedom of the will," the way we usually understand it. We are always under the pressure of *prevenient* grace in the justice struggle. We have no choice but to walk in God's way, to be pilgrims. The question of the freedom of the will is never decided on truly neutral grounds. To be or not to be—in the justice struggle—that is the question.

My approach here is neither a "radical monotheism" (H. Richard Niebuhr) nor a sheer "Christocentrism" (Karl Barth), but a Holy Spirit praxis presupposing God as always entering human history and conscience in a transformation of the will. God is revolutionizing humanity through the Trinity as a whole. We leave behind a merely monotheistic approach with the religious notion of a 1:1 relationship between an abstract God and the human being. Theological modernism is especially prone to this view. Schleiermacher was its most eloquent spokesman. The christocentric approach, on the other hand, is too much grounded in an orthodox ontologism of Chalcedon where a definite theory precedes everything else. Discipleship thought instead lets God shape the doctrine of God in new ways, not neglecting the creative activity of God or Christian tradition, but letting God first of all take over in God-walk, the human being falling in line with God's full activity in the justice struggle.[29]

What we learn on these grounds about the human being is direct and clear. It is focused in the eucharistic Word. There is first of all that aspect of the person with which we are all most familiar: the human being is created by the Creator God *in the image of God*. "Let us make the human being in our image, after our likeness" (Gen. 1:26). "God created the human being in the image of God— male and female God created them" (v. 27). Needless to say, the book of Genesis does not think in trinitarian terms (first introduced by Christianity after Messiah Jesus had come and offered the gift of the Spirit). But note that there is a plural involved: let *us* make the human being in *our* image.

The text does not offer any indication that the image of God is confined to the human mind, or reason, or will. It pertains to the wholeness of personhood. What the text yields is basically that the human being is constituted by the corporate character of male and female (v. 27). There is no romanticizing of the male/female relationship. A sober point is made—in the nontheological language of Emile Durkheim: The human being is *"homo duplex,* both I and we."[30] The analogy is one of mutual accountability—from the very beginning. The corporateness of God (accountability faithful to itself as I and we) calls for the *homo duplex*—where human beings are accountable to be faithful to each other.

By way of "extrapolating" from our human condition we might assume that in God there are male and female dimensions—because this is what human persons offer as "image." The point is important not merely for distinct aspects of God's being, but in terms of *accountability* as the raison d'être of shared personhood.[31]

Is there any point, however, in trying to uncover the pristine image of God in humanity defaced by sin? The serpent is reported as telling the woman: "For God knows when you eat of [the fruit] your eyes will be opened, and you will be like God, knowing good and evil" (Gen. 3:5). At the core of human sin is usurpation or self-negation. Usurpation is arrogating God's power and God's position to oneself and thus also destroying accountability with regard to God and neighbor. Adam "passes the buck" to Eve, and Eve to the serpent (Gen. 3:12–13)—shifting accountability. There is no reason to inject a notion of guilt at this point, especially not of guilt-feeling. The point is that throughout the human race the Adam/Eve "deniability" syndrome seems to be ineradicable. Human nature looks for the opportunity to usurp God's place and power. We all want to be so very *good*. We know the difference between good and evil. We know what is just and unjust among humans. But built into the best willing is the drive toward evil—like rot "built into" the apple. We deny our accountability.

As history evolved, usurpation did not always take the form of a radical wresting of power from God. There was at times a yielding of power to an alien other—for example, of the female to the male or—more rarely—vice versa. The ramifications that flow from sin are infinite. And thus in many respects it is not appropriate still to speak of the human person as the image of God, the *imago Dei.*

The rot is there. "I will what is right, but I cannot do it" (Rom. 7:18). So *our greatest virtues become splendid vices* (St. Augustine). St. Paul presses further: "For I do not do the good I want, but the evil I do not want is what I do" (Rom. 7:19). This is very much part of the *liberation* dimension of God's work (and human existence) because it is exactly in our best intentions that we need liberation from sin for participation in God's justice work. This ultimate defeat, *being pressed against the wall*, realizing that our best intentions are in vain, is perhaps the most frightening, and yet also the most saving spiritual experience. Sin at its core is a *lie*. It is always an attempt to create a pseudo reality, a reality of power, of sloth, or both, in any case an attempt to play God. Yet it does not "explain" sin. The human will inexplicably always abuses human existence. It pits one person against the other, Adam against Eve, Cain against Abel. The disorder of sin shapes up today especially as class struggle, race struggle, and sex struggle. Sin tries to void justice wherever it can. Sin forever tampers with the empowerment to be just. The core of the human being is justice. "Original sin" inexplicably is the act of each of us. Human beings, *created in the image of God*, accountable to God and the corporateness of human life in history, for no good reason prove immediately sinful, as soon as they appear on the scene. That is, we humans cannot remember a time when things were not "out of sync." We cannot imagine what a justice state might have been like.

Accountable teaching takes sin into account as it focuses on the person who comes to us as the image of God, Messiah Jesus, who is *the likeness of God* in the midst of sinful humans (2 Cor. 4:4: *eikōn tou theou*). Jesus puts before us godhead embodied in the flesh. Corporateness and thus also accountability for him constitute the fullness of humanity. In some respects, it is the opposite of the old notion of the *uni*personality of Christ. We are dealing today with the *multi*personality of Messiah Jesus. All persons are included, especially the powerless, the lost, the rejects, the special victims of usurpation, although not sinless themselves either and often also the victims of their own resignation.

To be human on grounds of the *multi*personality of Messiah Jesus means to be empowered to be just—to let creation and one's neighbor be themselves, to become stewards of creation and "keepers" of one's neighbor. Sin tampers with this empowerment. Inasmuch as the empowerment comes from God as Holy Spirit, an injury to God is involved.[32]

Human beings as male and female can reflect the multipersonality of God in Jesus. Their relationship becomes an occasion for justice. Sin originates at the point where a person is unable to let God, creation, and neighbor be themselves. It arrogates to oneself as individual what actually is accountability to many. The framework is a power struggle. We need to stress the inexplicable *perversion* of the will to arrogate to itself what belongs to another, God or neighbor, or to enervate the will of its resistance and resilience to oppression. There is a fierce and awesome inroad on God and neighbor, as often also a willful submission to otherness.[33]

The patriarchal interpretation of Eve as the origin of all evil, mixed with the Platonic idea of women identified with nature and (sinful) instinct, has had disastrous consequences for the relationships of humans toward each other as well as their natural surroundings. Non-Western and nonwhite peoples have suffered the same fate as women. They have been seen as representatives of unbridled nature, to be tamed, educated, civilized, and ruled over. This kind of domination-obsession often also results in the passive submissiveness of some of the oppressed. In our natural environment, domination has led to a disregard of the earth and its elements as part of our corporate humanity.[34] It is not by chance that Messiah Jesus kept company with women, and that the sparrow, the mustard seed, and the lilies of the field were to him capable of interpreting the reign of God.

"The Human One [Son of Man] came to seek and to save the lost" (Luke 19:10). This has to be spelled out with regard to those who are rejected by the strong—the poor, those who are being read out of the *homo duplex* structure, the "we" who are also the "I." The image of God is best understood at the point where in Messiah Jesus accountability is embodied. In view of the person accountable to God we realize that we definitely are *not* accountable, that we usurp God's power—that we are sinful. Messiah Jesus presents to God what humanity is truly like as created humanity. It expresses itself, we need to remember time and again, as justice/love. Yet in spirit-praxis the *imago dei* is not limited to Christ. Messiah Jesus foreshadows what we are to be. So in a sense the human being is the *imago futuri*. Human beings can image the future in hopeful ways, although we do not as yet know exactly what we will be.

Especially in view of Messiah Jesus as the image of God it

becomes clear who we are as accountable to God in corporate humanity. In willing God's will, Messiah Jesus becomes the truly sharing and accountable person. In him all are included in the structure of human selfhood. Here we come to understand justice as justice/love. God so rights the human condition in the liberator/reconciler that his reality *suffices* for what God wants. So God shows us amazing grace, grace greater than all our sin, making the struggle in history meaningful and effective, and enabling us to share in the coming of the kingdom. Human beings are not to be invited to live by "faith" as such, awakened conscience alone, but by *grace*, "grace under pressure," justified awakened conscience.

Faith has been fussed over too much in Christianity. It has been blown up into a giant balloon bound to explode some day. Faith in some sense can easily become another work. The works-righteousness of faith can be utterly frightening. Schleiermacher is a case in point. Christian teaching in him came down to *Glaubenslehre*, teachings of faith. In a sense, according to Schleiermacher, we are justified through the ideas produced by faith.

But it is just the other way around. We are "defined" as humans *by what God does for us* in history through Messiah Jesus. It is always a *world-transforming* work, not just a drop of grace into the sin bucket. It is effective atonement work going on in history.[35]

The created human always comes forth from the hand of the creator as good. But each one of us abuses good human nature in the context of sin. Grace does not annul good human nature, but evokes its divine intention—in struggle. So the truly human person is the accountable person: Created in the image of God, usurper or negator of that image, set right in Messiah Jesus—that is, graced by justice/love for participation in God's labor. Basic accountability is co-reason, con-science discerning good and evil under God's pressure of grace.

So what constitutes the human being is basically *accountability*, expressing itself in faithful relationships grounded in an elementary corporateness. Here first of all the image of God is at stake in the most intimate way. Here the human being senses right and wrong, good and evil, and distinguishes between just and unjust. It is through the Holy Spirit that God ultimately reaches into us and moves us. God's goodness shows in conscience, thus also in the goodness of human nature. God still contacts humankind, in spite of usurpation or resignation. Sin cannot undo God's work. It cannot destroy conscience. The human being *is* conscience (not pristinely *homo faber*, the tool-making animal; not *homo ludens*, the playing animal; not even *animal orans*, the praying animal making contact with God). The human being as conscience is completely predicated on God making contact with us as human beings, in spirit-praxis.[36]

Thus Christian anthropology is based on Holy Spirit—the self-realization of God in history traceable from Abraham and Sarah through Sophia to Jesus and continuing on in all historical struggles. Jesus says of the Holy Spirit that this Spirit "will take of mine and declare it to you" (John 16:14). We always stand in the tension between what God already is doing through the Spirit in the world in justice/love, and what we are asked to do by joining this work, although unable to achieve the perfection we and others expect of ourselves. Here we continue to learn "grace under pressure" as "justice under pressure." "The fruit of the Spirit is love, joy, peace, patience, kindness, goodness, faithfulness, gentleness, self-control" (Gal. 5:22f.). The entire gift of faith is offered under pressure, in the struggle of life, God's struggle for justice/love: "Those who belong to Christ Jesus have *crucified* the flesh" (Gal. 5:24). This is a life-giving discipline, not an asceticism-trip or a hankering for martyrdom.[37] The ongoing crucifixion in history is painful, but also a joyous experience. The cross is the Tree of Life. The eucharist here is the central access: "This is my body broken for you, my blood shed for you." Suffering turns into celebration; physical and spiritual hunger, into a common meal. It is in the eucharist that we are *most* human.

Because marriage is centrally tied to the sacrament of the eucharist, it is understandable why the church eventually came to speak of marriage as sacrament. Marriage embodies the image of God as sharing personhood very concretely. Who we are becomes transparent in accountable concreteness. Our life depends on such troth between human beings. In the corporateness of women and men, in the corporateness of being members of the body of Messiah Jesus, we *are* con-science. The single life is equally accountable. Yet it has its own dimensionality and its own rewards before God. In spirit-praxis ultimately all our relationships are sacramental.[38]

Ecclesiology in Accountable Teaching

Accountable teaching as enabling framework of discipleship makes things transparent in our faith. In God-walk we understand: the Holy Spirit and human persons in corporateness—that is, the church. In clear thought-flow, spirit-praxis gives rise to the notion of the church.[39] It is simply Christian anthropology "writ large." The church expresses in depth and corporately what it means to be persons. There is nothing mystifying about the existence of the church. The eucharist already divulged the church's "inmost secret." There is basically nothing more to the church than being the elementary accountability group before God.

Biblical metaphors of the church as people of God abound, "Israel of God" (Gal. 6:16), "household of God" (Eph. 2:19), "chosen race, royal priesthood, holy nation, God's people" (1 Pet. 2:9). Most distinct is the "body of Christ"—a very transparent metaphor. If Christ is the image of God (2 Cor. 4:4), the body of Christ is the humanity that embodies—on its level—the *homo duplex*, in fact, the plural character of living persons, of God and human beings. Here the multipersonality of Messiah Jesus has its corresponding reality. It is the elementary truth of the church— humanity centered in the eucharist. "Body of Christ" is a metaphor from 1 Corinthians 12:27. Unfortunately it is often in disrepute, for it has given rise to such vague notions as the "mystical body" of Christ—when all it wants to do is to point to the divine-human corporateness in Messiah Jesus.

One can offer other descriptions of the church. We can speak of it as new covenant, for example. "I will establish a new covenant with the house of Israel" (Heb. 8:8). Jesus is here the mediator of the new covenant (Heb. 12:24).

Whatever metaphor we use, in spirit-praxis there is always a caveat. In God-walk we learn soon enough, *you can't go home again*. Our own social location makes us understand that there is no way to return to the first century and *re-create* primitive Christianity, or the primitive church, for our time. Imitation is out of the question. In shaping the church the *innovatio Christi* is especially crucial.[40] Present-day churches need to be infused with a grasp of what the church as the *body of Christ* could be today—not re-creating the primitive church, which we usually romanticize anyway, but living by its Spirit. John Macquarrie makes a good point about the church when he quotes John Knox: "To be in Christ is to belong to a new corporate reality. . . . The 'new creation' has taken place, and the church is the historical embodiment of the new humanity."[41]

But then Macquarrie moves on to define the church as extension of the incarnation without making use of Knox's good insight about the new body of humankind. In God-walk, the notion of an extension of the incarnation cannot possibly arise. It is a speculative point. It lacks the realism of social location. God is not interested in repeating or extending the incarnation. What we need to stress is God's deprivation, God's impoverishment. Among humans God works toward captivation. God wants us to be gripped by the justice struggle waged together with Jesus as God's right hand. Here God's deprivation is the crucial point about incarnation. Messiah Jesus "emptied himself" (Phil. 2:7).

In Jesus something surprisingly new happens. One corporate selfhood is created out of the warring factions of humankind, Messiah Jesus having reconciled us to God "in one body through the cross, therefore bringing hostility to an end" (Eph. 2:16). The reality of this event moves on as the heart of God's justice struggle. The root metaphor of liberation-atonement reappears in all aspects of accountable teaching. Ultimately at stake is *shalom* between God and us and between our warring factions. God is working toward ever greater accountability—toward the church as a structure of corporate accountability that cannot be quickly discarded as religious whim or fancy.[42]

God's action in Jesus' life, death, and resurrection was not a bold move to get more political power, but God's share in the uprising of the poor people, the common folk, who had had enough of bloodshed, anarchy, and oppression. God for them was Immanuel, *God with us* in the struggle, sharing in the cross, vindicated in the resurrection. To the victims of injustice God was saying: enough is enough.

It is on these grounds that God takes the initiative to bring about a church. In a very bold move, God breaks down the wall between Judea and Samaria, Israel and Egypt. A new humanity is brought forth with shalom (justice/love) as center. Constituted by sinful human beings, the church is full of ambiguities, certainly short of outward perfection.[43] Yet God's initiative in creating a church functions as messianic event for the nations: "I saw no temple in the city, for its temple is the Lord God Almighty and the Lamb. And the city has no need of sun or moon to shine upon it, for the glory of God is its light, and its lamp is the Lamb. By its light shall the nations walk" (Rev. 21:22ff.). God-walk finally extends to the nations. The earth shall be remade in the beauty of peace.

There is also the great image of the river:

> Then he showed me the river of the water of life, bright as crystal, flowing from the throne of God and of the Lamb through the middle of the street of the city; also, on either side of the river, the tree of life with its twelve kinds of fruit, yielding its fruit each month; and the leaves of the tree were for the healing of the nations [Rev. 22:1-2].

The elementary issue at stake in the body of Christ is *the healing of the nations*. For that to happen there has to be a lot of healing of persons. Walls have to be broken down between God and the human being, in the human being itself, and between human beings.[44]

Any local church not oriented toward the healing of the nations, not understanding itself as justice church and peace church, misunderstands the body of Christ—and misunderstands our age in which the church needs radical new embodiment. The elementary framework of the church is ecumenical. It is also missional and messianic. It expresses itself as one, holy, and catholic. The *oneness* of the church is the center of the peace that justice/love brings to the nations. Its *holiness* is God's presence in this "city of God," our being set apart—that is, our being "set together" as corporate self for sharing in God's struggle in history. Holiness is the justice dynamics of the church. The *catholic* dimension of the church points to its global presence because God's peace is worldwide, built on the foundation of prophets and apostles with Messiah Jesus the chief cornerstone (Acts 4:11).[45] We believe in the one, *just*, catholic church.

God struggles for all this to be real in the local church as social location of peace and justice/love. The church embodies God's drive in Messiah Jesus to unite humankind in one city of God in history, bringing history to its consummation. In this regard many American Christians have internalized an enemy image: one is either on the side of the social gospel (activism) or on the side of spirituality (quietism), either on the side of the *vita activa*, or the *vita contemplativa*. As soon as christo-praxis is mentioned, up goes a red flag. The cool crowd says: "Just another social gospel!" The quietists charge: "Just another activism!" But there is no dichotomy between activity and contemplation in God.

The problem is that in the United States, on account of nineteenth- and twentieth-century theological liberalism, the notion spread that we could build the kingdom of God, the brave new world of God, on earth. Christo-praxis is not kingdom-building, but plain God-walk, walk together with God through the struggles of history. It is the justice struggle itself, often a Paris tango, two steps forward and one step backward, yielding little measurable progress, but even so the dance of prevailing life.[46]

For that very reason we need to stress the discipleship church. This is not in opposition to the institutional church. Both are tied into one unit. The discipleship church is the leaven of the institutional church, yet just like leaven not separable from the loaf. We have to keep struggling with the fact that there is much more to the church than institutional maintenance. The church is human beings as corporate selfhood gathering around the eucharist in sharing God's work in the world. As accountable teaching keeps listening to the eucharistic Bible, the "engine" of the church cannot be a "social trip." This is hard to grasp for our pragmatic American minds. I have heard it said many times in our struggle: "The only hands God has are human hands." From the perspective of God-walk, it is not true; it is make-believe. From the perspective of the class struggle, it is ambiguous: sometimes it turns out that way, sometimes not. Discipleship knows that Messiah Jesus is always God's right hand. That is the first hand that counts. We can only join our hands to Jesus' hand. That is what discipleship is all about.[47]

God as Holy Spirit is God working in history with this right hand of Jesus shaping and reshaping the human potential toward greater accountability—faithful relationships. That is how the discipleship church originates. We confess that we believe in the Holy Spirit and in the one, holy, catholic church. These two affirmations are *intimately linked together.* In creating the world and the human being to care for it, God limited godhead. There is a self-limitation of God involved especially in allowing human beings to be stewards of creation. All the distortion of the trust and challenge that human self-contradiction brings about *cannot thwart God's purpose.* The whole human enterprise with its tendency to self-destruct, especially now in nuclear holocaust, cannot stop God.

In the church we discern God's self-limitation and willing deprivation. The church is the place where human beings know that human perversion is not absolute, that God prevails. The historical enterprise is not a divine gamble. God does not cast dice with the universe (Albert Einstein). God also does not cast dice with human beings. The existence of the discipleship church bears it out. On these grounds we might want to say that God uses human hands as extensions of Jesus' hand. What we do in creation and history depends on God's out-stretched hand, on what God is already doing in Jesus. We need to join hands with God's hand.[48]

"Unresting, unhasting, and silent as light, nor wanting, nor wasting, thou rulest in might. Thy justice like mountains high soaring above; thy clouds which are fountains of goodness and love." In a seemingly different vein we sing: "Through the thick darkness thy kingdom is hastening." God moves toward humans through Jesus with an unhasting and yet hastening power and thus gathers the church.

The church knows the first point about history is not what human beings are doing, what the Kremlin or what Beijing, Washington, Cairo, Teheran, and Rome are doing. It is also not what the church is doing, but what God is doing.

God is in the process of forming a community of corporate selfhood, shaping and reshaping the human potential, making women and men a conscience. We put up a lot of resistance—often so much that God appears to be losing out. And yet as conscience tells us, God keeps inviting us to take the risk of sharing in that process. That is what the church in essence is all about: human beings through the Holy Spirit risking to share in God's struggle of bringing about corporate humanity.[49]

God is at work creating just humanity, anticipating the reign of God. There is little we can do but join God's enterprise. We are caught up in the awesome struggle over the character of human personhood. That is what the de facto course of history is all about. Creating new human beings for the just society is *God's work*. Our response will require much self-limitation. But in the agonizing struggle over the new piety, the new chastity, and the new social order, we just may be surprised—by justice.[50] Only in God-walk will we discover history that way, and this is what the corporate humanity of the church lives by. It extends from Adam/Eve through God's self-realization in Abraham and Sarah, Joshua and Deborah, David and Esther, to Sophia and thereby finally to Messiah Jesus. It is extended to all humans as shalom at Pentecost. That is what we do not see because of the peculiar blinding power of sin. In discipleship we do not ask: "Are you running with me, Jesus?" (Malcolm Boyd). For the church to be church it is the other way around. The heart of the church is asking, Are you running with me, Malcolm? Are you running with me, church?[51] The church is human beings who are running with a heart given by God. The corporateness of the church is unique in that it is a *given* that human beings cannot generate by themselves.

Eschatology in Accountable Teaching

How does one paint a bird in flight? Like any moving object, so too God's reign cannot be frozen into a static picture for us to behold. It is dynamic and ever-changing because it is rushing in, as it were, from the future. There are important things we can still learn if we are open to this future.

In God-walk we first of all recognize that from the perspective of God's coming rule we fail, and yet our sense of failure here is not the same as guilt-*feelings*. There is no point in feeling bad about our inability to usher in God's new order. God wants us to hold up our heads. God-walk is upright walk (*aufrechter Gang*).[52] "Look up and raise your heads, because your redemption is drawing near" (Luke 21:28). The basic repentance in view of the coming reign of God in history is not directed to guilt over any conscious shortcoming, but to "sleep." Most of the time we humans are spiritually and intellectually asleep. There is the parable of the five foolish virgins and the five wise virgins. "As the bridegroom was delayed, they *all* slumbered and slept" (Matt. 25:5). That is the root-parable of our lives. And if we are awake we run around with blinders at best, halfway sleep-walking through life, not seeing the full picture. That is also what St. Paul might have had in mind when he said: "You know what hour it is, how it is full time now for you to wake up from sleep" (Rom. 13:11). Sleepers awake!

The same issue has been dealt with in psychological research. Formerly, with Freud, we thought that consciousness is a wide-ranging dimension of our lives with subconsciousness as a relatively small area of a strange "underworld." Now psychologists assume that this underworld morass is the major part of our psychic life and consciousness only a thin veneer on top of it. Our underworld occupies us most of the time. That is why we are so much asleep, not really alert to reality. Repentance is basically this waking up from sleep, the awakening of conscience, seeing the full picture—if only for moments at a time. We usually do not grasp how things hang together in our lives. Open your eyes that you may see—that is what repentance means. Recognize especially the losers and lost of your world—those who are nonpersons in your eyes. Recognize also God's creatures whom we are hurting. Recognize the natural elements we are thoughtlessly poisoning. Accountable teaching of the reign of God grows out of awakened conscience, an awakened analysis of our context, our social location, our place in the whole cosmos.

There is much occasion for misunderstanding. Some might think we develop Christian thought *out of* our experience. Most of the time it is my modern temptation. Accountable teaching does not bank on the theory we bring *to* our experience, but it lets the poverty and the oppression into which God places Jesus and us determine new theory. In the section entitled "The Eucharistic Word" (pp. 150ff.), I referred to Marx and class analysis. Any use of such analysis grows out of the praxis in which we live. Because of our praxis among the losers we want to understand the brute power factor involved between the haves and the have-nots. Only then can we hope to succeed in grasping the overall reasons for the dilemmas in Durban, South Africa, or Durham, North Carolina. Class analysis grows out of God-walk, spirit-praxis.[53] It is rooted in analysis of the eucharistic scriptures.

What has it got to do with the coming of the reign of God? That God's rule is coming toward us, we sense at the eucharist. "For as often as you eat this bread and drink this cup, you give expression to the Lord's death [God's justice struggle in history] until the Lord comes" (1 Cor. 11:26). That is, the bread and the wine are the locale where the future of God rushes in.

Without the body of Messiah Jesus as worshiping community in which God comes to us from the future to be present, Christian life is impossible. We Christians gather for praise and adoration in rehearsing our eschatological life. I appealed earlier to the situation mentioned in the book of Acts: "Day by day, attending the temple together and *breaking bread* in their homes, they partook of food with glad and generous hearts, praising God and having favor with all the people" (Acts 2:46,47). In this movement of gathering for worship eucharistically (breaking bread), Christian spirituality is encompassed. It is corporate worship, corporate prayer, corporate witness—as empowerment from God's future where shalom, God's peace, will reign on earth.

There is a difference between cultivating the soul and God's historical struggle. The motto of God-walk is *struggle and contemplation*. Its heart is prayer—spirituality. In view of God's justice struggle it is *critical* spirituality. It has nothing to do with feeling one's religious pulse. It is immersion in God's Spirit focused in a notion such as that of St. Paul: "Likewise the Spirit helps us in our weakness; for we do not know how to pray as we ought, but the Spirit personally intercedes for us with sighs too deep for words" (Rom. 8:26). Here we find the subject and the subject matter of our spiritual life. We are not looking around in history to be able to control God at every corner or in every turn of events. We focus on Messiah Jesus in the eucharist where he draws near to and draws unto himself all the historical struggles of the poor and the soul-struggles of the lost. Our spirituality is determined by christopraxis and is therefore spirit-praxis.

The Holy Spirit, the Paraclete, as Resistance Spirit is also the Comforter. Resistant comfort and comforting resistance—this is the most taxing oxymoron of Christian praxis.[54] The church is not an armed camp (although we lustily sing: "Onward Christian soldier, marching as to war . . . "), a revolutionary cadre, or a political pressure group out for more political clout. The church is the church. It functions only too often willy-nilly as political pressure group, sometimes without realizing it. Let the church be the *just* church. As it shares in God's justice struggle it binds the wounds of those who have been bruised in the struggle, and those who feel wounded because they have failed to participate or cannot be part of the struggle. But it does so in ceaselessly trying to bring about a state of greater justice. Our sleepiness has to go.

It is obvious that there are other things that pain Christians. There are also our tears, for example. Yet there is no tear that God does not wipe away in the coming reign. That is the promise. Being the just church as Messiah-body mandates both struggle and comfort, care of soul as well as care of body, *diakonia*.[55] It is important to see the dynamics in terms of the full dimensions of God's coming rule:

> Put on the whole armor of God, that you may be able to stand against the wiles of the devil. For we are not contending against flesh and blood, but against the principalities, against the powers, against the world rulers of this present darkness, against the spiritual hosts of wickedness in the heavenly places. Therefore take the whole armor of God, that you may be able to withstand in the evil day, and having done all, to stand. Stand therefore, having girded your loins with truth, and having put on the breastplate of justice, and having shod your feet with the equipment of the gospel of peace [a peculiar kind of armor for the God-walk of peace!]; above all taking the shield of faith, with which you can quench all the flaming darts of the evil one. And take the helmet of salvation, and the sword of the Spirit, which is the word of God [Eph. 6:11-17].

From "war-language" the epistle quickly turns to soul-language:

> Pray at all times in the Spirit, with all prayer and supplication. To that end keep alert with all perseverance, making supplication for all the saints, and also for me, that utterance may be given me in opening my mouth boldly to proclaim the mystery of the gospel, for which I am an ambassador in chains, that I may declare it boldly, as I ought to speak [Eph. 6:18-20].

What is basically at stake in the worshiping community as Messiah-body, the corporate new humanity, is God-walk, walking toward the coming reign. It pertains to our liturgy as well as to our contemplation in the streets. This is what Ephesians calls "the mystery of the Gospel" (Eph. 6:19). The mystery is not something inarticulate. But it is a logical stop card, a mind-boggling otherness in a distinct shape. One always has to keep two things in mind at the same time in this context—as in any oxymoron. F. Scott Fitzgerald observed, "The test of a first-rate intelligence is the ability to hold two opposite ideas in mind at the same time, and still retain the ability to function."[56] This fits the oxymoron character of God-walk very well. It is part of the gospel-mystery. The doubleness is always trying to do justice to two poles of our life, without falling into Orwellian doublethink. God's truth about the coming new world is never monolithic. Occasionally we even have to keep *three* "opposite" things in mind, as in the Trinity, for example. And with the multipersonality of Christ, truth is even more multifaceted.

All of this doubleness, tripleness, and diversity, our attempt to grasp God's walk among human beings, only indicates that we are still on the way, pilgrims toward God's rule. We are gripped by the work of the Spirit hastening God's coming. But it is not the consummation itself.[57] In the creed we point not only to "sitting at the right hand of God," the sharing of God's work as God's right hand, but also to the coming again to judge the quick and the dead, the resurrection of the body, and life everlasting. The point is that history, though the turf of God's struggle for justice, is not the whole of life's meaning.[58] The question and answer from the *Heidelberg Catechism* (1563) with regard to the holy, catholic church bears repeating: "What do you believe concerning the Holy Catholic Church?" Answer: "I believe that, from the beginning to the end of the world, and from among the whole human race, the Son of God, by his Spirit and his Word, gathers, protects, and preserves for himself, in the unity of the true faith, a congregation chosen for eternal life. Moreover, I believe that I am and forever will remain a living member of it eternally" (question 54).[59] A *congregation* chosen for eternal life, God's coming reign. I will remain a *member* of it. Both the corporate and the personal are involved in this movement toward the future.[60]

As the struggle with the powers and principalities, the rulers of chaos, goes on in history, *there is no ultimate fulfillment within history*. There is only foretaste, a glimpse of things to come. The

Holy Spirit is presence of God as coming God, consummation in the sensing of this coming, waking up to God's rule.

What one experiences is God's movement in front of oneself, the dynamics of what is hastening "through the thick darkness"—in terms of the hymn referred to before. As the metaphors of Resistance Spirit and Comforter Spirit converge in the actual gift of the Spirit, the empowerment for God-walk comes time and again into our hearts and souls.

The mystery of God-walk is not the final consummation of all things beyond history. The mystery is the presence of God's coming rule as empowerment of God-walk in history. It is the presence of the coming God, appropriated as liberation from sin and all the powers of evil, and the prevailing of our life over death. The gospel is thus not pie in the sky—the offer of something in the distant future. It is history reshaped.

The mystery is that God's reign is "at hand" (Mark 1:15). The time is fulfilled: "If it is by the finger of God that I cast out demons, then the kingdom of God has come upon you" (Luke 11:20). The future reign is accessible in a concrete person coming to us in the eucharist—Messiah Jesus. What we receive in him is *embodied eschatology*, just as we understand God's deprivation (incarnation) as embodiment of God. Through the Holy Spirit this embodied reign is made present in the church. It is personally embodied "eternal," prevailing, life and becomes concrete ever again in the eucharist: "Whoever eats my flesh and drinks my blood has eternal life" (John 6:54). "Prevailing life means to know you, the only real God, and Messiah Jesus whom you have sent" (John 17:3).

The emphasis is Pauline as well as Johannine: "The free gift of God is eternal life in Messiah Jesus our Lord" (Rom. 6:23). The mystery of God reaches into the human condition here and now, and offers us purpose and meaning, justice and freedom, as anticipation of the reign of peace (shalom).

We are here up against another "oxymoron," the *now* and the *not yet*, the this-worldly and the other-worldly, the immanent and the transcendent. The mystery of God's presence in the Holy Spirit makes these things cohere. They do not fly off in all directions centrifugally, as it were, but hang together in the central dynamics in front of us: our humanity is anchored in God's shalom. What we experience as corporate humanity through Messiah Jesus in the church is what we will experience eternally in God's peaceable reign. We are compelled to be together with all of God's people when God reigns fully. The Holy Spirit empowers in us a heartfelt *desire* to be in solidarity with the "the least" of our neighbors.

This is not *realized* eschatology. Nothing is as yet fully realized. God is still *in the process* of self-realization. God personally is still changing together with us, taking up our struggles in the divine heart. It is *embodied* eschatology, part of the process of God—history moving toward the divine goal, shalom, in which God will be all in all.

We cannot say, at the point where history seems to deny final fulfillment forever, that actually the eschaton enters time, or that eternity becomes time—with nothing to be expected beyond time. History never "fulfills"—our reach is always beyond our grasp. But in spirit-praxis we sense that eternity enters history on God's terms to fulfill history where we fail. The oxymoron of empowerment by the Spirit, resistance and comfort, is the cause of clowning, and thus ultimately of laughter. Of all things human, laughter comes closest to perfection. What carries us on toward the coming reign of God is the Easter laughter.

Life is not a joke. But we can laugh about it. We can laugh about ourselves. If the human being is conscience, and faith is conscience activated, the point of life is eternal life making conscience laugh. Shalom in the face of the Pershing IIs and SS 20s seems as funny, awkward, and ineffective as a clown, and yet it will prevail. In conscience, we participate in the coming reign of God, we laugh for joy because it is near. So our willing and knowing is empowered to become future-oriented in peace, and therefore active, risky, and—in everybody's eyes—clownish. We do not take peace lightly, but we are lighthearted about it. The future is in good hands. God reigns in church and world, and creates the Messiah body, corporate humanity. Thus God also reigns in my personal life. I am chosen for eternal life—that is, prevailing life. The point of my life is communally mediated in the eucharist. Among sisters and brothers around the bread and the wine, life makes sense. We know under whose aegis we move: "For as often as you eat this bread and drink this cup, you proclaim the Lord's death until the Lord comes" (1 Cor. 11:26):

In our God-walk
Let us laugh.
Let us laugh together.
Let us laugh for God's sake.
Let us laugh all the way.

"When the Lord restored
     the fortunes of Zion,
   we were like those who dream.
Then our mouth was filled with
     laughter" [Ps. 126:1–2].

In faith, awakened conscience, the affirmation of the coming reign of God again turns into questions as we ask reality: Will it react on these grounds? Will it react to laughter—not any kind of laughter, but God's laughter, Easter laughter? That is faith as hope. As long as we know in part, love as justice/love fills the gap of our ignorance. Because we know so little, we try to be just. Because we know so little, we love so much. That is faith as risk—on grounds of empowerment for God's coming justice/peace—shalom.

NOTES

Introduction

1. It is understandable that David Tracy in his method immediately moves toward placing Christianity within the "religious dimension." It yields of course much insight to view Christianity as one piece of "that puzzling and ambiguous phenomenon, religion." But Christianity is thus placed among the normalcy phenomena of all religious experience and no immediate question is being asked about unique dimensions that might well have to be attended to first. Is it a foregone conclusion that Christianity is basically best understood as a religion? See David Tracy, "Theological Method," in Peter C. Hodgson and Robert H. King (eds.), *Christian Theology* (Philadelphia, 1985), 53, 57. If only for a moment we try to view Christian existence outside the realm of religion, we realize that there are options. Many are asking: What we have as Christianity in the West—is it still the genuine thing or some counterfeit? We have to move to a very self-critical point right away. The present volume from the outset is not based only on the historico-critical method, but on the historico/self-critical method.

2. Examples are the section on "Our Theological Task" in the *Book of Discipline of the United Methodist Church* (Nashville, 1980), 71–85, and "Towards the Task of Sound Teaching in the United Church of Christ," a seminar report included in my *Justice Church* (Maryknoll, N.Y., 1980), 139–54.

3. The sharp difference between the Christian way of life and the culture of the West has been movingly described by a Russian refugee, Tatjana Goritschewa, *Von Gott reden ist gefährlich* (Freiburg, Basel, Vienna, 1985), 107–27, esp. 121.

4. There is now wide agreement developing as to the existence of three basic options. The first edition of Peter C. Hodgson and Robert H. King (eds.), *Christian Theology* (Philadelphia, 1982) has liberation theologies functioning as a third option (24, 81, 232, 239, 323, 325, 332, 334, 335, and passim). But Hodgson/King did not proceed in terms of the options as calling for a new *paradigm* for theology as a whole.

199

5. In trying to find a sharp profile for liberation theology in Protestantism, it is imperative to steer clear of misleading terms. "Symbol" can be interpreted in all kinds of ways. Roger Haight (*An Alternate Vision: An Interpretation of Liberation Theology* [Mahwah, N.J., 1985]) makes a good case for keeping the notion of symbol in Catholic discourse and in the liberation context (8–12, 42, 59–60, and passim). But he ties it to Tillich's method of correlation, which immediately raises for Protestants the question whether the use of the notion makes one buy into a lot of liberal theology premises that ultimately do not bring about a radical turning. In Protestantism, a radical break with the post–Enlightenment is called for. I tried to raise this issue in an early response to Hugo Assmann. The decade since has underscored my conviction that few in liberal Protestantism are ready to contemplate the implications of a radical break with the liberal theology premises. This means ultimately that we are merely legitimating economics and politics, culture and society, the way they are—however many radical words we use. See my "On Liberating Liberation Theology," in Hugo Assmann, *Theology for a Nomad Church* (Maryknoll, N.Y., 1976), 9f.

6. *Women and Spirituality* (Totowa, N.J., 1983), 1.

7. There is a crucial decision to be made at this juncture. The option we are compelled to affirm is *God's* option for the poor. It makes all the difference in the world. It eliminates any hankering to move to the modern theology project with the desires to mediate God to our secularized consumer culture. Roger Haight (note 5, above) states the terms of the decision most clearly: "Gutiérrez too has proposed, and often repeated, that theology in the developed nations is fundamentally different from liberation theology. Like Sobrino, he sees northern theology as dominated by the problem of faith in a secularized and even materialistic consumer society and culture. How is one to mediate God to a satisfied society? The problem of Latin American and liberation theology is not the problem of God or faith in God. Rather it is the problem of the non–person, the oppressed and disenfranchised, and how Christianity responds to them in their situation" (p. 31). The God who stands by the poor is not mediable to consumer societies by God–talk: "The question of faith is not decided by an extended argument or a book that claims to have demonstrated that God is or that God–talk is meaningful. Rather it depends almost solely on whether Christian faith as a social or public phenomenon is meaningful" (ibid.). How are we to mediate God to a satisfied society? What else can we do to offer, instead of the idol "god" of Western civilization, the poor God who in Jesus proves to be bending low to every disfigured face, to every threatened creature?

8. The presupposition of *God-Walk* is that theology comes as a second step after praxis or spirituality. I agree with Carol Ochs that the "process of

coming into relationship with reality is spirituality" (*Women and Spirituality*, 10).

9. Eberhard Hübner, *Theologie und Empirie der Kirche* (Neukirchen–Vluyn, 1985) is a beautiful tour de force of the Protestant praxis issue in the northern hemisphere. Even Schleiermacher, Hübner makes clear, knew the priority of praxis over theory. Praxis is much "older" than theory. In some respects, liberation theology can never say more than that. So what is new? Schleiermacher chose to walk with the cultured among the despisers of religion. In the Hübner book, praxis of the poor and praxis together with the poor appear nowhere, not even on the horizon of the argument in this context. It proves that not only tensions between North and South are strong in this respect, but also among different options in the North.

10. Susan Thistlethwaite provides a telling criticism of my use of "Messiah Jesus." She wonders whether the term really links "our primary identity as Christians with the history of Judaism and with Jewish thought. Jesus is *not* Messiah for Jews" (*Metaphors for the Contemporary Church* [New York, 1983], 92). How can I not agree with the point? Yet Jesus *was* Messiah for some Jews. They had no other word to make the crucial ground of their God–walk clear. It was a messianic praxis they had entered, the christo-praxis. I cannot distance the Jewish community from an event that happened in its very own past. I cannot deny the data. I have no right to undo what early Jewish Christians felt to be true. *Their* Jewish identification of Jesus with Messiah has created our present Christian dilemma. To move away from the oxymoron here expressed would mean to surrender Jesus' Jewishness, I believe. No one regrets more than I the mad superiority by which Christians have idolized their Jesus. But nothing is gained for understanding by dissociating him from the Jewish Messiah. There must have been an intensely felt liberation among some Jews when they realized that Messiah was one of them, the poor, the outcast, the marginal. The most magnificent Jewish figure is being identified with the rejects and wretched of the earth. It does not figure, and yet it figures.

11. Carolyn Walker Bynum, *Jesus as Mother: Studies in the Spirituality of the High Middle Ages* (Berkeley, 1982), 256–62.

12. Matthew Fox (ed.), *Illuminations of Hildegard of Bingen* (Santa Fe, 1985), 92.

13. "Instruction on Certain Aspects of the 'Theology of Liberation,' " *Origins: NC Documentary Service*, 14:13 (Sept. 13, 1984), 199–200.

14. Alasdair MacIntyre, *After Virtue: A Study in Moral Theory* (Notre Dame, 1984), 61.

15. For the earliest beginnings, see Gerd Theissen, *Sociology of Early Palestinian Christianity* (Philadelphia, 1978), 31–95.

16. Alistaire Kee, *Constantine Versus Christ* (London, 1982), 135.

17. Ibid., 136.

18. Ibid., 137.

19. Ibid., 138.

20. Ibid., 139.

21. Ibid., 140.

22. See note 11, above.

23. Elisabeth Schüssler Fiorenza, *In Memory of Her: A Feminist Theological Reconstruction of Christian Origins* (New York, 1983), 152, 128, 138.

24. Clarence Jordan, *The Cotton Patch Version of Luke and Acts* (New York, 1969), 95–96.

25. David Tracy, *The Analogical Imagination* (New York, 1981), 208.

26. Ibid., 212.

27. Goritschewa, *Von Gott reden*, 86.

28. Ibid., 50.

29. Ibid., 87.

30. Karl Barth, *Dogmatics in Outline* (New York, 1949), 13.

31. We dare not misrepresent the basic engagement of Barth's. For Anglo-Saxon Christians, the church struggle that determined Barth's outlook from 1933 onward is often nearly incomprehensible in its profound effect on Barth. He initially objected to large numbers of Christians in Germany who did not even inquire into the threat of the movement known as German Christians. It is often intimated that Barth was focusing on the internal hassle of the church only and was not addressing the state at all. The point is that countless church members as part of the movement called German Christians were either already an *arm* of the state, or were in the process of becoming such. The horror for Barth was that the Protestant Church was widely no longer the church of Jesus Christ, but an extension of the state. Therefore *theological existence today (theologische Existenz heute)* was the issue at hand. The church institution, the *ecclesia*, thrives on doctrine. Where doctrine collapses, the institution is also in danger of collapsing. Barth was still oriented in the Constantinian *Grosskirche*, the church of the *corpus Christianum*. Because of the peculiar structure of the German church struggle, Barth never had to make the God–walk dynamics the starting point of his thinking. In the midst of so much fake God-talk, Barth developed the counter-talk of theological existence. It was for him not just a matter of the church having to save the independence of proclamation and theology. The question was the sovereignty of the Word of God in proclamation and theology. Was there any *God*ness at all breaking through to the church? See Karl Barth, *Theologische Existenz heute* (Munich, new ed., 1984), 72.

32. Barth feared that the Word of God might be taken away from the

German church the way it was taken away from the church of St. Augustine, the church of North Africa (ibid., 77f.). Much of this still has validity today in the United States. We also know of the clash between the counterfeit church and the true church. It is our clash we need to attend to. But today we cannot do it on the level of mere theology—which meanwhile has become suspect itself. For Barth it was possible for the church to *be* church (p. 82) on account of good theology. What is missing for the North American situation is the discipleship moment. We cannot tie the continued existence of the church just to theology revitalized. The christo-praxis challenge is inescapable and comes first. Which God do we as Christians offer to the secular culture, the matinee idol or the poor God?

33. Friedrich Schleiermacher, *The Christian Faith* (Edinburgh, 1928), 76.

34. Ibid., 127.

35. The very crucial issue that will accompany us from now on is the adequate grasp of the liberation process in North America. What attitude do we take toward liberation thought from the Third World? The dominant stance is reaction/response. At least this is the way a large segment of the American churches viewed the Detroit conference on Latin American liberation theology (Detroit I, 1975). Ever since, *response* has been the lodestar of North American (and European) assessments of Third World thought. Obviously response is important and dare not be excluded. But we make it the be-all and end-all only at our own peril. The issue is to understand the Moloch of North American oppression within which we ourselves are caught. Any effort toward a liberation shape of dogmatics has to keep it in mind all along. We need to show how new dogmatics grows out of a particular God–walk. But the end–effect of shaping the new dogmatics is to gut the old structure of dogmatics that props up the present social and political configuration. We need to develop a North American vision of our own, a genuine North American model, whatever the cost. Our North American problem in many areas is that we merely react. L. Fletcher Prouty, writing about the CIA, states very much the principle that pertains to a range of things we do as Americans in relationship to the world as a whole: "The response method of anything is a trap. The most frustrating and debilitating thing about it is that we have no objectives, no goals" (*The Secret Team* [Englewood Cliffs, N.J., 1973], 68). Beginning with the Civil Rights era, the black church in the U.S.A. was able to point to God's justice struggle on the side of the poor. See James H. Cone, *Black Theology and Black Power* (New York, 1969), 108f. The framework is, of course, much wider. In the mid-1970s I sketched the overall framework in brief: "Unless we in the U.S. pass through the needle's eye of the black, red, feminist, Chicano and other liberation experiences in the one America

where we live, we will not enter the kingdom of liberation in *both* Americas" (in Sergio Torres and John Eagleson [eds.], *Theology in the Americas*
[Maryknoll, N.Y., 1976], 146). Looking back, I can still subscribe to what I
wrote at that time. Yet I also see how little difference we have made within
the churches, the divinity schools, and our culture. Perhaps we tried to
cover too many bases. Perhaps now even liberation theology language, not
just religious language in general, is being used to keep the real conflicts of
society concealed. More than five decades ago a good American, John
Dewey, described the peculiar North American phenomenon of the function of religion: "Nowhere in the world at any time has religion been so
thoroughly respectable as with us, and so nearly totally disconnected from
life. . . . The glorification of religion as setting the final seal of approval on
pecuniary success, and the adoption by the churches of the latest devices of
the movies and the advertiser, approach too close to the obscene" (John
Dewey, *Individualism Old and New* [New York, 1930], 14). Much of white
religion in the U.S.A. promotes the energetic struggle for pecuniary success. What I did not elaborate thoroughly enough in the mid-1970s was the
sharp distinction between God and idol. We will make that distinction the
major orientation point of our efforts. Living under the pressure of the
American empire is to suffer the full power of the idol that keeps us in
bondage. The first task of dogmatics is to show the illusory nature of the
idol and to smash it. Yet even to raise the issue is to invite immediate scorn.

36. Barth did not want to speak *to* the situation, as though the situation
were of importance in itself. But he did want to take the situation seriously
(*Theologische Existenz heute*, 83). In this regard his theology was a highly
contextual theology too that made a tremendous difference in 1933,
though what Barth wanted to guard was *theological existence*. The moment of discipleship was not as such part of the picture. Barth pitted
theological categories against counterfeit categories. Today "Irangate" has
made us aware again of the strange temptation of the modern state to make
totalitarian claims on persons and to enlist Christianity for its cause.

37. What we find in Barth in 1933 is utter concentration of revelation in a
narrow point. The Nazi development had not popped out of the blue for
Barth. He was able to look back on years that had led up to that moment.
The sudden accession to power by the Nazis created, however, a type of
frenzy in Protestantism. At that point there was little time left. So Barth
coined the notion of "theological existence" and hurled the key categories
of neoreformation thought into the teeth of an ever hungrier beast. He was
confronted with notions such as German Christians (*Deutsche Christen*),
empire bishop (*Reichsbischof*) and young reformer (*Jung Reforma-
torisch*). Barth appealed to catechism, confessions, and above all the Bible,
Jesus Christ, and the Word of God. The struggle took place on the level of

theological categories. There was no other way at that time. "Discipleship today" was not Barth's point, or a query as to *who* exactly it was whom the church was to hear. The name Jesus Christ was entirely sufficient.

38. We need to focus liberation theology very carefully at this point in terms of the North American challenge. Rebecca S. Chopp has written a thus far unsurpassed summary of what is at stake. She asks: Is liberation theology really different from modern theology? She answers no and yes. In one respect, she believes "liberation theology continues—albeit in a radically reformulated manner—the fundamental nature of modern theology" (*The Praxis of Suffering* [Maryknoll, N.Y., 1986], 149). It is difficult to nail the issues down in brief. Perhaps it is best to begin with her basic claim: "In sum, we might say that liberation theology is as anthropocentric as most of the rest of modern theology: Christianity is interpreted and lived in relation to the human subject" (p. 150). We need to question liberation theology as a continuation of the modern theology project. For God-walk any anthropocentricity is suspect, whether modern or ancient. The best way I can explain the liberation theology project in the light of the Chopp analysis is to say that by the time her book was written, the paradigm shift had come just so far. The next liberation task is to rid Christian thought of modern anthropocentricity. In principle, I have to agree with the Chopp analysis of six assumptions that govern modern theology: "(1) The human subject is a meaning–seeker; (2) the human subject must be brought to higher consciousness; (3) history and nature are both characterized by the interrelation of cause and effect; (4) faith is located in personal experience and neither contradicts nor is reducible to scientific or historical knowledge; (5) tradition itself demands continual reinterpretation and change; (6) theology has an interpretive role, mediating the relationship of human existence and Christian tradition" (p. 149).

But we also have to examine each point critically. (1) The human subject cannot be all that central—ever. (2) Higher consciousness is not the major issue, but altering of consciousness. (3) History and nature are both littered with the debris brought about by cause and effect theories. (4) Faith is not the primary concern, for faith is simply the reconstitution of conscience. (5) Tradition is much less an object of interpretation than a dwelling place of faith. (6) Theology is subject to reexamination and no longer plays a primary role. It is a second step.

What makes the Chopp approach difficult is that (correctly from the viewpoint of modern theology) there are only two options for human subjects: meaning-seekers or meaning-makers. Modern theology is cursed with the assumption of *human* initiative in all things: either we seek or we make. *Tertium non datur*. But besides being meaning-seekers or meaning-makers, we are also *meaning-takers*. The first thing that God-walk makes clear is that *we* do not generate primal Christian thought. Our first thought in God-walk is a *given*. To be able to live in terms of a complete *gift* of meaning—that is how God-walk begins. There is a radical difference to be noted also in regard to the newness of liberation theology. One of the reasons Chopp finds that liberation theology appears as a new paradigm compared with modern theology is "its orientation toward transformation rather than understanding as the reconciliation of human existence and reality" (p. 151). Here again, *tertium non datur*: either reconciliation or transformation. Yet are not both anteceded by fascination? That is, fascination with the gift—the gift of justice? We find the same alternative in David Tracy who speaks only of *revelation* (disclosure) and *transformation* as options (*Analogical Imagination*, 87, n. 37). But the liberation paradigm has already moved beyond the alternative. Chopp of course hits the nail on the head when she says that "liberation theology asks a quite different question from that of modern theology, the question of massive public suffering" (p. 151). However, the *gift* of meaning, God personally, appears *within* massive public suffering. This is not a transcendence from beyond history. This is historical transcendence: God as gift within the historical process. God personally does the transforming and reconciling. We do not have to worry it into existence. What we can do is *resist* the powers that want to transform and reconcile in God's stead—surrogate gods.

39. It is crucial not to cover up in Christian thought the harsh reality of the poverty struggle. As soon as we get to this point, the smoke screens go up and one can hardly move on with reflection on praxis. Sometimes critics would like to remove even the ground under our feet in the argument. In an essay, "God-Walk and Class Struggle" (*Circuit Rider*, 9:6 [June 1985]), I underscored the inescapable lot of poverty for millions. One letter writer (*Circuit Rider*, Oct. 1985) responded that my argument implied we were keeping the poor out of our community. Yet, the writer said, 99 percent "of the hungry in our land are loners who chose not to become involved in any church or friendly fellowship. They may not have been sought out, but they were not kept out" (p. 20). Most of the poor in the Third World are in economic distress because the political conditions are such that they cannot but be poor. This is also true for many of the poor in the U.S.A. Our task is to find out why conditions are such that human beings starve and live in poverty. We soon discover how the economic system works in favor of the rich and the rich countries. In letters responding to my essay there is also the intimation that the option for the poor foments revolution. I can only state that where the poor are oppressed, herded like cattle away from their ancestral homes (in South Africa, for example), revolutionary conditions exist as a matter of course. Christian thought does not have to invent them. But it has to face them. For (in spite of all the lamentations to the contrary)

revolution has a lot to do with the struggle for justice against injustice. It makes no sense to try to relativize the revolution or to speak of the vast gap between God's revolution and human revolution. I am no longer sure that the notion of "God's revolution" makes sense. The point is: it is human beings who make revolution. God wades into the human mess. But God tends to God's own dynamics in these matters. The challenge is to see the seriousness of revolution—a very human answer to structural sin, but in any case an answer. Christian thought cannot run away from these historical dynamics. And yet the churches will not want to jump on the bandwagon of revolution either. Some of the traps might be illustrated by the more recent history of communism in the U.S.A. One has to honor—and understand—the tremendous sacrifice and commitment of countless party members during the 1940s and 50s. Vivian Gornick, (*The Romance of American Communism* [New York, 1977]) beautifully recalls the traumas, tragedies, failures, and losses as well as the gains of those years. These very dedicated communists believed: "Everyone knows the revolution is around the corner" (p. 111). To some, "every major and minor struggle on the floor of the factory was a preparatory battle for the revolution" (p. 127). "The revolution was everything" (p. 144). We have to recall the utter dedication of rank and file party members: "For thousands of Communists, being a Communist meant years of selling the *Daily Worker*, running off mimeographed leaflets, speaking on street corners, canvassing door-to-door for local and national votes, organizing neighborhood groups for tenants' rights or welfare rights or unemployment benefits, raising money for the Party or for legal defenses or bail bonds or union struggles. Only that and nothing more" (pp. 109f.). Much of their activity parallels church witness: "It was exactly like the church" (p. 167). Communism was the substitute church. Of one member it is reported, the party meant "a generalized but deeply felt identification with all those who were 'hurting' under capitalism" (p. 179). Identification led to a deeply felt corporateness: "And we all did it for the same reason: we were accountable to each other" (p. 110). The *mutual accountability in identification with the oppressed* brings us almost to liberation theology. In some respects, nothing in liberation theology reflects a Christian *proprium*. Much of this has been tried before.

The Gornick book is also a documentation of the tremendous disillusionment with the revolution. It was *not* around the corner. It therefore fudges the issue of Christian thought when revolution is introduced as part of the primary rationale of liberation theology. Liberation theology in North America cannot move from some abstract concept of revolution to "theological reflection." Otherwise we would do no more than repeat the communist move in the 1930s. What is more, we need to start with our praxis situation, not with revolution as theory. Liberation theology grows out of the turmoil of the pastoral situation in social location with the poor. Initially it becomes no more than a hermeneutical lens through which we view Bible and tradition.

Studying the lives of those who have become martyrs in the present struggle aids us in understanding. Practically on our U.S. doorsteps, there was the assassination of Archbishop Oscar Romero, the murder of Ita Ford, Maura Clark, Dorothy Kazel, and Jean Donovan. Less known is the death of Father Stanley Francis Rother (1935–1981). Henri J. M. Nouwen writes a beautiful epitaph. It was a pastoral situation that evoked his death: "Stan came as a pastor, a shepherd, to Santiago Atitlán, and he remained a pastor to the very end. He stayed far from politics and politicians. . . . Without wanting or deserving it, Stan's pastoral commitment increasingly made him an enemy of those who had power. In the context of the struggle of the poor for dignity, lending a hand to an Indian peasant becomes a political act. Stan knew that. That is why he said: 'Helping these people could very easily be considered subversive.' If that is subversive, then Stan was willing to take the risk—although with many precautions—to be considered as such. The political situation causes immense violence, the violence causes deep human suffering, and the suffering calls for pastoral care and healing—independent of who is to blame. It was this care for the people, at all times and in all circumstances, that would lead to the deaths of Archbishop Oscar Romero, Ita Ford, and many others. It would also be the source of Stan's martyrdom" (Henri J. M. Nouwen, *Love in a Fearful Land: A Guatemalan Story* [Notre Dame, 1985], 57). There could not be a more telling God–walk story. The Rother martyrdom tells the basic truth.

Nouwen also shows how the eucharist (together with prayer) functions as focus of the meaning grasped in suffering (p. 95). The task of Christian thought is to understand how "the body and blood of Christ" are central to God's justice struggle. Chalcedon teaches us that God and humanity are unmixed in Jesus, and yet inseparable. But it does not clarify for us in what sense God in person is immersed in the immense suffering that continues after Jesus' death. God–walk makes sure we understand the unity of Jesus' divine/human personhood as sustained by God's solidarity with unjust suffering. God is not merely person *in the divine Logos* (as Chalcedon instructs us), but God is also person in the nonperson. God is person and nonperson. Because the high and mighty cannot tolerate that kind of "power" (it questions empire power of every hue), they need to destroy it, put it out of the way. God's justice struggle at this point cannot evade the power struggle. Stan Rother's death explains it all. The christology arising from christo-praxis is so important because for a Westerner trained in

Chalcedonian Logos-christology, God will primarily be sought among "the high and the mighty." And we will still end up with a high and mighty Pantocrator Christ, all the medieval crucifixes notwithstanding. The watershed moment we face today relates to a completely new sensibility. People are invited by God to see God among the suffering, the poor and oppressed. Otherwise the destruction of the environment and the devastation of history will continue. See my essay, "A New Spirituality: Shaping Doctrine at the Grass Roots," *Christian Century* (July 30–Aug. 9, 1986), 680–81.

40. Since the time I wrote *Liberation Theology* (New York, 1972), I have learned to scrutinize the significance of both liberation and theology more fully. I have been compelled to become more deeply immersed in the liberation dynamics. As far as theology is concerned, I have become more and more distanced, skeptical, and self-critical. Theology is a word that runs wild. Usually it is understood as the be-all and catch-all of the thought of Christian thinkers. Liberation theology has generally offered a clarification: theology at best is only the second step—following praxis. I believe it is fair to say that within the new grassroots dynamics that are shaping up in the teaching formation within some U.S. churches, God-walk issues in new doctrine—that is, basic faith arguments, accountable teaching. The task of theology would then be to reflect on discipleship in the church as it produces wisdom language that seeks to guide the thought of the community. So the sequence would be: (1) praxis; (2) doctrine; (3) theology. This book is also theology. But it is first of all an attempt to show how Christian thought arises in a person or community. It deals with the genesis of Christian thought, with common discoveries of faith that can be taught and "passed on"—to become "traditions." I try to describe the difference between doctrine and theology on new grounds—social analysis from a new social location. As far as *liberation* theology is concerned, it functions in this book initially as hermeneutical lens. With attention to God as person *and nonperson*, God involved with the poor and losers, how does the dogmatic tradition shape up? I am not trying to add a private find of my own, *another* theology. I am trying to discover how, with the hermeneutical lens of liberation theology, the church as a whole, corporately, can arrive at a new dogmatics, a body of teaching that will guide our life in terms of mutual accountability, not hierarchically from the top down, but from below, from the grassroots. All that *God-Walk* will be able to do is to scratch the surface, to take a little step here or there. It is pioneering time. These are "early days," the days for listening to the poor.

41. One example. Gordon Kaufmann has again characterized theology as God-talk: "And inasmuch as theology is, after all, *talk*,—talk about God—theology does well to listen carefully to what the linguistic philoso-

phers have to say about the possibilities and the limits of human talk in general, and especially about the 'deep grammar' of our language about God. There is a great deal to be learned from philosophy about the nature of theology, and thus about the proper tasks of theology and the methods that theologians can employ. In short, philosophy can teach us much about the sort of vocation that theology can be and how that vocation can best be carried out" (Gordon D. Kaufmann, "Theology as Public Vocation," in Theodore W. Jennings, Jr. [ed.], *The Vocation of the Theologian* [Philadelphia, 1985], 54). Here of course we become aware of the dilemma in our field. Kaufmann makes the move to philosophy, lets philosophy offer significant categories, etc. So we hardly get to the problem of "nuclear theology": How does a Christian thought originate in the first place? This book is ultimately wrestling with little more than this question—the question of "genesis."

42. John Macquarrie, *God-Talk* (New York, Evanston, 1967), 33.

43. The contribution of liberation theologies tries to nail down the issue from the opposite direction. José Míguez Bonino ("Theology as Critical Reflection and Liberating Praxis," in Jennings, *Vocation of the Theologian*) speaks of a search for models through which the "blinding effect of a social location can be overcome." This is something the liberation theologian has to solve "not merely in theoretical terms but in actual life" (p. 42). For Míguez Bonino, God is the "fundamental reference" (p. 42). God has a particular social location in Christ, which has to be kept in mind when we seek to appropriate Míguez Bonino's definition of theology: "Christian theology . . . is not a reflection on social praxis in general but of social praxis as experienced and acted out by Christians" (p. 45). Míguez Bonino makes crystal clear that we cannot eliminate the God-factor in this social praxis. That factor also stands out boldly in his book *Toward a Christian Political Ethics* (Philadelphia, 1983): "God's . . . power is affirmed in the midst of conflict. God is engaged in a struggle" (p. 97). Latin American liberation theology and North American liberation theology coincide at this point. I understand my *God-Walk* to be in full agreement with Gustavo Gutiérrez in his, *We Drink from Our Own Wells* (Maryknoll, N.Y., 1985). We both begin in "a way of following Christ" (p. 52). All of this distinctly backs off from developing a liberation theology taking its cue from liberal theology. See my introduction to Hugo Assmann, *Theology for a Nomad Church,* 1–23.

44. David Tracy's review of praxis-oriented Christian thought is still the best I am aware of and from which I am still learning (*Analogical Imagination*, 69–79). The question remains, however, whether he represents the praxis issues in the liberation theologies in their full ramifications. Many liberation theologies and political theologies surely work the issues the way

he describes it. There is a *lot* of liberal theology in some liberation theologies (see Chopp, *Praxis of Suffering*, 149). Tracy comes close to understanding a major move away from liberal theology in liberation theology when he argues: "Is it not the case that Christian faith, hope, and love are first praxis realities for a transformed agent and community before they are expressed in cognitive claims or right beliefs? In that sense, is it not the case that orthopraxis does in fact ground orthodoxy?" (p. 76). Yet there remains a nagging problem. Are not orthopraxy as well as orthodoxy both *our* human part of the God-walk? What about *God's* own part? How does God ultimately meet us? This is also a praxis issue. Obviously we can agree with Tracy that "all good theory is grounded in the authentic praxis of intellectual integrity" (p. 77). But does that get at the gist of the Christian praxis issue? My problem with Tracy is that he basically seems to come down on a paradigm of "movement from the relatively abstract to the relatively concrete" (p. 87). It would appear in christo-praxis to be just the other way around: we need to move from the body, the concrete, to the relatively more abstract.

45. Gordon Kaufmann claims: "Theology is also a reflexive discipline and must include a theory of itself in connection with its theory of God" (in Jennings, *Vocation of the Theologian*, 55). As true as the statement is, a major task still extant is the analysis of the *genesis* of the theological theory of itself and its theory of God.

46. Langdon Gilkey makes a pertinent observation: "Theology represents a Christian *theory* about existence and the God to whom it is essentially related. It is Christian understanding, and it characterizes our *thinking*, whereas Christian life or faith characterizes our *existence*, the way we are and act" (in Jennings, *Vocation of the Theologian*, 91). Yet how are thinking and existence related? How does Christian thinking grow out of existence? These are some of the issues that need tackling anew. Is it really the case that theology relates itself first of all to other *theories* and only indirectly to concrete situations in actual life (ibid.), if theology is "a function of the church" (p. 90)—as also Gilkey wants it to be?

47. *Keeping You Posted* (United Church of Christ Newsletter, New York), May 1, 1984.

48. Loyd D. Easton and Kurt H. Guddat (eds.), *Writings of the Young Marx on Philosophy and Society* (Garden City, N.Y., 1967), 414f.

49. Matthew Fox (ed.), *Illuminations of Hildegard of Bingen* (Santa Fe, 1985), 64.

50. *The Charlotte Observer* (Nov. 30, 1976).

51. While this book was taking shape in the struggles of a particular southern social location, another departure from the usual way of shaping dogmatics appeared: Geoffrey Wainwright, *Doxology* (New York, 1980).

Wainwright grounds Christian thought in liturgy: "My own vision of faith is firmly shaped and strongly colored by the Christian liturgy" (p. 1). *God-Walk* pushes the issue one step back to the genesis of Christian thought in christo-praxis as social location also of worship. In the future, it appears dogmatic work will again be much more determined by the church dynamics that calls forth Christian doctrine in the first place. Yet I am less sanguine than Wainwright about what systematic theology in North America might still accomplish in terms of the expectations of most churches. Wainwright says of his work: "This book may be taken in two ways. It is primarily intended as a systematic theology written from a liturgical perspective. It can also be considered as a theology of worship" (p. ix). I will not claim that systematic theologies will no longer be written, but I think we need to examine very carefully the nature of systematic theology. The current use of the term reflects a rather modern outlook. Since the days of Friedrich Schleiermacher, systematic theology was possible because of a basic systematic principle—for example, the feeling of absolute dependence or (in Paul Tillich) the principle of correlation. That systematic principle was possible only because of a presupposed unitary anthropology and unitary worldview. Both no longer exist. Everything "universal" has collapsed. New dogmatics has become much more difficult than a systematic theology—a system. I have examined the problem in "Vom Ende der Systematischen Theologie," Hermann Deuser et al. (eds.), *Gottes Zukunft—Zukunft der Welt* (Munich, 1986), 502–10. In that article as well as in *God-Walk*, I have been groping toward an "archeology" of Christian thought. Geoffrey Wainwright senses the increasingly pioneer-type situation. But I wish to dig for the roots of worship itself in social location.

52. We dare not forget our being influenced by the societal state we find ourselves in. Christopher Lash (*The Culture of Narcissism* [New York, 1979]) writes: "Unfortunately the attempt to restore a sense of collective worship cannot restore the unity of belief that once gave life to such forms" (p. 163; see also pp. 319–49).

53. *Proposed Services of Marriage: Test Document* (Church Leadership Resources, Office for Church Life and Leadership, United Church of Christ, St. Louis, 1982), 26.

54. Obviously the discussion of these issues goes far beyond the United Methodist Church or the United Church of Christ. In a more "interdenominational vein" the issue has been analyzed by John Shelby Spong, "Can the Church Bless Divorce?," *Christian Century*, 101:37 (Nov. 28, 1984), 1126–27. Spong describes "a liturgy designed to offer to God the pain of a divorce." Focusing on a concrete divorce service, he reports: "Because the man and the woman remained committed Christians, the church which

had been a central focus of their marriage somehow also had to be part of their separation" (p. 1126). But does the whole reality of God's justice struggle really call for a rite of divorce? Or are we not absolutizing a personal human struggle, though very painful and wrenching, in a narcissistic way? The churches' failure to minister adequately to divorced persons cannot be compensated for by a new invention of "rites."

55. Mel Krantzler, *Creative Divorce: A New Opportunity for Personal Growth* (New York, 1973).

56. Dietrich Bonhoeffer, *The Communion of Saints* (New York and Evanston, 1964), 155: "But since where the Body of Christ is the *sanctorum communio* is, this makes marriage the smallest sociological unit of the *sanctorum communio*. In fact it can be present in marriage to the highest degree." Here Bonhoeffer lays the groundwork for making the connection between marriage and the eucharist.

57. We cannot stress enough our society's shallow mentality concerning these matters, which in turn impacts the church. One example is Robert J. Ringer's, *Looking Out for #1* (New York, 1977). "Vanity made the revolution; liberty was only a pretext" (Napoleon).

58. The abortion controversy belongs here as an extension of the argument. In recent years Christians have increasingly realized that reverence for life is all of one piece. Franz Alt, a German TV reporter, in 1983 published a book on the Sermon on the Mount, *Peace is Possible*. In 1985 he followed it up with *Love is Possible*. He ties nuclear ethics and sexual ethics together within the context of liberation theology mandates as he sees them (Franz Alt, *Liebe ist möglich: Die Bergpredigt im Atomzeitalter* [Munich, Zurich, 1985]). Referring to the Vatican Instruction criticizing liberation theology, Alt claims that the Vatican hardly notices how the rich nations stand in need of liberation theology (p. 43). This is the same emphasis as in *God-Walk*: the need for liberation theology among the rich. In the arms race, the rich nations arm themselves to death, the others starve themselves to death (ibid.). In the rich nations, the main dilemma has two dimensions for Alt: "The possible destruction of 'big' humankind through nuclear bombs and the destruction of the 'little' human through abortion are—ethically—not separable. In both instances reverence for life or the refusal to revere life is the issue" (p. 64, my translation). Reverence for life is a concomitant of God's justice struggle. In the U.S.A. we are almost backing into it now as we ponder the full implications of more liberal legislation on abortion. See, for example, Linda-Marie Delloff, "A Pro-Choice Protest of a Pro-Choice Protest," *Christian Century*, 102:37 (Nov. 27, 1985) 1084–85. There is still much debate ahead of us. But we are learning more and more how empire has made us obedient tools of its death machine all around. What occasionally seems like individual free-

dom of choice is only the other side of the death syndrome with which empire reigns supreme. Fundamentalists are off base in wanting to give the state the power to rule over a woman's body (the same state that feels free to risk millions of lives in a nuclear war and that applies the death penalty to "expendables"). But they are on base in their commitment to life. Our churches have failed to create support structures for unwanted children and their families. See Ginny Ernest Soley, "To Preserve and Protect Life," *Sojourners*, 15 (Oct. 1986) 34–37. Reverence for life is reverence for the future, the mother, and the whole of corporate humanity.

59. The reason why we immediately get tied to the Bible (with liberation theology as our hermeneutical lens) is that here the choice between God and idol is key for the human being. It is exactly at this point that we learn from Latin American liberation theology: "To know Yahweh is to do justice and compassion and right to the needy. . . . The essence of the idol is in this: We can approach it directly. It is entity . . .; it is not the implacable moral imperative of justice" (José Porfirio Miranda, *Marx and the Bible* [Maryknoll, N.Y., 1974], 57). The "God of the Bible" (p. 66) is unavoidable: "I am no longer alone. . . . I am always in relationship with another" (ibid.). Transcendence here does not involve ontology: "Transcendence does not mean only an unimaginable and inconceivable God, but a God who is accessible only in the act of justice" (p. 48). Miranda appeals to the Bible, so that the difference between God and idol becomes inescapable: "The unique character of the God of Israel is irreducible to ontological questions, no matter how many efforts and analogies the philosophy derived from the Greeks might make in the belief that it can understand everything in terms of being. The Western absolutization of the ontological point of view makes us believe that this instrument of cognition is superior to that of the Bible" (p. 60). It is pointless, however, to place all the blame for the idol on Greek thought. In the West we have simply begun to subsume any kind of religious experience under the term "God": "We do not mention or allude to different gods by different names anymore. Instead we simply use the one word 'God' to refer to any and every type of religious experience, even to experiences that are quite contrary to one another" (Juan Luis Segundo, *The Liberation of Theology* [Maryknoll, N.Y., 1976], 45). So it is reasonable not to focus just on the Greek view, although we usually fall back on it: "Yet even now, when Greek philosophy is a museum piece, that old notion of God continues to dominate not only certain strains of popular thought but also scholarly theological tracts" (p. 46).

60. Implied here is a view of the authority of scripture that excludes domination: "The paradigm that no longer makes sense to feminists is that of *authority as domination*. . . . The emerging feminist paradigm trying to make sense of biblical and theological truth claims is that of *authority as*

partnership" (Letty M. Russell, "Authority and the Challenge of Feminist Interpretation," in Letty M. Russell [ed.], *Feminist Interpretation of the Bible* [Philadelphia, 1985], 143f.).

61. The struggle with correcting tradition dare never cease: "We must be told that at a certain moment in history the Church stopped listening to the voice of Christ and began to listen to the voice of the ruling classes and their selfish interests. We need these seemingly harmful hypotheses to wake us from our ideological slumber" (Segundo, *Liberation of Theology*, 42). Sheer repetition of tradition will certainly never help: "Formal orthodoxy is not a sufficient guarantee against idolatry. One can recite all the creeds of theological history and still believe in an idol" (p. 47). Wrestling with tradition also aims at getting straight the distinction between God and idol.

62. There is always the internal critique of tradition by the Jesus event. See Juan Luis Segundo, *Faith and Ideologies* (Maryknoll, N.Y., 1984), 45.

63. *Book of Discipline of the United Methodist Church,* 80.

64. We need to make explicit to ourselves how we experience life in all respects. This is the basic human dimension. As Christians we are totally part of it. There is no special Christian humanity. Increasingly, human beings feel themselves as part of nature, the vast evolutionary process that now might be stopped by human hubris through willful ecological destruction. One of the suggestions for survival is to do away with the tragic sense of life: "When the existence of many species, including the human, and the continuity of the biological environment are threatened as they are now, mankind can no longer afford the wasteful and destructive luxuries of a tragic view of life"(Joseph W. Meeker, *The Comedy of Survival* [New York, 1974], 37). Meeker comes down on comedy vs. tragedy as a policy for clean living: "The comic point of view is that man's high moral ideals and glorified heroic poses are themselves largely based upon fantasy and are likely to lead to misery or death for those who hold them" (p. 26). *God-Walk,* shaping an oxymoron notion of God, is unable to make such an easy choice between tragedy and comedy. Some things are tragicomic and others are comitragic. The Christian experience of life is a tragicomedy. We will want to clown our way through it, but with some method to our madness. With Meeker all values seem to go out the window: "The most respected tragedy further assumes that some truth exists in the universe which is more valuable than life itself. There must be abstract ideas and values which are worth dying and suffering for, otherwise the hero's painful quest for spiritual purity and enlightenment becomes absurd" (p. 37). Although there are no values worth dying for—in that direct sense of dying—there is one value worth living for: God's justice. That God's justice struggle occasionally presses persons into "tragic" situations is part of history. But there is usually a "way out." The tragic dynamics of God's justice struggle

is not an end in itself. It is certainly not the case that in Jesus some truth exists that is more valuable than life itself. Jesus is truth as life. Jesus means, in practice, that human life prevails. Life is that valuable. Yet it is not life for life's sake, but for the sake of God's justice. I can perhaps clinch the analysis by a brief comparison. Meeker makes a good point: "Warfare is the basic metaphor of tragedy, and its strategy is a battle plan designed to eliminate the enemy" (p. 38). As counterpoint I might be able to say: God-walk is the basic metaphor of tragicomedy, and its map shows the road of conscience toward God's justice. "We commend ourselves to every person's conscience in the sight of God" (2 Cor. 4:2). What is more, Pogo always wins when it comes to the enemy: "We have met the enemy, and they's us."

65. If we grasp the elementary tragicomedy of life, we perhaps have laid the groundwork for facing the basic implication of method in liberation theology. We have made a choice for *homo ludens* over *homo faber*, the "making" animal, self-making, meaning-making, "making" at any cost. The fierceness of class struggle is all around us. But the Christian cannot tackle it on its own terms. The law of this struggle for the Christian is not determined and defined by the struggle itself. To understand what is going on we have to take social analysis seriously. Yet we cannot reduce dogmatics to social analysis. Dogmatics is indeed steeped in a social location. Which experience becomes part of its rationale? Simply put, it is tragicomedy within the class struggle. It needs to be underscored that here the sheer liberal stance does not offer us any strength. "To many secular leftists, even the stances taken by the progressive churches are full of contradictions. Thus progressive churches seem more aware of the suffering of black South Africans than of the role the United States plays in aiding South Africa's destabilization of Angola, more sympathetic in their understanding of the feminization of poverty than willing to come to terms with the class basis of that poverty. To secular leftists, then, the antipathy to the concept of class struggle, the emphasis on reconciliation, the belief in the possibility of convincing the powerful to change their ways and become more sensitive to the needs of the poor disqualifies even the progressive church from serious consideration as a source of transformation" (William K. Tabb [ed.], *Churches in Struggle: Liberation Theologies and Social Change in North America* [New York, 1986], xvi). What we have as experience is ultimately tragicomedy in class struggle. Dogmatics obviously can deliver only a few things. What it can do is make clear the mandate of *resistance* to empire-domination over church and society at the point where God is used to bless America—as empire. In the present situation there is no more important mandate for the churches than to resist the beast from the bottomless pit that has put itself in God's place. Yet they can do it only as they are steeped in the *liberation process*—which is

found where the poor respond to God's justice work in history. We find this certainly not "all over the map." We do find it among the black poor, American Indians, women, Hispanics, and others who bear the brunt of the economic burden and suffer the loss of human dignity. It is easy to write about these things. But the long decades of our attempt to struggle with the liberation dynamics have seen the rich become richer and the poor poorer, so that now 10 percent of the U.S. population owns 82 percent of its wealth. All the liberation conferences have not changed that. Where lies the problem? We are simply not very clear in North America about the nature of our own struggle. This is the struggle against the class that can foist on us the nuclear arsenal of death a hundred times over, the class that supports empire-domination. Resistance to empire-domination is the same as resistance to the ruling class.

66. The difficulties of debating liberation theology experience are partly related to misperceptions of its origin and influence. Black theology was very much North American liberation theology from the beginning. Even so, for example, Michael Novak writes: "It is the tragedy of liberation theology that it has been born in a part of the world in which democracy has long been fragile, not least because its underlying base in a free, inventive, and creative economy has been sadly lacking" (Michael Novak, *Freedom With Justice* [San Francisco, 1984], 193f.). To discuss the matter entirely in terms of Latin American thought or Third World efforts makes it easy for any writer to dismiss the issue at hand. The core question remains: Is there class struggle also in North America and, if so, what does dogmatics do about it? Relative inattention to our own North American challenge makes it easy for Novak in all his writings to dismiss the issue of liberation theology out of hand. As regards Novak's most recent comments on liberation theology, see Robert McAfee Brown, "Liberation as Bogeyman," *Christianity and Crisis*, 47:5 (April 6, 1987) 124–25.

67. Obviously the word "experience" is used in many ways. "Some people call that which they have done wrong all their lives, their experience" (Elisabeth Müller-Luckman, *Die grosse Kränkung* [Hamburg, 1985], 85, my translation). That is certainly also true of theologians. Christian experience is basically nothing but the awareness of Jesus' presence in history as God's right hand in the struggle for justice. This is the divine tragicomedy in class struggle. The first thing the experience calls for is rejecting the religious underpinnings of empire-domination. God does not legitimate our brutal society in its denial of human dignity.

68. *Book of Discipline of the United Methodist Church*, 81.

69. There is a clear tradition underlying this approach. We have to begin our examination of conscience in the biblical matrix. See Robert Jewett, *Paul's Anthropological Terms* (Leiden, 1971); Claude Anthony Pierce,

Conscience in the New Testament (London, 1955). On the subject as a whole, see the significant Duke University dissertation by Barry Harvey, "Piety, Power, and Politics: An Appraisal of the Notion of Conscience as a Discursive Nexus for Systematic Theology in the Writings of Paul Lehmann" (1987).

70. Barth, *Dogmatics in Outline*, 12.

71. Ibid., 21.

72. Karl Barth, *Church Dogmatics*, I/1 (New York, 1949), 208f.

73. Ibid., 245.

74. The debate in the United Church of Christ, 1983–1987, proves the point. See *New Conversations*, 8:1 (Spring 1985), a publication of United Church Board for Homeland Ministries, New York. The strength of this debate is predicated on the wide participation of grassroots members. Here is no doctrine handed down from the top, but doctrine being shaped at the bottom. It shows that new doctrine can grow out of corporate discipleship. At the same time, it proves that the new teaching insights do not arise from abstract argument, but from concrete engagement of grassroots Christians. Although there is a drive toward unity and an attempt to grasp how it can be handled creatively, we are still confronted with a difference in camps. The whole situation is one of "between times."

75. *New Conversations*, 29. We are at least at a point in the United Church of Christ where we know the terms of the struggle, also as regards the need for the church to be a confessing church. The issue of justice is not an optional interest. It is the question, To what extent do Christians want to covenant with each other in regard to God's truth and confess it?

76. From a completely different angle, Joseph Hough and John Cobb have raised similar issues. Their focus is totally on ministerial education (Joseph C. Hough, Jr., and John B. Cobb, Jr., *Christian Identity and Theological Education* [Chico, Calif., 1985]). Their chapter on the nature of Christian truth and the nature of the church is a beautiful statement of two theologians. Yet to what extent is it rooted in the actual life of the church? They helpfully state that images of the church "portraying ideals disconnected from reality are not the sort of images we need" (p. 48). But how do better images originate and take hold effectively? Do we expect ministers fresh out of the seminary to implant them in the people? As long as churches do not commit themselves to principal doctrinal understandings of these images, we simply pit new theology against old theology, and wait and see how things will work out on the way from seminary to church. The premise of Hough/Cobb is very strong: "Christian identity is no abstract or formal concept. Christian identity is forged by the living practice of Christians in their world" (p. 49). But the living practice of Christians needs to be looked at in terms of how it actually functions. We

live as Christians by what the basic doctrines of our faith affirm. We can state, for example, together with Hough/Cobb, what we think about the poor: "God is God for the poor, and the people of God are the people for the poor—living, working, and moving on their behalf" (p. 59). But we also need to ask: Where is this view anchored? Unless Christians bind each other on this score and make each other accountable for it time and time again, it does not really matter. The 1968 Medellín documents were commitments of practically the whole Catholic Church in Latin America. In praxis each church begins to realize how the very nature of doctrine is changing in the process of new insights. The way this works in the United Church of Christ is that we face the reality of God's own poverty. In Jesus, God shares the lot of the poor: "For you know the grace of our Lord Jesus Christ, that though he was rich, yet for your sake he became poor" (2 Cor. 8:9). The whole christology core of the church's teaching is challenged, I believe. I have attempted to show the interaction between what Hough/Cobb call "the living practice of Christians" and the formation of doctrine within the United Church of Christ in "A New Spirituality: Shaping Doctrine at the Grassroots," *Christian Century*, 103:23 (July 30-Aug. 6, 1986) 680–81. The Hough/Cobb proposal does not intend to impose ideals on us. Yet it cannot help ending with a series of *musts*: "For example, if Christians are to understand themselves as globally connected, then worship must broaden their horizons to a fully global context. . . . If we are to act for a unified world, our worship must direct us to God as the creator and redeemer of an interdependent creation, who values all living things. If we are to act for the poor, we must worship the God who has revealed herself as for and with the poor" (p. 75). It is difficult to explain the problem of these *musts* in a sentence or two. Hough/Cobb present a *postulation* of what the church ought to be. Perhaps I should say: Let us praise them for it. Yet I would be less than candid if I were not to say that only on the basis of sound teaching, for which Christians make each other mutually accountable, will we likely see change. Images of the church need to be based not on moral "musts," or demands, but on the *enunciation* of who God is in Christ, and how the cosmos and the human being are constituted. Unless through worship we discover that we become what we already are in Christ, we are put under new law, a new legalism. It is the indicative of doctrine that antecedes imperatives of any shape or hue. I do not know whether or not we can manage to inject this factor into ministerial education. My notion is that serious ministerial education takes place where there is serious doctrinal struggle. Merely offering another new theology among the many we already have will be of no help. Liberation theology functions merely as hermeneutical lens through which we examine Christian doctrine anew and reshape it. There are other lenses that are used in the struggle of understanding. See Geoffrey Wainwright, *Doxology* (New York, 1980): "But there is still a sense in which the rite and its accompanying 'story' constitute a pre-reflexive matrix in which doctrine takes shape and develops" (p. 293).

77. As an instance of the bilateral approach, see James E. Andrews and Joseph A. Burgess (eds.), *An Invitation to Action: The Lutheran-Reformed Dialogue, Series III, 1981–1983* (Philadelphia, 1984).

78. The whole strength of the present situation is that we do not have to go it alone in one country or in one church. The principal point of *God-Walk* rests on the same foundation as the work of Gustavo Gutiérrez, *A Theology of Liberation* (Maryknoll, N.Y., 1973): "To support the social revolution means to abolish the present status quo and to attempt to replace it by a qualitatively different one; it means to build a just society based on new relationships of production; it means to attempt to put an end to the domination of some countries by others, of some social classes by others, of some people by others. The liberation of these countries, social classes, and people undermines the very foundation of the present order: it is the greatest challenge of our time" (p. 48). But we can do only one thing at a time. The dogmatic task in the United States is to undo any legitimating of human omnipotence by the omnipotence of God. There is no way to get God to justify the present Northatlantic exploitation of human beings, animals, and the earth. See André Gorz, *Ecology as Politics* (Boston, 1980).

79. *Book of Discipline of the United Methodist Church*, 80.

80. Alfred Lorenzer, *Das Konzil der Buchhalter* (Frankfurt, 1981), 98, my translation.

81. Ibid., 99.

82. As North Americans, in the development of liberation theology we do not have a basic reference point like the Latin Americans. There is no North American Medellín (1968). That does not mean, however, that we all have to fend for ourselves. We have to begin in the context of our various denominations as they relate to the historical process (see notes 74 and 75, above). Principally, however, the move is very similar to the one in Latin America: "Medellín marks the beginning of a new relationship between the theological and pastoral language on the one hand and the social sciences which seek to interpret this reality on the other. . . . But this language is only a reflection of a deeper process, a new awareness" (Gutiérrez, *A Theology of Liberation*, p. 136). It is this deeper process to which I am also appealing.

83. Ernesto Cardenal's, *The Gospel in Solentiname* (Maryknoll, N.Y., 1978) was the first of several volumes that again brought that point home. Also see Philip and Sally Scharper, *The Gospel in Art by the Peasants of*

Solentiname (Maryknoll, N.Y., 1984); and Milton Schwantes, "Von unten gesehen: Die Bibel als Buch der Befreiung gelesen," *Evangelische Kommentare*, 19:7 (July 1986) 383-87.

84. A description of the countermove is found in Guillermo Cook, *The Expectation of the Poor* (Maryknoll, N.Y., 1985), 108-18.

85. See Monika K. Hellwig, *The Eucharist and the Hunger of the World* (New York, Paramus, 1976), 71.

86. Gutiérrez, *We Drink from Our Own Wells*, 33-53.

87. We need to take this a step further than did Dietrich Bonhoeffer, *The Cost of Discipleship* (New York, 1953), 153-56.

88. We are still only in the beginnings of our efforts to recover the key role of the eucharist, although a new awareness of the issue goes back several decades. A strong early focus was John A. T. Robinson's *Liturgy Coming to Life* (Philadelphia, 1960): "As it begins, in the offertory, with the thrust of the secular into the heart of the sacred, so it ends with the releasing of the sacred into the midst of the secular" (p. 71). There is already a vast expansion of this notion in Tissa Balasuriya's, *The Eucharist and Human Liberation* (Maryknoll, N.Y., 1979): "The churches are linked throughout the world. Earlier, they generally had an influence for domesticating peoples within capitalism and imperialism. Now, they can be powerful agents of human liberation—if they really want to be so. The theology of the Eucharist must become planetary. *We need a global spirituality*" (p. 142).

89. There is no way of avoiding the social location issue for dogmatics also at this point. So far, there has been no serious question asked along these lines in the systematic theology field. As a consequence, there has been much self-deception. Part of the problem has been the continuing linkage of Christian thought to philosophy as a priority. The existentialist era has done much damage: "Heidegger is involuntarily—but with great effectiveness—the great ideologue of the bourgeoisie and the establishment. That he should dominate Rahner, disconnected as Rahner stands from the Bible, is not at all surprising. But that in the last analysis he has been able to bridle the efforts of Bultmann to escape the 'wisdom of the world' constitutes an unsurpassable demonstration of how the enslavement in which the world holds us reaches its greatest effectiveness when it makes this slavery not even able to see that it is slavery" (Miranda, *Marx and the Bible*, 249f.).

90. The range of the challenge here is staggering. See Nicholas Lash, *Voices of Authority* (Shepherdstown, W.Va., 1976), 25-42.

91. *New Conversations*, 28-29, 43-47. In recent United Church of Christ debates, a group of 39 theologians chose especially tradition as reorientation point for the new approach in teaching accountability of the

church: "What is needed, we believe, is a sustained rethinking of our theological tradition (as reflected in the various traditions behind the United Church) to see how that tradition can be reappropriated in faithful and fresh ways as a discipline and resource for our life of faith" (*New Conversations,* 2). Opposition to "the 39" came largely from a UCC group called Christians for Justice Action (CJA): "We wonder whether fear of change and mistrust of the Spirit are the motivating factors in calls to return to past creeds and confessions as contemporary norms" (*New Conversations*, 43). Much of the opposition operates against what it assumes to be a neoorthodox view of tradition. An alternative view of the eucharistic character of the scriptures is not in the field of vision of the opposition. As a consequence, creeds and confessions are mostly looked down upon as doctrinal straitjackets, in great distance from any dynamics of interaction with the scriptures as justice power. In this way we will never break through some of the major roadblocks on the way to liberation. There is a generally freewheeling notion in many North American Christian minds that assumes liberation can happen apart from denominational struggles over structure. Yet from the word "go" any Protestant approach to liberation in North America is tied into the actual polity commitments of the denominations. Ultimately members of a denomination can always hide behind them when the situation becomes critical. Yet they could also open the door to new understandings of the corporate shape of Christian life. The rhetoric of associating with basic polity commitments is often deceptive, however. The Christians for Justice Action also claim: "Of course, it is basic that Christians should know what they believe. And we need to affirm the truth as it has come to us through history, creeds, and confessions if we are to be in dialogue with other faith groups" (*New Conversations*, 46). But that is not the issue. The tough question is whether in any denomination we are willing to express accountability to each other in matters of liberation as *polity intent* and not just as private intent. There is now much talk in the UCC about "theological ferment." The 39 faculty members had not been interested in ferment, but in doctrinal content. There is an immense voluntarism of good will all around. Friendly gestures abound. Yet all this does not amount to something of value for the church as *church*, unless we are willing to commit our good intentions to constitutions and by-laws of our respective denominations. Otherwise we are always in a never-never land, the sweet by-and-by, with our heads in the clouds. Social location in liberation is intimately tied to denomination. An academic religionist mentality does not want to admit it. As a consequence, we are making no headway in liberation. In Protestantism, no one wishes to be governed by "canon law." But that does not mean there is no need for some "canon" in constitution and by-laws. As one examines the Christians for Justice Action material further, in regard to affirming the truth "as it has come to us through history," the statement "does not appeal to religious anarchy, but suggests that there is a valid way to identify authentic faith today" (p. 47). In terms of various identification points, the statement of Christians for Justice Action (1) "acknowledges the authority of scripture and searches it as a source of truth for our day," (2) "receives with gratitude and learns from the creeds and confessions of those who have gone before," and (3) "seeks to identify the Spirit working in the world and to affirm, be blessed by, and work with it" (p. 47). It needs underscoring that we are encouraged to read the scriptures only as *a* source of truth for our day. Need not Christians for Justice Action review their stance relative to the whole framework of Protestantism? We can say all kinds of things, and do all kinds of things, without the scriptures as "canon." But can we be *church*? Is not the approach of Christians for Justice Action ultimately just another form of the autonomous theological liberalism even they themselves want to get beyond? Are they not inviting us here to acknowledge the model of liberal Protestantism as *binding*? Here lies the crucial difference for understanding most of the present debates in Protestantism about liberation. We are often still confronted with models of the past that no longer fit our present-day context. Many of us take pride in the fact that some denominations have no ordination "requirements." Yet the fundamental issue lies much deeper: Are we willing to take seriously the mutual accountability factor also in regard to tradition? As long as this is not clear, there is little possibility to grasp the sharp difference between scripture and tradition as well as their interdependence. Christians for Justice Action usually retain some neoorthodox framework: "At the same time we cannot rest in the past but must move on to be about the business of continuing reformation in areas of belief and action" (p. 43). Neoorthodox thought as neoreformation thought was able to impress on us the needs for continuing reformation. Yet we need to keep in mind that it kept us out of the socio-historical and socio-political realm to a large extent, at least in its more popular forms in the churches. Some of the social involvement of the churches had its mainspring in earlier church movements. In any case, the urgency of the scripture/tradition dynamics is not easily grasped within the framework of the *continuing reformation* model as far as the underside of history is concerned. A further difficulty is that interdependency dynamics of authority in the church will not be grasped adequately apart from the eucharist tied into the underside of history. In church authority matters we dare not be locked into a roster of technical points we can list abstractly and pick apart in debate with each other without being part of the social location of Jesus himself. Only if we indwell the Jesus reality radically in this very social location will we be able to become more fully accountable to each other. The critique by Christians for Justice Action touches the issue: "While there is an apparent openness to some social and structural change, the suggestion of theological or belief change appears to cause great uneasiness" (p. 43). This is not a very accurate or clear perception. The question is: On what grounds is there to be belief change? On grounds of the tradition that helps us check out the integrity of the change? Or on sheer subjectivistic and privatistic grounds? Openness to structural change implies openness to belief change if it is anchored in the eucharist—God's own justice struggle for the whole world. Christological change is what the hermeneutical focus of liberation theology is ultimately all about.

All this is to indicate how in one denomination the scripture/tradition dynamics can be tackled. But all denominations caught in the liberation process have to go through this struggle in similar ways. If this is not part of the picture, an argument about liberation theology as hermeneutical focus in North America is in vain. It is difficult to see why we cannot be as faithfully engaged in involving our tradition in clarifying our struggle as, for instance, our sisters and brothers in South Africa. See Allan Boesak, *Black and Reformed: Apartheid, Liberation and the Calvinist Tradition* (Maryknoll, N.Y., 1984).

92. J. T. Müller (ed.), *Die Symbolischen Bücher der evangelisch-lutherischen Kirche* (Gütersloh, 1928), 386, my translation. For the standard English translation, see Theodore G. Tappert (ed.), *The Book of Concord* (Philadelphia, 1959), 365.

93. Harvey Cox, *Religion in the Secular City* (New York, 1984), 192.

94. Frederick Herzog, "God-Walk and Class Struggle," *Circuit Rider*, 9:6 (June 1985): 4f.

95. We face here a general problem prevalent also outside the church. See Yves R. Simon, *A General Theory of Authority* (Notre Dame, London, 1980), 16–22. There is nothing especially unique about the authority dynamics of the church except the person of Jesus—which implies a lot of uniqueness.

96. Even where the framework is seen in broad terms, the basic tendency toward intellectual assent is deeply ingrained in modern Christian thought. See Paul Tillich, *Systematic Theology* (Chicago, 1951), I:36ff.

97. A valiant attempt to clarify the neoorthodox position was made by Hermann Diem, in his *Dogmatics* (Philadelphia, 1959), 41–111.

98. The more succinct Karl Barth became in making his point, the clearer the problem of his use of tradition stands out (Barth, *Dogmatics in Outline*, 61, 85f.). His stance is here very orthodox. It is not surprising that Karl Barth frequently is categorized as part of the neoorthodox camp or that Dietrich Bonhoeffer charged him with "revelation positivism."

99. John Macquarrie, *Principles of Christian Theology* (New York, 1977), 6.

100. Ibid., 5.

101. Ibid., 6.

Chapter 1. Theo-Praxis

1. Walter Kaufmann (ed.), *The Portable Nietzsche* (New York, 1954), 95. I ought to say something about my use of the word "God." This word has lent itself well to the vast Western manipulation of the transcendent. We need to confront the major challenge of distinguishing between our *projection* of a god on the screen of the transcendent (the idol) and the *affection* of all our elementary relationships through the encounter of a claim. We are beings who are "affected" long before our ideas are projected. I might say, we are beings who *are* projected before we ourselves project. Within the context of God-walk we are led to call "God" only what affects us in our conscience as a justice claim—an absolute claim we cannot escape. We *take* meaning from this God. There is a great difference between meaning-taking and meaning-making. In most respects, the "God is dead" notion of Nietzsche does not touch the God of God-walk. The God who died belonged to human meaning-making. What happens to us in the heart of creation is not dependent on our meaning-making (or tool-making issuing in an idol).

2. James C. Livingston, *Modern Christian Thought* (New York, London, 1971), 65f. The basic analysis of the reality of God in this section is based on the Livingston outline. Livingston offers a clear access to the historical framework.

3. Ludwig Feuerbach, *Principles of the Philosophy of the Future* (Indianapolis, New York, Kansas City, 1966), 5. The original was published in 1843.

4. James H. Cone, *For My People: Black Theology and the Black Church* (Maryknoll, N.Y., 1984), 69. Much of the present chapter owes its basic outlook to my early encounter with the black struggle that sensitized me to the difference between God and idol. A saying in the black community became for me a moment of truth: "Whites have a different God."

5. Jon Sobrino, *The True Church and the Poor* (Maryknoll, N.Y., 1984), 14.

6. Ibid., 30. The arguments on God and theodicy in this context are strikingly clear in Sobrino. They make a lot of sense viewed from the Latin American context. The notion of building the kingdom, however, has a peculiar ring in North America. It is tied to all kinds of liberal schemes of improving conditions that have little to do with the reality of the God of the

Bible. So I stay away, together with Sobrino, from trying to *explain* the nature of God. What we cannot escape is facing the reality of the God of the Bible. The crucial point in this regard is to make sure we always keep in mind the difference between God and idol. Here José P. Miranda's, *Marx and the Bible* (Maryknoll, 1974) has led the way: "The essence of idol is in this: We can approach it directly. It is entity, it is being itself" (p. 57). My preference would be to say that the idol is a figment of the imagination we approach directly as though it were God. Some idols are tied to ideas only, others to stones, wood, or other materials. The idol is something we can manage and control. The idol is the controllable God, the puffed-up God. "Puff Graham," said a newspaper publisher in a memorable phrase. And so the Billy Graham cult was born. "Puff God," says the religionist. And an idol is born.

7. An overview of the North American Enlightenment dynamics is given in Henry Steele Commager's *The Empire of Reason* (New York, Toronto, 1977).

8. This formulation probably does not express Miranda's "implacable moral imperative of justice" (*Marx and the Bible*, 57). On Christian grounds, we encounter more than just a command from somewhere in the Bible. We are part of a community that meets the reality of God in Christ in its life as body of Christ. Miranda is focused on "no other god than the God of Jesus Christ" (p. 58). But how do we come to meet this God? I do not see how Miranda's prioritizing states the situation adequately: "*It is not a matter of excluding cultus but rather of this very clear message: first justice and then cultus*" (p. 58). Does it make sense in the Christian community to separate cultus from history? This is of course what has happened for centuries. But it is exactly this dualism that has brought us to the impasse we are in. What constrains us to act justly is God's own justice struggle in Christ. It takes place in history and consequently in the church in history. The point is that this does not function as imperative, but as indicative. It is not a must or an ought. God's justice struggle is the air we breathe and the elements we partake of in the eucharist. We are not *commanded* to share in it. We cannot help *being* part of it.

9. Ralph Ellison, *Invisible Man* (New York, 1953), offered the term.

10. David Tracy, *The Analogical Imagination* (New York, 1981), 78, and passim.

11. For early understandings of the *sensus communis*, see Anthony, Earl of Shaftesbury, *Characteristics of Men, Manners, Opinions, Times* (Indianapolis, New York, 1964), originally published in 1711, and Friedrich Christoph Oetinger, *Inquisitio in Sensum Communem et Rationem* (Stuttgart, 1964), originally published in 1753.

12. *The Heidelberg Catechism* (Philadelphia, 1962), 9. Originally published in 1563.

13. There is a hiatus between some North American thinking and Latin American thought on this score. Tracy, in *The Analogical Imagination* (p. 290), critiques the Miranda perspective: "For an example of exegesis sensitive to the prophetic-social but insensitive to alternative interpretations emphasizing the dilemmas of the solitary individual, see José Miranda, *Marx and the Bible*." There is first of all a different hermeneutical premise operative. Miranda does not predicate his ideas on the philosophical scheme of the symbolic. That does not mean, however, that he leaves out the individual. He agrees, for example, with the statement of Pierre Bigo that "the supreme delicacy of charity is to recognize the right of the person being given to" (p. 62). Here certainly the dignity of the individual person is not slighted. God-walk empowers us to see the individual in new ways.

14. Juan Luis Segundo, *Faith and Ideologies* (Maryknoll, N.Y., 1984), 37.

15. Ibid., 20.

16. Ibid.

17. We are touching now on very crucial issues. Here we make decisions also on the very origins of ministerial education. The educational process here grows out of wrestling with the reality of God in the eucharist. As regards the pioneering suggestions made by Hough and Cobb (see Introduction, n. 76, above), I hope they would be considered seriously with the understanding that the *genesis* of Christian thought itself is at stake in these reflections. Latin American liberation theology in particular and Third World theology in general are part of the picture. But it is now first of all a question of how adequately we understand our own North American mind. Hough and Cobb suggest two categories, the *practical Christian thinker* and the *reflective practitioner*, as foci of what they want to set up as the new model of the *practical theologian*—over against the missionary, revivalist, pulpiteer, builder, and pastoral director. In a strange way Hough and Cobb are still tearing asunder what, I think, God has joined together. It is very difficult to see an ultimate logic of faith in such sentences as: "Some tension remains between reflective practice and practical Christian thinking. On the one hand, practical Christian thinking calls for bold vision, aggressive leadership, and strong commitment to genuine Christian practice. On the other hand, reflective practice calls for involvement of the whole community in practical thinking. . . . These tensions will finally prove to be creative. The leadership of the practical Christian thinker must be consonant with the church's self-understanding as a human community. The reflective practitioner's practice must be grounded in the identity of the church and reflection on the implementation of that identity for life in the world" (*Christian Identity and Theological Education* [Chico, Calif., 1985], 90f.). It is difficult to see why the practical Christian thinker and the

reflective practitioner should be torn apart. A tricky dualism or dichotomy has crept into the picture. "Practical Christian Thinkers reflect not only *about* practice. They also reflect *in* practice" (ibid., 85). The whole point is that the Christian thinker is also a disciple and never "off duty" in that regard. So I wish Hough and Cobb could have pressed the issue of practice further to the praxis root of discipleship. Genuine *Christian* thoughts are not available apart from discipleship. We have to reflect *in* practice if we want to have Christian thoughts at all. Christian thought grows out of discipleship. Discipleship gives rise to Christian thought and teaching. If I understand at all how Hough and Cobb use the term "internal history" (ibid., 82), I should think they would want to consider that its *reflection* grows out of reflection-in-*action*. There is really no vision (ibid., 85) of Christianity that does not grow out of the situation of what Hough and Cobb call the practitioner. As long as we think we can bank on the Christian thoughts of others without experiencing the birthing process of Christian thought in ourselves, we cannot know what Chrisitianity is all about. It is a question of the inner citadel and the outworks. Without realizing that doctrine itself has to be changed, a lot of the good expectations of Hough and Cobb will come to naught.

18. Hough and Cobb stress the need to recover internal history and Christian identity. "Indeed, no problem is more urgent for the church than to recover its ability to direct its practice consciously in a Christian way. Its main need now is to renew identity and to act according to that identity, and for such renewal and action, leaders are required" (*Christian Identity*, 84). As a step toward that goal, Hough and Cobb wish critically to examine our internal history as Christians (ibid., 97ff.). They cannot do it without developing a theology. To what extent do they really relate it to the churches? To what extent does it grow out of the churches? It is hard to tell. The core issue here is that Hough and Cobb develop a Jesus who becomes accessible in "the memory" of Jesus (ibid., 82f.), which is to be fused with internal history as they see it. Yet, to put it plainly, although there is memory of Jesus, there is no realpresence of Jesus. In my view, the whole relationship to God has to be seen from a different angle. We have to start from the ground up if we want to get at the internal history. We have to discover how human inwardness and Jesus' realpresence converge. Of course some readers will say: All that is at stake is merely a different theology. I am not so sure. It is first of all a question of how seriously we take reflecting *in* practice. Here the *dogmatic* issue comes to the fore forcefully, I believe.

19. See Horst E. Richter, *Der Gotteskomplex* (Hamburg, 1979), 23. We have not as yet adequately assessed our Enlightenment heritage. The reason why dogmatics plays no role in Hough and Cobb is, I believe, their

unbroken Enlightenment commitment or, at least, their exclusion of problems of the Enlightenment heritage. From the Enlightenment onward we have "a rationalizing denial of the depowering (*Entmachtung*) of God" (*Gotteskomplex*, 28, my translation). Human beings wanted God's power, assumed it unto themselves, but still tried to make God responsible for this shift—a strange self-contradiction. The Richter book is a vast unraveling of the difference between idol and God. Unfortunately, through modern philosophy, most of us pure academics are caught in the subtle idolatry of modernity. Unless this development is reversed in the educators' guild in the church, ministerial education will not be capable of making the shift that Hough and Cobb are envisioning.

20. A painting by the Meister of Messkirch—Southern German painter (ca. 1560). Art Museum, Basel (Switzerland).

21. *The Book of Discipline of the United Methodist Church* (Nashville, 1980), 55.

22. Harvey Cox, *Religion in the Secular City* (New York, 1984), 229.

23. John Macquarrie, *Principles of Christian Theology* (New York, 1977), 87.

24. *The Hymnal* (Authorized by the General Synod of the Evangelical and Reformed Church, Saint Louis, 1940), 130.

25. Adolf Deissmann, "Christianity and the Lower Classes," *Expositor*, 7 (1909) 224.

26. Ian G. Barbour, *Issues in Science and Religion* (Englewood Cliffs, N.J., 1966), 366f.

27. Jürgen Moltmann, *Gott in der Schöpfung* (Munich, 1985), 92ff.

28. Ibid., 97.

29. Richter, *Gotteskomplex*, 43.

30. Barbour, *Issues*, 455.

31. Macquarrie, *Principles*, 218.

32. Ibid., 219.

33. Ibid., 206.

34. Jim Wallis, *The Call to Conversion* (San Francisco, 1981), 104.

35. Theodor Roszak, *The Making of a Counterculture* (Garden City, N.Y., 1969), 245.

36. Teilhard de Chardin, *The Phenomenon of Man* (New York, 1959), 120.

Chapter 2. Christo-Praxis

1. Albert C. Outler (ed.), *John Wesley* (New York, 1964), 316.

2. We need to be aware at this point of the immense labors of Jon Sobrino, *Christology at the Crossroads* (Maryknoll, N.Y., 1978). His liberation approach is a model of clarity. He makes it immediately clear

that his starting point is the historical Jesus (p. 3). And he is not happy about the approach that grounds christology in cultic worship, the liturgy of Word and sacrament. In one respect he almost seems to agree with the starting point in worship: "Once one does accept the presence of the living, resurrected Christ, then faith *knows* of the existence of the historical Jesus in and through the liturgical experience" (p. 6). But is it altogether that simple? What it means for Sobrino to start with the historical Jesus is very clear. The historical Jesus "is the person, teaching, attitudes, and deeds of Jesus of Nazareth insofar as they are accessible, in a more or less general way, to historical and exegetical investigation" (p. 3). But very few of us really start with the historical Jesus only. One might say that Albert Schweitzer's *The Quest of the Historical Jesus* (New York, 1948), is such an attempt. But he too had an additional factor in mind when he said that the "abiding and eternal in Jesus is absolutely independent of historical knowledge" (p. 401). How does the abiding and eternal get into the picture? The same with Sobrino. How does the use of the word God as reality in the present get into the picture? He cannot possibly derive it only from biblical language when, for example, he speaks of the "verification" of God (*Christology*, 55). Obviously there is the danger that liturgical experience can be filled with illusion and deceit. But so are other experiences, even historical ones. Therefore, my presupposition here is that at least the God-factor is introduced through worship. The reader will want to recall that here I see the eucharist in social location, as I have been trying throughout this work. It helps clarify what Sobrino wants to do in the *hermeneutic circle* as first step: "We must first reconsider the relationship between our conception of Christology and Christian ecclesial praxis at a given concrete moment in history" (p. xxi). So Sobrino certainly does not begin without some reference to *ecclesial praxis*; no one writing a christology does. I believe we need to spell that out, but with the realization, of course, that there is no foolproof way of doing it. The spelling out is also historical and therefore finite and limited, subject to error. Sobrino speaks of various types of hermeneutic: existential, transcendental, historical, revolutionary, practical, etc. "The important point for us here is to note to what extent a given hermeneutic outlook has an impact on the concrete elaboration of a given Christology" (p. 20). The basic inner dynamics of the hermeneutic is a *preunderstanding*, in my view. That pre-understanding for Sobrino is "the possible reconciliation between God and what is not God" (p. 20). The way this plays itself out is that for Sobrino Latin American theodicy is "concerned with the practical problem of building up and realizing the kingdom of God in the face of captivity" (p. 36). It is along these lines that liberation makes itself felt, its most comprehensive concept being the *kingdom of God*. We are here facing a difficult decision. Having stated the preunderstanding issue and the starting point, what next? Christianity is not making much of a dent now on North American society. If it were not for the 11:00 A.M. Sunday worship hour, probably no one would notice it existed. It makes little difference in the moral conduct of the nation. The Christian terms have been duly absorbed in the cultural stream. And the Christian faith is widely nothing more than opium for the people, a drug helping to maintain societal tranquility. In this situation scholarship cannot simply turn its prayer mills. It needs to make sure that its findings have bite. In North America just to alight on the kingdom of God concept does not have bite. It is also not clear historically that Jesus said all these things about the kingdom of God Sobrino works with. We need to know what social location we place ourselves in and what kinds of things we need to know or *can* know in this location. I think that Sobrino puts more into his social location than the *historical* Jesus. He states, for example, "We do not know what Jesus thought explicitly about himself. We do not know for sure whether he saw himself as the Messiah or the Son of man. . . . All we can get at is his *relational* self-awareness: i.e., what he thought about himself in relation to the kingdom, and the decisive importance of his own person in its arrival" (p. 70). Or, "The Gospels simply do not provide us with enough data to figure out what Jesus thought about himself exactly" (p. 73). I myself am not so sure what it means that we cannot get at what Jesus thought about himself in relation to the kingdom. Sobrino's view on this score is fairly simple: "It is my belief that it is by observing the relational character of a person that we plumb the depths of that person; and the same holds true for the person of Jesus" (p. 74). The problem I see here is that it is difficult to plumb the depth of a person *in the past*, especially where we have no personal writings. What we have reported to us in fairly clear terms is the *shape* of the public ministry. There is a historical configuration. For a brief moment of history a new reality breaks forth—as the reporters of this event see it. I am content to leave it all to Matt. 6:33: "Seek ye first the kingdom and its justice . . . and everything shall fall into place (shall be added unto you)." Here suddenly something broke through in history that until then had not been seen as the inside of history. And from their preunderstanding in their social location the first witnesses united the shape of this history with God. That is, they did not *manipulate* the matter that way. The presence of God in their lives made them understand the mystery of their history and perhaps the mystery of the kingdom of God: God is involved in a justice struggle. On this basis all other things will fall into their place. Justice, I believe, here means: affirming human rights on grounds of God's rights. It is care for soul and body, salvation and liberation. So I would hope we would not need to press the overused "kingdom of God" phrase. In the U.S.A. we have run out of steam when it comes to the kingdom of God idea. Said H. Richard Niebuhr fifty years ago: "In institutional liberalism as in institutional Evangelicalism and Protestantism the aggressive movement of the kingdom of God in America had apparently come to a stop" (*The Kingdom of God in America* [New York, 1937], 197). The problem with a sheer christology of the historical Jesus, a christology from below, is that it sees God as acting in the past and the future, but right now *we* are acting, not God. I tend to blame this on the exclusion of the eucharistic method. In one way, all we know in Christianity is the *now*. The starting point is the presence of God in Christ where, in the eucharist under the broken bread and shared wine, God confronts us with the shape of Christ's public ministry (crowned by the cross and sealed by the resurrection) and thereby with God's justice struggle. Sobrino's position comes through loud and clear in sentences such as, "God's will is historical rather than eternal" (p. 129), or, "Becoming a good human being in the process of discipleship means not only bringing about the kingdom but also staying open to the need to do this in ever new ways" (p. 126). Why should God's will not be both historical and eternal? And why should we be the ones that bring about the kingdom? Naturally "it would be wrong to conclude . . . that here and now today, when the parousia does not seem imminent, the most correct ethical attitude is one of passive waiting for the kingdom" (p. 134). Is there not a *tertium quid* between passive waiting for the kingdom and bringing about the kingdom? True, Jesus and his immediate followers were "actively working on its behalf" (p. 134). But it was in the sense that the followers were *sharing* in his work. It was the *christo*-praxis—God's own praxis—that counted. There is no reason to assume that this has stopped.

My problems with Sobrino's "christology from below" lie in the fact that we stay on an *anthropological* and *ethical* scale most of the time. He does not see the God-factor as part of the picture from the word "go." To begin just with the faith of Jesus and his fidelity may initially produce a moving human story. But it is not only ultimately, but also from the very beginning, the story of God. For the North American christology situation, I have a hard time starting the other way around, because liberal theology already for so long started that way. And where did it get us? We keep second-guessing Jesus *and* ourselves. The thing to do in North America is to stay away from making the anthropological and the ethical primary the way Sobrino seems to do it in thoughts like: Jesus "concretizes his morality" (p. 123), or, Jesus' "faith is not simply a fidelity to God. It is a fidelity to his mission" (p. 90). I would (together with Sobrino) say that Jesus' "interest is in the justice of God" (p. 122). As a next step, though, I would not worry about *persons* being capable of "doing the work of justice proper to God's kingdom" (p. 122). The North American christological point to make is that *God* is about the kingdom work and we need to share in it. I do not think a reference to the fourth Gospel is out of place here: "My Mother/Father never stops working and I keep working too" (John 5:17). *God* constantly relates in fidelity (to use Sobrino's phrase) to this person. God constitutes a new selfhood in Jesus as God confronts us with the shape of this public ministry crowned by cross and sealed by resurrection. On the human level this selfhood is constituted by a peculiar solidarity with the poor and the oppressed. Obviously the faith of Jesus is not unimportant. Yet Jesus in the shape of ministry, death, and resurrection first of all represents a structure of corporate selfhood that functions as the new self. This is not a matter of self-*understanding* but of human structure. The losers, the outcasts, are also represented in the new selfhood. In this regard, Jesus is a *multi*personality, not just a unipersonality (as in the Chalcedon christology). I have suggested the possibility of an inside-out christology instead of one from above or one from below. The joy of creativity in the inside-out approach is that we too "affirm a truly historical *logos*" (p. 83), but do it through its eucharistic presence. There is also a "return to Scripture" (p. 82), but with the understanding that it is the eucharistic scripture. In the eucharist we are celebrating an *ongoing* activity of God. It is true that "the Chalcedonian formula presupposes certain concepts that in fact cannot be presupposed when it comes to Jesus" (p. 82). Obviously we use "definitions" of divinity and humanity just like Sobrino. Yet we need to begin with what the presence of God in Christ through the eucharist already suggests as ongoingness of God's work in history. In other words, we cannot read God off of historical records. It is good that the sciptures offer us time and again new understandings of Jesus' "relational nature to the Father" (p. 82). Yet that does not yield the relational nature of the Mother/Father to the Son. On grounds of *God's* relationship to Jesus some of Sobrino's issues do not even arise or they turn out to be pseudoissues—for example, "the urgency to be like Jesus" (p. 111) or "the mere imitation of Jesus" (p. 132). Christo-praxis is first of all that of Jesus. We are invited to join in it, not to imitate it. There is no need to be *like* Jesus. My hope is that Sobrino could take some eucharistic method into account. The present *work* of Christ indicates who the person is because the work perpetuates the shape of the public ministry crowned on the cross and sealed in the resurrection (see John 5:17).

3. In North America we have the peculiar struggle with liberal theology. First of all, for many persons liberation theology and liberal theology sound very much the same. Having not thought through the issue, some use the terminology even interchangeably. Yet there is a fundamental

difference. See my Introduction to Hugo Assmann's *Theology for a No-mad Church* (Maryknoll, N.Y., 1976), 1–23. There is a tendency to assume that liberation theology says much the same things about Christ as does liberal theology. In North America it cannot do so. We can clarify this in regard to Tom F. Driver's *Christ in a Changing World: Toward an Ethical Christology* (New York, 1971). He claims his book is addressed to *liberal* Christians—"among whom I count myself" (p. ix). The approach comes down to minimal ethical imitation. Christ functions here basically as symbol. Neither the historical Jesus nor the risen Jesus has very much to say. Christ "is the changing pattern of our relationship to a living God. The christological task is to discern the features of this pattern in present-future time, and the only way to do this is to take with radical seriousness our ethical expectations" (p. 75). Some very strong convictions are expressed: "I believe we cannot come to a genuine theological appreciation of plural-ism and relativity until we have disposed of the notion that there is only one Christ for all time" (p. 59). This makes for a very liberal perspective: "What we have, thank God, is a plurality of Christs, a number of evolving Christs increasingly engaged in cross-cultural and ecumenical interaction" (p. 75). Driver stands against the faith of the churches: "The churches seem to believe that since there was only one Jesus there is only one Christ for all time. The churches say that, in Jesus, God has already done the one thing necessary for our salvation" (p. 76). "This is what I mean by imprisonment of God in the likeness of Jesus" (p. 77). Tearing Christ and Jesus apart, the way Driver seems able to do it, is impossible for liberation theology as I understand it. Imprisonment of God in the likeness of Jesus is also an impossible idea. Jesus is regarded as the Christ in that this concrete person expresses justice in its most complete way. Banking on Hegel, Driver claims that because infinity is an aspect of every finite occurrence, the infinite commitment of God to finitude in Jesus *does not indicate something done once and once only for all time* (p. 65). As Jesus had his finitude, so we have ours (p. 66). That makes working together with the risen Jesus absurd from the outset. It introduces an arbitrary factor. I can practically relate to Christ any way I want to. I can create Christ as a figment of my imagination. It is an imaginary figure. Yet initially it was only the *title* offered the *person* called Jesus because of his work. It is not surprising that with Driver's presuppositions we get one speculative move after another. "If God in Christ had done something 'once for all,' that would be a betrayal of us who move in time. I have no need of a time-stopping savior who would rescue me from the flux of finitude" (p. 166). I do not see why God could not have done something "once and for all" while doing other things more often. But everything in Driver gets fixated on the infinity-finitude tension (in good Tillichian fashion): "The mistake was to have concluded (or insisted) that an infinite commitment of God to human finitude can occur once and once only" (p. 60). The mistake? No biblical writer insisted that an *infinite* commitment of God to human *finitude* can occur once and once only. The biblical God makes commitments to finitude all along and all the time. That God's activity in history continues in terms of Jesus of Nazareth is a precious confidence of Christian faith. In the logic of Christian thought it is practically unintelligible when Driver states: "It is a fundamental error, and a costly one, for theology to seek the truth of God and the truth of Christianity exclusively in Christ past" (p. 47). I believe the real challenge for liberation theology is finding the adequate relationship between *Christ past* (p. 47) and Christ *present-future* (p. 75). This is the core of the necessary response to liberal theology. It is clear to me that Driver is only one instance of the liberal approach. Orthodox christology makes a good case for Christ past, but does not worry about Christ present and future in the process. Driver tries to make a liberal case for Christ present-future, but loses Jesus in the process. He also expresses the hope that Christ "was and is an active agent in the real world" (p. 6). This seems possible, however, only if we allow that God raised Jesus from the dead into the present in such a way that he is always active as God's right hand in history giving expression to the justice struggle of God. Orthodox christology is always in a hammerlock and cannot allow Jesus to do much in history right now. So I can underscore some Driver concerns: "Jesus is not a mere form waiting now in some ecclesiastical robing room until God shall put it on again at the end of time for a second coming" (p. 59). My point is: Jesus is by no means inactive now. Yet orthodox christology, like liberal christology, does not join christology and the eucharist: the Christ past and the Christ present engaged in historical *action*. Driver accurately sees that some things no longer work in christology: "So I propose not to start from the top or the foot of any pedestal" (p. 16). In other words, *no christology from above and no christology from below!* But then, christology from where? Where do we start? Driver's summary of his approach is instructive: "We do not seek, then, a 'high' christology, and by the same token we do not seek a 'low' one. We seek a christology having little or nothing to do with the vertical imagery of high and low, while having much to do with the lateral movement of history and the time tracks of experience" (p. 19). Driver does lay his hands on the crucial problem. But he certainly does not tie christology and eucharist together. So there is no concern for the risen Jesus working on earth—just as in orthodox christology *at this point*, though the orthodox of course believe in the risen Jesus reigning in heaven.

In reference to Jon Sobrino, Driver speaks of Sobrino's christology as provocative but inadequate, because it presents Jesus as an examplar "normative for Christian discipleship" (p. 44). The inadequacy according to Driver is built into the Sobrino approach because in his *from below* perspective there is little he can say about Jesus' *present* agency (as risen). The resurrection for Sobrino is historical in that it opens up the eschatological future. Here we are at the center of all this reflection about Christ. God-walk wishes to affirm, *the resurrection is historical in that it reinforces God's present justice struggle.* In eucharistic christology the point is that Jesus risen *reinforces God's presence.* Against all this Driver could claim that it leads "to the degradation of other religions and indeed of all experience that is not identifiably 'Christian.' That text in the Fourth Gospel which makes Jesus say, 'No one comes to the Father except by me' (John 14:6) should be repudiated, along with the rest of that Gospel's elitist, christocentric anti-Semitism" (p. 65).

It is important in some way at this point to make clear why an analysis of an example of North American liberal christology is significant. (1) It is next to impossible for the Third World to get an intelligent response to its theological struggle from the First World, because it is not at all clear with what kind of *Christ* First World theologians are responding. (2) We will never arrive at a satisfactory consensus on Christ among First World theologians, because of our First World pluralism. Yet we have to make clear to ourselves and to others the utterly conflictual situation among us in this regard. (3) We can serve our Third World sisters and brothers best by fighting our own battles and by making clear to them that we have our own liberation struggle. (4) As much as I also oppose "elitist christocentric anti-Semitism," I cannot bow to Driver's repudiation of John 14:6. All that Jesus wanted to say, I suggest, was that *no one comes to the Mother/Father but through the Mother/Father—struggling concretely for justice in you as in me.* What Jesus embodied was what counted. It was a most *theo*centric statement. Not God in the *highest*, but God in the pits, God in the dumps, God on the underside of history, even the seamy side of life—where life is most threatened. Orthodox language would tempt us to say: God *condescends* to the lowliest place. Liberation language can only counter: God *bends* to the most threatened face. God is already present; God does not have to descend. There is no guarantee of immediate solutions. The struggle goes on. But we know who is at the center of the struggle. (5) I do not see that North American liberal christology has made even a first concerted step in the direction of the underside of history. We either tend to stress the cultic Christ of the orthodox two natures or the myriads of liberal cultic Christs. The whole liberation theology struggle in North America cannot be over social ethics issues primarily, or sociology. It is over christology. In terms of God-walk it is a struggle over christo-praxis, or the relationship between christo-praxis and christology.

4. John Macquarrie, *Principles of Christian Theology* (New York, 1977), 277.

5. *Expositor*, 7 (1909), 224.

6. Elisabeth Schüssler Fiorenza, *In Memory of Her* (New York, 1983), 129.

7. The vast debate on these issues comes down on discovering just how much of Jesus still "functions" for us in the first place. One way of doing this is to distinguish between the *that* and the *what*. David Tracy summarizes it beautifully: "Paul's dominant proclamation-orientation leads him to rest content with the pure *that* of Jesus with little concern for the what of Jesus' life and ministry in favor of the eschatological reality of cross and resurrection. And yet Paul's eventlike 'that' as the that-it-happens-now grounds his theology and his proclamation in none other than the same Jesus of Nazareth, just as surely as do the narratives of the ministry in the synoptics. . . .John's narrative becomes not so much a story as a verbal icon or a listening through music" (*The Analogical Imagination* [New York, 1981], 286). God-walk needs to argue that the debate is leaving out an important dimension. Also in the *what* there is a peculiar *that*ness involved, which the emphasis on the *that* usually leaves out. Mere *that*ness is something Jesus is condemned to as nonperson. And extinction next? We get into an area we usually do not think about in terms of our empire hermeneutic. I hardly know of an adequate analogy to clarify the point in terms of the uncanny *that*ness here involved. God's solidarity with outcasts and losers often seems to let Jesus shrink away from history entirely. Perhaps we should recall that after Alice in Wonderland drinks from the little bottle on the table that causes her to shrink, she wonders if she would "shrink any further: she felt a little nervous about this; 'for it might end, you know,' Alice said to herself, 'in my going out altogether, like a candle. I wonder what I should be like then?' And she tried to fancy what the flame of a candle looks like after the candle has been blown out" (Lewis Carroll, *The Annotated Alice* [New York, 1960], 32). Becoming a nonperson through identification with nonpersons is in the eyes of many also a "going out altogether." This is the root issue in christo-praxis. Tracy outlines the attendant arguments very well. One can know through the historico-critical method "with a certain degree of historical probability some facts about the 'historical Jesus' " (p. 300). Yet the historical Jesus as such is not what we are after. "It is not 'the historical Jesus' but the actual Jesus remembered by the community and confessed in these narratives about Jesus which must bear the theological weight" (ibid.). "It is not the 'historical Jesus' but the confessed, witnessed Jesus that is theologically relevant" (p. 301). It is the actual Jesus as eucharistic Jesus—where there is nothing left to cling to but the nonperson. Lest there be misunderstanding,

it should be underscored that the eucharistic Jesus is the historical Jesus remembered as nonperson, but now in his risen presence affecting us by reinforcing God's presence. I repeat from n. 3, above: God *bends* to the most threatened face. Here is the center of that bending reality of God. To rephrase an old saying: *Bent down so low that low will bother God yet more.*

8. Macquarrie, *Principles,* 300.

9. Ibid.

10. Ibid., 301.

11. Esther and Mortimer Arias, *The Cry of My People* (New York, 1980), 20.

12. Julian N. Hartt in Peter C. Hodgson and Robert H. King (eds.), *Christian Theology* (Philadelphia, 1982): "On the convictional level, Christian expressions of experience are indissolubly linked with images rather than with concepts; doctrinal formulations tend largely to operate with concepts and often function as theories" (p. 117).

13. Philip Schaff, *The Creeds of Christendom* (New York, London, 1977), 32.

14. It needs to be clearly understood that with regard to faith, God, and the person of Jesus, North American Christianity confronts a challenge fundamentally different from the way Latin American liberation theologians and, for that matter, many other Third World theologians see their task. In my Introduction to Hugo Assmann's *Theology for a Nomad Church* (Maryknoll, N.Y., 1976), I pointed to the basic stumbling block in accepting the general Latin American thrust: "The strange circumstance now arises that Assmann's approach transcribed directly as applicable to our culture will be absorbed by liberal Protestantism as just one more *situational* theology. Assmann understands the situation in quite different terms. But the situation *as such* in liberal Protestant thought is also the reference point: 'Its "text" is our situation, and our situation is our primary and basic reference point' " (pp. 9f.). In Latin America generally, our sisters and brothers are struggling with the subjective component, faith, or an anthropological starting point. In North America the issue is basically the character of God and christology as both relate to history.

15. We have to keep this in mind when we try to grasp the methodology orientation of Latin American liberation theology. Nothing is to be gained in North American Protestantism by following the path of Juan Luis Segundo, *The Liberation of Theology* (Maryknoll, N.Y., 1976): "One element is permanent and unique: *faith*. The other is changing and bound up with different historical circumstances: *ideologies*" (p. 116). Jesus cannot help us very much in this issue, according to Segundo: "When Jesus talked about freely proffered love and nonresistance to evil, he was facing

the same problem of filling the void between his conception of God (or perhaps that of the first Christian community) and the problems existing in his age. In short, we are dealing here with another ideology, not with the content of faith itself" (ibid.). But when, in this context, we look around for what the *content* of faith might be, we hardly get even a minimal answer. On the one hand, there is not much liberation to be derived from the Christian scriptures: "We could maintain that liberation was the only theme of the New Testament, I suppose, but only if we were willing to go in for a great deal of abstraction" (p. 112). What are we left with? "Faith . . . is the total process to which man submits, a process of learning in and through ideologies how to create the ideologies needed to handle new and unforeseen situations in history. The Scriptures can and should be examined and studied from both points of view since both processes are in the sacred writings and do not compete with each other over content. This means that fighting one's way out of bondage in Egypt is one experience and turning the other cheek is another experience" (p. 120). As much as we search, *content* keeps evading us, unless we would wish to see content in some vague way in turning the other cheek. At least in our North American situation we cannot proceed that way. Too much of the Euroamerican baggage of liberal theology keeps haunting us as it still impinges on us time and again, even in recent publications.

16. Ernst Troeltsch (1865–1923) is perhaps the best prism for discovering the pros and cons on the European side of the Euroamerican syndrome. In his essay, "The Significance of the Historical Existence of Jesus for Faith," he shows how the Friedrich Schleiermacher/Albrecht Ritschl/Wilhelm Herrmann line on a new approach to Christianity from the Protestant perspective surrenders much of tradition. He himself ends up with a minimum content of faith. If one really pushes it hard, it comes down to little more than "Christian belief in God and the person of Jesus." If we ask, exactly what is the content of belief in God or in Jesus, there is little we are told (Ernst Troeltsch, in Robert Morgan and Michael Pye [eds.], *Ernst Troeltsch: Writings on Theology and Religion* [Atlanta, 1977], 191). What becomes so controlling in the approach is that the individual can fill belief in God and the person of Jesus with almost any content she or he wants to. Troeltsch rejects the Nicene tradition and the atonement/Reformation tradition as well. What he wants to retain in small measure is the historical Jesus. He summarizes his position: "No matter what emerged later from this earliest form of the Christian community as a Christ cult, the original motive is clear. The need for community and the need for cult had no other means than the gathering to worship Christ as the revelation of God. The dogma concerning Christ which emerged from this Christ cult was only meant to show and give access to the one eternal

God in Christ in order to create a new community. . . . The original motive responsible for the emergence of faith in Christ and for linking the new belief in God to the Christ cult is still operative under different forms and conditions today. It is a law of social psychology that individuals with merely parallel thoughts and experiences . . . can never simply co-exist for long without affecting each other and joining forces. Out of the myriad connections community groups with higher and lower strata are everywhere produced and taken together these need a concrete focus. This law holds for the religious life too" (p. 195). As Troeltsch moved toward the law of social psychology, he was on a good track of research, but did not push far enough. He still wanted to stay in control of the subject matter. No question is asked about the reality-configuration in the subject matter itself. Here Troeltsch would have had to move from *social psychology* (subjective orientation) to *social analysis* (objective reality). He was quite content to confine his social location to a small circle of academic historians. The time apparently was not ripe for him to move beyond that circle.

17. This is not the place for an extensive confrontation with 19th-century Protestant thought in terms of its 20th-century counterpoint. For all practical purposes, it is summed up by Robert Morgan: "Barth and Troeltsch in particular are difficult to read without strong feelings of aversion—and gratitude for the other. Troeltsch's reasonableness on the historical questions and his recognition of their significance is very impressive. On the other hand it is difficult for a theologian with strong roots in the classical Christian tradition to read *The Significance of the Historical Existence of Jesus for Faith* without being profoundly thankful for *Church Dogmatics*" (Morgan and Pye, *Ernst Troeltsch*, 217). With this summary the stage of the polarity in our situation has been set. For God-walk grounded in co-reason there is no way to avoid the historical question. In this sense Troeltsch still has a tremendous contribution to make: "Troeltsch was prepared to accept the consequences of insisting upon the importance for Christianity of the picture of Jesus mediated by historical research" (p. 222). Reason has to make up its mind which configuration of reality in the life designated by the name Jesus it wants to receive signals from, for direction and orientation. At the same time it has to be clear that it all cannot be done without the community called the church. That is the truth of the Barth approach. The question here becomes, though, whether we demand *assent to beliefs* or discover a *consent of reliefs* (removal of the oppressive, burdensome, painful, or distressing). We can also put it differently. Is it ultimately faith seeking *understanding* we are oriented toward, or faith seeking *accountability*? It may be that sound perception of the originating event of Christianity has been so tampered with during the

history of the church that we are no longer able to get the matter straight. Troeltsch thought that we somehow had to be involved in apologetics in order to see the problem. Apologetics may be a dead-end road. But that does not mean the dynamics involved are absurd. Robert Morgan speaks to the point: "It is . . . one thing to argue that Christian theology ought not to proceed by way of apologetics, and quite another to claim that the whole enterprise of tying knots between faith and knowledge is misguided" (p. 226). Without apologetics, it ought to be possible to show how faith and knowledge interface and coincide. We cannot go the way of Barth's *Church Dogmatics* and reject reason. We also cannot follow Troeltsch by apotheosizing reason. We need to move to another universe of experience and discourse—the underside of history. The subject matter itself forces us to do so.

18. It cannot be stressed enough how little the liberation dynamic has made an impact on the North American scene, with the exception of feminist thrusts and black and other ethnic demands we rejoice in. The center of the churches and theology have remained untouched, unreconstructed. There is smoke screen on top of smoke screen . . . almost ad infinitum. The idea that for white America some broad liberation theology has become a new focus for Christian thought is preposterous. We usually do not even understand the minimum that tough social analysis would compel us to acknowledge about our North American situation. We have to learn the *basics* of liberation before we can get any further. What are the basics? We cannot get at them without reflection on the earthly Jesus. Segundo (see n. 15, above) moves too quickly into the notion of ideology in scripture. There certainly is also ideology in scripture. But we first have to grasp the reality-configuration that underlies the ideology. Otherwise we cannot even discern what the ideology is. In order to discover the ideology, *we have to have at least one nonideological factor by which we can measure what the ideology might be also in the scriptures.* When Jesus utters the cry: "The time is fulfilled, the kingdom of God is at hand; repent, and believe in the gospel" (Mark 1:15), the question of course suggests itself: What is the gospel, the good news, in the first place? What is so important about this cry? Who needs a kingdom of God? What is it for? We cannot understand without some social analysis (and some "social psychology," as Troeltsch would say).

19. We have almost reached midway in this book. In terms of social analysis there is little that in principle needs to be added. What historically is mediated to us is a precious historical configuration of the lowly shape of Jesus' public ministry that offers us a new insight into reality. There is the corporate selfhood that bends low toward each threatened creature—which at the same time erupts in opposing empire, oppressive power that

threatens human dignity and the dignity of every creature. So we raise the question time and again: Is there sacred space in reality where we can rediscover the dynamics of this historical configuration? It is especially at the eucharist that this question arises most compellingly.

20. There is so little we really "know" in Christian thought. And what we "know" little of, God is probably the most difficult of all. It ought to be very clear that behind the words of this book also lies Auschwitz, not only as inescapable memory but first of all reality. Yet we gentiles do not honor Auschwitz by pouring the word in printer's ink all over the pages of our books. It accompanies me as a deafening silence all the time. Only Jews can address it authentically, as only blacks can address slavery authentically. Anne Roiphe, in *Generation Without Memory: A Jewish Journey in Christian America* (Boston, 1981), writes: "It seems absurd to conceive of God's participation or presence in the world of the camps and the trains. To think of God as the master of cruelty is to take the first and irrevocable step in denying His existence. If God was silent, as some say, that too is without excuse. If God had some plan in His mind that required the Holocaust to take place, such as warning the world of the evils to come, that betrays an incredible disregard for human life. It shows more sadism than is tolerable in a God, even in a God invented and designed by man. If the event of the Holocaust is to Jews as the Crucifixion is to Gentiles, then it is a cross too many had to bear. It is a Good Friday without an Easter Sunday. It makes a mockery of man's prayers" (pp. 175f.).

21. Today it is crucial that it be understood how the poor in history and the impoverishment of creation go hand and hand. Liberation always has an ecological implication and thrust. The work done by the UCC Commission for Racial Justice is trail-blazing in this regard. Under the leadership of Benjamin F. Chavis, Jr., it published a significant analytical study of how in the United States toxic waste sites have tended to be developed near minority and ethnic population centers: *Toxic Waste and Race in the United States: A National Report on the Racial and Socio-Economic Characteristics of Communities with Hazardous Waste Sites* (Commission for Racial Justice, United Church of Christ, New York, 1987). Some of the spadework for the study went back to the PCB protest in Warren County, North Carolina, under the leadership of Leon White. See Jenny Labalme, *A Road to Walk: A Struggle for Environmental Justice* (Durham, 1987).

22. See Morgan and Pye, *Ernst Troeltsch*, 197ff. In some respects we have not advanced beyond the dialectics between Jesus' person and Jesus as cult symbol. From James M. Robinson, *A New Quest of the Historical Jesus* (Naperville, Ill., 1959) to Helmut Ristow and Karl Matthiae (eds.), *Der historische Jesus und der kerygmatische Christus* (Berlin, 1962) the key issues reappear. The question is ultimately from which social location

are questions being addressed to texts. *God-Walk* tries to steer away from excessive concentration on Jesus' teachings (heralded widely through Adolf Harnack, *What Is Christianity?*, [New York, 1957]), concentrating instead on the shape of the public ministry.

23. *Time* (Oct. 22, 1979), 68.

24. Philip Wylie, *Generation of Vipers* (New York, Toronto, 1942), 300f.

25. Michael B. McGarry, *Christology after Auschwitz* (New York, 1977).

26. Friedrich Schleiermacher, *The Christian Faith* (Edinburgh, 1928): "Christianity cannot in any wise be regarded as a remodelling or a renewal and continuation of Judaism" (p. 61).

27. Dan Cohn-Sherbok, *On Earth as It Is in Heaven: Jews, Christians, and Liberation Theology* (Maryknoll, N.Y., 1987): "Thus for both Jews and liberation theologians the establishment of the kingdom of God is a process in which all human beings have an important role" (p. 114).

28. Schubert M. Ogden, *Christ Without Myth* (New York, 1961), 154. I do not discover a basic christological change in Ogden's *Faith and Freedom: Toward a Theology of Liberation* (Nashville, 1979), also not in his *The Point of Christology* (San Francisco, 1982), in itself a marvelous book. My question remains. How do we get together Jesus as "Liberator" (127) and "authentic self-understanding" (130) in regard to Matt. 25:31–36 where Jesus' words, "you did it to me" (168) reflect a unique selfhood of Jesus? See also Ogden's *On Theology* (San Francisco, 1986), 150: Christian theology *must* be a theology of liberation. Without a unique selfhood of Jesus?

29. Ibid., 161.

30. Ibid., 162.

31. Karl Barth, *Christ and Adam* (New York, 1957), 29.

32. Edward Huenemann, unpublished paper presented to the Duodecim Society, Oct. 9, 1981, 4.

33. Macquarrie, *Principles*, 321.

34. The significance of the creation for God's work of liberation is a theme that needs pursuing far beyond the immediate confines of this book. In some respects, liberation is *the* work of God in God's ongoing creation-activity; see Matthew Fox, *Original Blessing: A Primer in Creation Spirituality* (Santa Fe, 1983). Expansion of reflection into the dimension of creation will be important in order to find the place in nature where the historical configuration of the shape of Jesus' public ministry coincides with God's ongoing work. For indications of new thinking in this direction, see Günter Altner, "Vom Sein zum Werden: Zum Dialog zwischen Theologie und Naturwissenschaften," *Evangelische Kommentare*, 20:4 (April 1987), 190–92; Holmes Rolston III, "Shaken Atheism: A Look at the Fine-Tuned Universe," *Christian Century*, 103:37 (Dec. 3, 1986) 1093–

95; Fritjof Capra, *The Turning Point: Science, Society, and the Rising Culture* (Toronto, New York, London, Sidney, 1982); Marilyn Ferguson, *The Aquarian Conspiracy* (Los Angeles, Boston, 1980); and Roger S. Jones, *Physics as Metaphor* (New York, Scarborough, 1982).

35. St. Anselm, *Cur Deus Homo* (La Salle, Ill., 1951), 239.

36. Ibid., 242.

37. Ibid.

38. Ibid., 244.

39. Ibid.

40. Ibid., 245.

41. Cohn-Sherbok, *On Earth*, 35.

42. Ibid., 62.

43. Ibid., 115. Although there is an overlapping of concerns between Jewish religion and liberation theology, there are also still vast differences. Says Cohn-Sherbok: "Despite the common ground we have explored there are important theological differences between Judaism and liberation theology. As in the past Jews today would regard the liberationist's adherence to traditional christology as misguided. For the Jew, God is an absolute unity; God is indivisible and unique, containing no plurality. Given this understanding, the doctrine of the Incarnation must be rejected. The belief that Jesus was both man and God continues to be considered a blasphemous heresy. Contemporary Jewish thinkers also reject trinitarianism in any form; there is simply no way to harmonize the belief in Jewish monotheism with the conception of a triune God. Similarly, Jews of all degrees of observance deny the liberationists' claim that Jesus was the Messiah. For Jews, Jesus did not fulfill the messianic expectations: he did not gather in the exiles and restore the Law; he did not rebuild the Temple; nor did he bring about a cataclysmic change in human history. Further, Jews deny that Jesus had an extraordinary relationship with God and that he can forgive sins" (p. 112). Obviously a wide chasm continues to exist. For Christians, it is impossible not to take seriously all those points Cohn-Sherbok says Jews must reject. From a Christian liberation perspective, all doctrines in any case dare not be parroted conceptually, but have to be reexperienced in their genesis. There is a range of reality to which Christian metaphors need to be addressed as questions to see whether reality will "behave" in new ways. Anne Roiphe, in *Generation Without Memory*, makes the point that she cannot simply take over concepts of Maimonides dealing, for example, with God being the creator, making and willing all things (pp. 181f.). In christo-praxis we first have to walk the faith, walk the commitment. Theology is only a second step, organizing the Christian teachings that grow out of praxis. We need to begin to dialogue with regard to the *genesis* of our faith-ideas. The end results in *concepts*

will always keep us at a distance from each other. *We need to be liberated from oppressive God-concepts and reexperience God's reality in the brokenness of life.* To take our place at the underside of history is the first step. Only thus can we hope to do justice to the historical/self-critical method and forgo control.

44. Cohn-Sherbok, *On Earth*, 35.

45. Schüssler Fiorenza, *In Memory of Her*, 130.

46. Ibid., 132.

47. Ibid., 135.

48. Cohn-Sherbok, *On Earth*, 33.

49. In many respects we are lacking the right terms to express our God-walk, especially vis-à-vis dialogue with Judaism. The notion of incarnation has become so overwhelmingly obtuse in most theological jargon that Christians themselves are usually mystified as to the root-metaphor meaning of the term. So the objections and reservations of Cohn-Sherbok urge us to sweep in front of our own doors. Obviously Christian praxis is not the same as Jewish praxis in all respects. I believe we need to be open for different experiences of God's own God-walk through history. The sheer deprivation of God mediated to us through Jesus as God pursues divine involvement in history is difficult to express in words. We need to be open to what it tells Christians of God. Incarnation is a big problem today, a metaphysical conundrum, a mystification, which is what many are hankering for. *Deprivation* is no issue at all, something nobody wants generally. It is an offense, just as it was in St. Paul's day (1 Cor. 1:23). The problem today is that we are not adequately presenting to the Jewish community what for Christians happened in Jesus of Nazareth. We have to understand some of the reasons for the dilemma that has been delivered to us by the previous generation. Reinhold Niebuhr is a good case in point in this respect. "He was preaching one Sunday in the 1940s in a little chapel near his then-summer home in Heath, Massachusetts, when his friend and neighbor, Supreme Court Justice Frankfurter, remarked: "I like what you said, Reinie, and I speak as a believing unbeliever." Niebuhr replied: 'I am glad you did. For I spoke as an unbelieving believer.' . . . Sharing more and more of his time with secular, agnostic, and frequently Jewish intellectuals, Christianity was placed in brackets, the brackets of civility" (John Murray Cuddihy, *No Offense: Civil Religion and Protestant Taste* [New York, 1978], 35).

50. There is much we can learn from Jewish tradition as far as corporate selfhood is concerned. See Roiphe, *Generation Without Memory*, 182f.

51. *The Book of Discipline of the United Methodist Church* (Nashville, 1980), 57. Here lies of course a sharp division with much of Judaism. "Christianity asserts that we cannot liberate ourselves by our own effort"

(Cohn-Sherbok, *On Earth*, 22). Why is God in Christianity experienced so differently? Auschwitz might offer a clue. Germans have no way of liberating themselves from that past. German reparations to Israel certainly do not wipe out the crime. It still stands between us in its raw brutality. Only God also at the underside of history can evolve something new. What humans do does not suffice to wipe the slate clean.

52. *Book of Discipline*, 57.

53. Paul Tillich, *Systematic Theology*, (Chicago, 1957), 2:178.

54. Ibid., 179. We need to view the whole issue of justification in a much wider context, not just the religious. See John Howard Yoder, *The Politics of Jesus* (Grand Rapids, 1972), 215–32.

55. Tillich, *Systematic Theology,* 2:179.

56. Ibid.

57. Ibid., 178.

58. Ibid., 173–76.

59. Ibid., 173. In the older formulations of the doctrine, we spoke here of the *ordo salutis*. As we compare, say, John Wesley with Paul Tillich, we see how Christian thought has pressed the issue further. We do not think so much of component parts of salvation, but of a unitary process with different dynamics of functions. See, in contrast to Tillich, Ole Borgen, *John Wesley on the Sacraments* (Grand Rapids, 1985), esp. 121–217. Today we are much more inclined to think of a *processus salutis*, not saying so much "one grace, different functions" as "one justice, different dynamics."

60. Tillich, *Systematic Theology*, 2:174.

61. Ibid.

62. Ibid., emphasis added. Troeltsch had the idea that the essence of Christianity changes. My point has to be that core Christian reality comes across differently at different times. It is a *processus salutis* that we are tied into. What the Reformation struggled over as grace, the liberationists struggle over as justice. The core point is that it is Godself that moves in the *processus salutis*. It reaches each generation differently according to the needs of human beings in a particular age.

63. Here is an issue that, in the end, still remains wide open. The ontological challenge cannot be avoided. The question is whether we analyze ontological structures in nature and the universe and then impose them on Christian thought, or whether we discover in the light of the historical configuration at the beginning of the Christian movement structures that respond to the historical configuration. Leonardo Boff, in *Jesus Christ Liberator* (Maryknoll, N.Y., 1984), speaks of "a christic structure . . . within human reality" (pp. 248ff.). It is one of the virtues of this great book not to have avoided the ontological structure issue. So when we deal with the atonement, for example, we are dealing with more than

just a configuration of historical events. The very nature of the universe, the very heart of creation, is at stake in the atoning processes. Yet we need to see the needed approach as a reversal of the Tillich approach where the ontology of nature and history determines the Christian project.

64. William E. Diehl, *Christianity and Real Life* (Philadelphia, 1976), 70.

65. *The Book of Discipline of the United Methodist Church*, 57.

66. *The Heidelberg Catechism* (Philadelphia, 1962), 64.

67. *Book of Discipline*, 57.

68. Diehl, *Christianity and Real Life*, 34.

69. Ibid., quote from Peter L. Berger.

70. Ibid., 35.

71. Ibid., 16.

72. It calls for thinking through our several traditions in new ways. It relates first of all to a grasp of the practical grounding of our thought, as indicated, for example, in Thomas A. Langford's *Practical Divinity: Theology in the Wesleyan Tradition* (Nashville, 1983). For the historical background of the Methodist practical divinity, see Howard A. Snyder, *The Radical Wesley* (Downers Grove, Ill., 1980).

73. *Time*, Dec. 27, 1976, 31.

74. Monika K. Hellwig, *The Eucharist and the Hunger of the World* (New York, Paramus, 1976), 11.

75. It is the significance of Third World wrestling with the eucharist that makes us especially think in this direction. See Tissa Balasuriya, *The Eucharist and Human Liberation* (Maryknoll, N.Y., 1979).

76. *The Book of Discipline of the United Methodist Church* (Nashville, 1980), 59.

77. As to the significance of the community for faith appropriation of the meal, see Markus Barth, *Das Mahl des Herrn: Gemeinschaft mit Israel, mit Christus und unter den Gästen* (Neukirchen-Vluyn, 1987).

78. Dennis C. Smolarski, *Eucharistia: A Study of the Eucharistic Prayer* (New York, Ramsey, 1982).

79. Tad W. Guzie, *Jesus and the Eucharist* (New York, Paramus, 1974).

80. Rolf Christiansen (ed.), *Alle an einen Tisch: Forum Abendmahl* (Gütersloh, 1981).

81. Ibid., 63.

82. *Pastoraltheologie* (1983), 91–93. My paragraphs following here are a summary of Christiansen's text, mainly a direct translation.

83. Ibid., 84.

84. It is important to grasp the risen Jesus as reinforcing the presence of God. See Gustave Martelet, *The Risen Christ and the Eucharistic World* (London, 1976).

85. The eucharist can also be understood as the ceremony at the center of

the world. Here we see into the heart of creation. Here we hear the heartbeat of the universe. There is considerable analogy in ceremonies of other faiths. See John G. Neidhardt, *Black Elk Speaks* (New York, 1961): "But anywhere is the center of the world" (p. 36).

86. For the use of the term in general, see Louis Pauwels and Jacques Bergier, *The Morning of the Magicians* (New York, 1968), 400ff.

87. Emile Mersch, *Théologie du Corps Mystique* (1946), 1:170.

88. Matthew Fox (ed.), *Illuminations of Hildegard of Bingen* (Santa Fe, 1985), 64. See also Tom Hansen, "Meditation on Water," *Anima* 11 (Spring 1985) 147–52.

89. It is a basic pattern in the universe that involves other patterns. See Capra, *Turning Point*, 94.

90. *Theological Education* 17 (Autumn 1980): 5.

91. Ernesto Cardenal, *The Gospel in Solentiname* (Maryknoll, N.Y., 1976), 28.

92. A paraphrase of Ernest Hemingway's "grace under pressure." See Arthur Waldhorn, *Ernest Hemingway* (New York, 1972), 5, 224.

93. There is a vast misunderstanding of how Schleiermacher functioned in legitimating the status quo. Richard Crouter, in "Schleiermacher and the Theology of Bourgeois Society: A Critique of the Critics," *Journal of Religion*, 66:3 (July 1986), claims I do not offer an adequate understanding of the relationship between Schleiermacher's theology and politics. My concern has always been to show Schleiermacher's world-construct, his relationship to his social order as a whole. Of course Schleiermacher stressed the principle of equality practically most of the time. The issue is: Who determines what equality is? The rhetoric does not matter. It does not matter that we mouth this word. The principle of equality is determined differently depending on which social order we align ourselves with. Which social order did Schleiermacher support?

94. The Reagan debacle in the Iran-Contra affair has underscored it all again. See Gary Wills, "What Happened?," *Time* (March 9, 1987) 40–41. The Jim Bakker affair in the realm of religion has underscored the bank-ruptcy of our public life: "Clearly the Bakkers' level of compensation suggests that PTL has become more entertainment, or show business, than religion—or more precisely, perhaps, entertainment masquerading as reli-gion" (*Durham Morning Herald*, "Bakkers' Salaries Were Not So High" [May 4, 1987], 4).

95. Fox, *Illuminations of Hildegard of Bingen*, 90.

96. Ibid., 92.

97. Ibid.

98. Ibid., 104.

99. Ibid., 105.

100. Throughout this chapter the theodicy issue has been a major component of the background that projected the dynamics of the argument. Basically God-walk makes us turn the *si Deus, unde malum?* question around, so that it now reads *si malum, unde Deus?*—if this be evil, what about God? As a framework of the question, the empire hermeneutic had to be always on my mind. Inside the most powerful nation-state of the twentieth century, how do we escape being controlled by it and being co-opted in its drive to control? As I was growing in understanding the need for pursuing my argument, I kept referring to Bertram Gross, *Friendly Fascism: The New Face of Power in America* (Boston, 1980); Morton H. Halperin, Jerry J. Berman, Robert L. Borosage, and Christine M. Marwick, *The Lawless State: The Crimes of the U.S. Intelligence Agencies* (New York, 1976); and Ernest Becker, *Escape From Evil* (New York, London, 1975). There is a continual flow of literature that deals with the overall framework even transcontinentally in the First World. One excellent example is Leroy S. Rouner, ed., *Civil Religion and Political Theology* (Notre Dame, 1986). The liberation theology literature itself is becoming so vast that it is nearly impossible to deal with it all. The point has also been reached where one bibliography seems to be compelled to best the previous one. For an excellent overview and a helpful select bibliography, see the two volumes by Deane William Ferm, *Third World Theologies* (Maryknoll, N.Y., 1986), an introductory survey (vol. 1) and a reader (vol. 2). See my review of the two books in *International Bulletin of Missionary Research*, 11:2 (April 1987), 92–93.

Chapter 3. Spirit-Praxis

1. On attempts to avoid developing a systematic principle for liberation theology, see Phillip Berryman, *Liberation Theology: The Essential Facts about the Revolutionary Movement in Latin America and Beyond* (New York, 1987), 60ff.

2. It will be helpful from the beginning of this chapter to keep in mind the interdependence of ecclesiology and pneumatology. See Leonardo Boff, *Church: Charism and Power* (New York, 1986), 144ff.

3. For the opposite position, see José Miranda, *Marx and the Bible* (Maryknoll, N.Y., 1974), 227.

4. It will call for a comprehensive new assessment of the relationship between biblical thought and natural science. See Holmes Rolston III, "Shaken Atheism: A Look at the Fine-Tuned Universe," *Christian Century* (Dec. 3, 1986) 1093–95. A pioneer attempt addressing a wide range of issues on this point is Matthew Fox's *Original Blessing* (Santa Fe, 1983). With specific emphasis on ecology, see Hoimar v. Ditfurth, *So lasst uns*

denn ein Apfelbäumchen pflanzen (Hamburg, Zürich, 1985).

5. For the role of the God of Israel today, see Robert T. Osborn, "The Christian Blasphemy," *Journal of the American Academy of Religion*, 53:3 (1986) 351f. I owe much to the quiet persistence of Osborn's work.

6. Marc H. Ellis, "Notes Toward a Jewish Theology of Liberation," *Doing Theology in the United States*, 1:1 (1985) 5–17.

7. Robert McAfee Brown, "Notes on 'Notes . . . ,' " *Doing Theology in the United States*, 1:1 (1985): "It is in the doing of justice that God is truly known" (p. 22). And first of all in God's own doing of justice.

8. Richard Shaull, "Revolutionary Change in Theological Perspective," in John C. Bennett (ed.), *Christian Social Ethics in a Changing World* (New York, 1966). From the very early stages of reflection on the liberation process, the triune activity of God has been appealed to (p. 26). The argument in notes 8–23 draws on the significant Munich University dissertation by Craig L. Nessan, "The North American Theological Response to Latin American Liberation Theology. Validity and Limitations of a Praxis-Oriented Theology" (1986).

9. The corporate meal of the eucharist under the aegis of spirit-praxis compels us immediately to take note of what eating actually amounts to throughout the world today. For the difference between "affluence-eating" and eating in want, see Tom Barry, "The Justice of Eating," *The Inter-Hemispheric Education Research Center Bulletin* 9 (Spring-Summer 1987), 1–4.

10. Much of the critique of liberation theology has focused on its Marxist leanings without raising the issue of ultimate control in theological use of other thought systems. See James V. Schall, *Liberation Theology in Latin America* (San Francisco, 1982): "The conclusion . . . is that Marxism is necessarily conformable with Christianity" (p. 34). Whether a system of thought was conformable with Christianity has been a question in regard to Aristotle in the Middle Ages or Whitehead in modern times. The crucial point is whether God remains in the driver's seat, so that Christianity orients itself in what God is doing. Or does it tell God how to drive?

11. We need to question the notion that liberation theology is practically condemned to offer a liberation other than God's. See Marc Kolden, "Marxism and Latin American Liberation Theology," in Wayne Stumme (ed.), *Christians and the Many Faces of Marxism* (Minneapolis, 1984), 130.

12. See Stanley Hauerwas, *Truthfulness and Tragedy* (Notre Dame, London, 1977): "The stories that produce truthful lives are those that provide the skills to step back and survey the limits of our engagements. Nations, no less than individuals, require such stories. . . . To accept the

Gospel is to receive training in accepting the limits on our claims to righteousness before we are forced to" (p. 98). The crux here is whether we accept the limits on our claim to righteousness by accepting the gospel as corporate gospel placing us in new social location with God including all of humanity, also the rejects, or whether we retain our self-orientation in our culturally conditioned self.

13. We easily assume a two-kingdom doctrine here. See William H. Willimon and Robert L. Wilson, *Rekindling the Flame* (Nashville, 1987): "We are in the world as Christians. This means we may take political stands; but they must be amenable to our prior commitment to Christ. We contend for justice, but justice that is continually reinterpreted by our commitment to Christ" (p. 29). Yet our commitment to Christ and our contending for justice cannot be two separate things, because Christ is justice, God's right hand of justice. Our commitment to Christ is our contending for justice.

14. As long as we do not stress the ongoing initiative of God in the liberation process, we obviously will continue to contribute to misperceptions of liberation theology. See Michael Novak, *The Spirit of Modern Capitalism* (New York, 1982): "The poor may have things wrong. Their opinions are not necessarily God's, nor do they necessarily carry the warrant of truth" (p. 185). Since the days of confirmation instruction, all of us ought to have known that much. It is a sign of the occasionally low-level debate that the argument among critics turns on these obvious points.

15. Obviously some might want to reject Marxist praxis as "the Trojan horse of liberation theology" (Carl E. Braaten). Yet one still would not have to reject almost automatically any notion of praxis. Obviously one might note that the concepts of *sola gratia* and *sola fide* are not part of the liberation theology emphasis. See Carl E. Braaten, "The Gospel of Justification Sola Fide," *Dialog*, 15 (Summer 1976) 208. Yet *sola gratia* and *sola fide* themselves grow out of praxis too. So, for example, faith needs to be examined in terms of praxis-genesis first.

16. We do not have to fall back into old habits at any point. To those who carefully examine liberation theology from an inside Catholic view, some emphases seem to recall ancient aberrations. See Daniel Berrigan, *The Mission* (San Francisco, 1986): "But it seems to me that certain of the liberationists are as tempted as anyone else to become obsessive Pelagians—theorists of the 'one way,' our way" (143f.). It is exactly Holy Spirit praxis that obviates the Pelagian temptation, or at least ought to.

17. John Macquarrie, *Principles of Christian Theology*, 152.

18. Some liberation theology is occasionally criticized for trying to correlate the themes of liberation and salvation. See Dennis P. McCann,

Christian Realism and Liberation Theology (Maryknoll, N.Y., 1981), 186. Yet they belong together in that creation is the theater of liberation and sinful history the place of salvation. As creator, God directs humanity toward liberation, as reconciler toward salvation.

19. It is also not wise to draw a sharp line between redemption and emancipation, as though the first were God's doing and the second the human being's. See Donald Bloesch, *Essentials of Evangelical Theology* (San Francisco, 1979), 2:165.

20. Macquarrie, *Principles of Christian Theology*, 102.

21. There need not be any misperception on this point, and certainly not any misunderstanding. In spirit-praxis the way to God is based on concretion. It is always God's own concretion and self-realization. There is no way to God but God. We meet no second God in Jesus. The one God comes to us through Jesus. Yet it is not Jesus as Jesus who is the way to God. There is no way to God; God is the way. It was still difficult to express in primitive Christian terms at the time. Even so there comes a point when the figure of Jesus disappears, so that God can be all in all (1 Cor. 15:28). See Gustavo Gutiérrez, *We Drink from Our Own Wells* (Maryknoll, N.Y., 1984), 54–71. Here spirit-praxis is detailed in terms of Latin American liberation theology.

22. Macquarrie, *Principles of Christian Theology*, 335.

23. The impression is often given that liberation theology is the same as social ethics. In principle, nothing could be further from the truth. Liberation theology is a hermeneutical focus, just like any other theology. It is unfortunate that thus far we have been unable to "handle" this fact "technically." For the identification of liberation theology and ethics, see Richard John Neuhaus, "Liberation Theology and the Captivation of Jesus," in Gerald H. Anderson and Thomas F. Stransky (eds.), *Mission Trends No. 3* (New York, 1976), 56.

24. Liberation theology as a hermeneutical focus is undergirded by its social location, a definite spirituality environment. In very plain terms it is "The Church as Sacrament of the Holy Spirit." See Leonardo Boff, *Church: Charism and Power,* 152.

25. Ibid., 154.

26. Elisabeth Schüssler Fiorenza, *In Memory of Her* (New York, 1983), 134.

27. Joan Chamberlain Engelsman, *The Feminine Dimension of the Divine* (Philadelphia, 1979), 81.

28. Ibid., 99ff.

29. Gustavo Gutiérrez, *We Drink from Our Own Wells*: "In many instances, our very questions will be reformulated" (p. 34).

30. Emile Durkheim, *Sociology and Philosophy* (New York, 1974), viii.

31. *Theological Education*, 16:1 (Autumn 1979), published "Theological

Education and Liberation Theology: An Invitation to Respond," a statement by twelve white male theologians with responses of seventeen theological educators. There is probably no other place where liberation theology as new hermeneutical focus needs more testing than in the seminaries and the divinity schools. It would be foolish to claim: if liberation theology does not work in the seminaries, it won't work in the churches. The point is: if future ministers do not wrestle with it seriously during their years of training, church members will hardly ever be confronted with it seriously and will take the media's lightweight stories about it for gospel truth. We had intentionally (in keeping with the pristine stage of the liberation theology debate in the United States at the time) cast the issue in the *question* mode. Yet even that was held against us. Virgilio P. Elizondo commented on the piece: "Every time it gets to a crucial point, it avoids the real issues by posing a question, rather than stating bluntly the conviction of the authors. The core statement and subsequent development are like a jet that begins to take off with great power, but then weakens quickly and fails to take off" (34f.). In the First World, it needs just as careful an analysis of what the issues are as in the Third World. I, for one, had stated my new findings many times before, bluntly. Perhaps it had brought me satisfaction, but had it brought change? What is it that is really at stake in First World ministerial education? Elizondo offers two important suggestions. (1) As universities and seminaries we have to be "willing to tighten our belt, to freely give up many of our privileges and comforts so as to enter into real solidarity with the poor." (2) "We must not just analyze and condemn, we must work together with the technicians of civilization to envision, plan, and build a radically new civilization based upon new heroes, new symbols, new values, and a new way of life" (p. 35). The key is certainly a new praxis. And yet it does not appear by fiat. From praxis grow the new values and the new way of life. What has grown up thus far is the realization that ministerial education is based on an obsolete anthropology grounded in obsolete christology. What is missing is accountable teaching on the human being, just as accountable teaching about Jesus is missing—in view of the new social location. There is a vast bouleversement of elementary relationships involved that even after nearly a decade of debate (or two decades) we have hardly grasped. The situation in many respects is still very much where Richard D.N. Dickinson saw it in 1979: "When one looks across the whole spectrum of theological education in North America one cannot be sanguine. The concern expressed in the invitation is manifest only feebly and in only relatively few institutions; there are few pioneers. And even where the concern is apparently deep and pervasive, the achievements are admittedly modest" (p. 33).

32. How pristine the whole debate in ministerial education at this point

still is becomes clear when we reflect on God's activity that underlies the christological bouleversement in which a new anthropology is rooted. Time and again we have tried to indicate that it is justice activity. Some of the critique in *Theological Education* took the line that we ought to distinguish between involvement and detachment in our teaching and come down more on the side of detachment in reflection. C. Douglas Jay suggested: "Intentional groups may properly be identified with particular causes, or strategies for their pursuit; but educational institutions . . . assume responsibility for, among other things, critiquing all serious ideological options. I submit that this calls for a measure of disinterestedness or detachment which may be incompatible with the wholehearted crusade for justice which the document seems to call for" (p. 38). Ultimately liberation theology, as perceived in God-walk, has nothing to do with a *crusade* for justice, but everything with the *cascade* of justice God is already providing for at the underside of history and on grounds of which God invites us all: "Let justice roll down like waters" (Amos 5:24). Short of that, involvement might turn out to be no more than field work. In the words of C. Douglas Jay: "Some things can only be learned through commitment and involvement; this is part of the justification for field education as an essential part of the curriculum for a theological school" (p. 38). God-walk makes field work and critiquing all serious ideological options join together in God's justice activity, foremost in a divinity school or seminary. We are not involved in history principally through field work, but through God. There is no way of escaping the activity of God—not even in a divinity school. Ministerial education, as a rule, presupposes only the vaguest anthropology, the lowest common denominator. As a consequence, teaching suffers severely.

33. Even in the most stellar books on authority today usually the immediate struggle of the Christian with God is not part of the picture. The authorizing of human existence is not such a hot issue. We are often confronted with some objective construct. Nicolas Lash, *Voices of Authority* (Shepherdstown, W. Va., 1976), after some reflection claims: "So far in the course of this opening chapter I have not explicitly taken into account any specifically theological considerations" (p. 10). Similar comments could be multiplied from other authors. The *anthropological* dilemma of Christian teaching seems overlooked as a relevant factor at the point of entry in authority discussions. Thus some ideological self-image of near perfection usually prevails to make self-justification easy and "self-evident."

34. It is important to work with this issue in the most concrete way at the grassroots level. See Jenny Labalme, *A Road to Walk: A Struggle for Environmental Justice* (Durham, N.C., 1987). Labalme in this small

booklet carefully reviews the PCB protest of the citizens in Warren County, North Carolina: "During a sultry fall in 1982, citizens here launched one of the largest civil rights demonstrations in the nation since the 1960s" (p. 2). For our solidarity with all of creation, see Jürgen Moltmann, *Gott in der Schöpfung* (Munich, 1985), 34–39.

35. It is important to listen to Evangelical critiques with regard to biblical foundations especially on this point. In regard to the importance of the Bible as the rule of God-walk, we can readily agree. It is elementary and nonnegotiable. The difference comes at the point where Evangelical theory is immediately imposed on the elementary point. Donald G. Bloesch states: "It can be shown that nearly all the great theologians of the past, both Catholic and Protestant, were concerned to demonstrate their faith in lives of witness and service. While emphasizing the priority of faith and doctrine over life, they nonetheless expressed their faith not only in the personal relationships with others but also in the social arena" (*Theological Education*, 17). Bloesch obviously assumes that "the priority of faith and doctrine over life" is part of the hermeneutical focus all *have* to agree to. In 1979 we certainly had not worked out much of the detail. Yet by now it is clear that we are struggling hard against the priority of faith and doctrine (both *human* expressions too) as foregone conclusion—a conclusion that has not been *shown* to be true in terms of both the genesis of faith and the genesis of doctrine. It is again an open question: How does Christian thought arise? How does a doctrine arise? The genesis of doctrine is little understood. Bloesch claims: "Where these theological giants differ from the liberation theologians of today is that they saw the primary purpose of the church as the saving of souls from divine judgment and hell rather than the improvement of the human lot here on earth" (p. 17). I do not believe it is quite biblical to make the gospel out to be concerned merely with soul-saving and not life-saving. Be that as it may, the basic objection I need to make here pertains to the theological giants argument. The Reformers used to argue somewhat bluntly: popes can err, bishops can err, etc. Today we might have to argue: theological giants can err. The angle of grasping the gospel may have changed. Of Luther, Bloesch writes: "The civil righteousness that can be attained by political means must not be confused with spiritual righteousness" (p. 17). It is unfortunate that Bloesch does not reflect the liberation struggle witnessed to in the Bible. The issue there is first of all not about human righteousness, whether spiritual or civil, but about God's righteousness. The whole liberation challenge is in any case first of all about a new grasp of God. So we have to disagree with the basic orientation of Bloesch: "Yet to insist that our primary concern be ethical obedience rather than purity in doctrine is misleading and counterproductive" (p. 16). Here again is one of those

instances where there is an almost immediate identification of liberation theology with ethics. I understand the reasons. Yet it is also too easy for finding an object of opposition. The issue is not primarily our ethical obedience, but God's own justice obedience, the way God is faithful to the divine purpose for creation as a whole and humankind in particular. It had been said in several contexts before that this was the core issue in North America. Yet it seemed convenient to caricature much or some of the serious Latin American struggle with the basic challenge and to end up with: good riddance. . . . The pain I have felt for years is that the "praxis" challenge of liberation theology has been dealt with much too sovereignly in North America. Even if one wanted to ignore human misery all over the globe, it is difficult to understand why the "classical" theologians did not sense that there was a flaw in the beautiful systems—something "rotten in the state of Denmark."

36. An elementary premise is missing everywhere, or almost everywhere, in the critiques of the liberation theology. The issue raised is ultimately about the character of God. Because that issue has been neatly shelved in most cases, liberation theology cannot advance within the model of ministerial education as we now know it in the West—that is, within the churches of the North Atlantic community. Harvey Cox makes the point very well: "What the document calls for, I believe, cannot be accommodated within anything like the present structure of theological education in North America without far-reaching changes" (*Theological Education*, 26). Short of these changes, we have to make clear what the issues are (over and over again). What is at stake ultimately is also the doctrine that Bloesch is so concerned about. It may be that christological reformulation is going on, growing out of new praxis that parallels pre-Chalcedon days. Bloesch and others need to hear that the West has imposed on ministerial education a cultural model that may distort the truth of the gospel, that at least needs to be examined in terms of the historico/self-critical method, and that cannot automatically be taken for granted as gospel truth. At the same time we need to take heed that we do not lose ourselves in the battle of words (logomachy). John H. Cartwright needs careful attention by all of us: "There is the tendency in contemporary theological circles to theologize about the gospel of liberation as an end-in-itself, thereby making of liberation a gospel of words—merely another in the long line of theological fads that ebb and flow" (p. 22)

37. It is also not groveling or self-hate. Martin E. Marty objected to the first line of our statement in *Theological Education*: "We are white male North American church practitioners and theologians" (p. 7). Marty's problem: "It connotes to me a kind of groveling and self-hate that cannot be of use to anyone else. One wishes a Jesse Jackson would walk into the

room and ask the writers to say, 'I am somebody!' " (p. 46). Does everyone who identifies himself as a white male today suffer from self-hate? I doubt that Marty would repeat his remark now that some more facts are in. Yet we need to listen carefully to Marty's critique. We can all learn from it, not merely from his first objection. His points are all very worthwhile pondering. Yet I would like to bring down my several difficulties with Marty's objections to my puzzlement over "I am somebody!" It would be unfair to say, this is what I heard my theology professors say. The fact is, this is what I heard *some* of my theology professors say. At stake is the issue of "control." The other side of this coin is walk in the Spirit, spirit-praxis. Parenthetically I should mention that it was a lot of fun to unlearn some of the John Wayne habits of the heart these past years. The main point, though, is the spirituality dimension of "control." Luther translated (I need to paraphrase just a little) Ps. 39:5, "What nobodies are all human beings who live that securely!" Those of us who are in the driver's seat of ministerial education have a lesson to learn here, I think. And we are just in the very beginnings. Spirit-walk is also giving up "control." It is in part sharing in the ongoing crucifixion in history. Those of us who reflected on the relationship of liberation theology and ministerial education did make false starts. And yet we kept on delving deeper into our own wells. Our major well was the Bible. Of this book Martin E. Marty makes the one decisive point: "Because of the situation of much of the biblical message among the poor, there are special reasons to give modern poverty a special place in imagination for the act of hearing" (p. 45). The challenge is to view this point as central in the hermeneutical focus that is liberation theology. Just what happens to an anthropology grounded in christo-praxis and fleshed out in spirit-praxis? For some of us the "I am somebody" Marty would like to hear from us is being transformed into *amor, ergo sumus*, I have been taught "grace under pressure," "justice under pressure," therefore *we* are. Whenever our critics have helped us move closer to the Bible, we have gained a litttle more light. John C. Bennett summarizes all the helpful support in this regard in very plain terms: "There are a great many themes in the Bible but if this theme [poverty] is neglected what is said about the others often seems hollow" (p. 15). I am greatly encouraged by support of sisters in the struggle. Our separate challenges meet ultimately in the anthropological obfuscations of the Christian tradition. Among those who form the wall of protection around us, Katie G. Cannon saw our effort as to our dilemma as "painfully disturbing and hopefully promising" (p. 19). Barbara Brown Zikmund felt that a part of her responded "cynically" to our effort: "Theological education is too old, too rich, too male, too concerned about standards and implications to make any very significant changes" (p. 66). Another part of her, however, "leans into these questions with feminist enthusiasm. . . . I believe that the presence of women in theological education is already bringing about change" (p. 67). I also count Barbara Brown Zikmund among those who form the rampart. Note that I did not say a word about gratitude. I simply need to acknowledge the presence of others in the same struggle as an empowering fact and—a challenge.

38. Schubert M. Ogden offers us once more a key to the crucial anthropological difference. If we get over this hump, we will be a long way toward understanding that there is a new option: Are we in ministerial education reflecting merely on a theoretical construct or are we developing teaching in the midst of God's real presence in solidarity with the losers as well as the lost in history? Ultimately we need to know whether our God-walk, including our worship, leads to new teaching—that is, whether there is anything to the *lex orandi, lex credendi.* Says Ogden: "Insofar as theological reflection necessarily involves any prior commitment, it is not committed either to the truth of the Christian witness or to the ongoing struggle of the poor and oppressed for liberation, but is committed simply to understanding the meaning of the Christian witness and to assess its truth, and hence to the ongoing struggle of any and all human beings to know the truth that will make them free" (*Theological Education*, p. 50). Here again we have this strange two-kingdom doctrine at the heart of anthropology, as though the ongoing struggle of the poor and oppressed had nothing to do with the ongoing struggle of any and all human beings, as though in God they were ultimately not the same.

39. It is clear to me that under the present circumstances any teaching on the church, any doctrine, cannot offer "solutions" in the literal sense of the word. All I am proposing is to find the fortitude that enables us to live with problems—creatively. I do not know of any doctrine of the church that at this time would intimate it might solve the dilemma of the church, for example, ecumenically or globally. Yet I hope that we can point out a direction God-walk might take. In this regard I am doing little more than drawing out the implications of *Justice Church* (Maryknoll, N.Y., 1980). I also find it encouraging that a number of the thoughts that grew into this section are in principle supported in Leonardo Boff, *Church: Charism and Power.*

40. Since my *Liberation Theology* (New York, 1972) it has become even more important to me to develop the notion of the *innovatio Christi.* The medieval thought of *imitatio Christi* implied that wisdom arises only from one configuration of pain. So we need to imitate it. In being related to God's pain, creativity can arise from all pain. Creativity is born of pain. That is what *innovatio Christi* in large measure wants to say. See Elaine Scarry, *The Body in Pain* (New York, 1985). The elementary understand-

ings in regard to the *creativity* of pain on which *God-Walk* is based recently benefited from a dialogue with Gerhard Sauter. I learned very much from it. God's reality, I concluded, can best be perceived as moving between the *creativity* of pain (*theologia vitae et resurrectionis*) and *suffering* pain (*theologia crucis*). We often say, there is no growth without pain. The thrust of God's activity in Jesus is *vita creativa*, not so much *vita activa* in general. There is also the *vita passiva* involved, yet always in the service of life. The affirmation of life first of all stresses the creation and re-creation of life. Liberation concerns itself with this angle of creation. See my "Praxis Passionis Divini," *Evangelische Theologie*, 44:6 (November/December 1984), 563–75; and Gerhard Sauter, " 'Leiden' und 'Handeln'," *Evangelische Theologie*, 45:5 (September/October 1985), 435–58.

41. Macquarrie, *Principles of Christian Theology*, 389.

42. There is always tension between *ecclesia* (structure) and *koinonia* (communion) when it comes to grasping what church is. Also in crisis situations we cannot disregard the structure, be it in persecution or political resistance, for example. The Catholic Church in Poland in some respects might be a case in point at this time. Although greatly appreciating his tremendous stress on communion in his struggle, I always regretted that Bonhoeffer did not at some crucial points bring out the interdependence between structure and communion. See Dietrich Bonhoeffer, *Life Together*, (New York, 1954), 21ff. and passim.

43. We need to see that what brings us together in the church is not we ourselves, but Christ, and the creativity of all pain. Dietrich Bonhoeffer's *Life Together*, in some of its unsurpassable insights, makes this utterly clear: "Because Christ stands between me and others, I dare not desire direct fellowship with them" (*Life Together*, 35).

44. See my *Liberation Theology*, 69–95.

45. It is impossible today to wrestle with the catholicity of the church without taking into account the base communities in the Third World. However difficult it might be in North America to find analogies, the issue has to be faced. See Leonardo Boff, *Ecclesiogenesis: The Base Communities Reinvent the Church* (Maryknoll, N. Y., 1986); Guilllermo Cook, *The Expectation of the Poor: Latin American Basic Ecclesial Communities in Protestant Perspective* (Maryknoll, N.Y., 1985); Juan Luis Segundo, *Theology and the Church* (Minneapolis, Chicago, New York, 1985). For our difficulties with analogies, see Daniel Berrigan, *The Mission* (San Francisco, 1986): "For our base communities, we have only the Catholic Worker, Sojourners, Jonah House, a few other lights, and small ones at that, in a vast darkness. We have never had the reins of apocalypse thrust in our hands, the words shouted at us, 'You're in charge. You make sense of things. Bring the world under control. . . .' Nor will such an event

conceivably happen in our lifetime. So we muck along as best we might, making do; so many in prison, many serving the poor, many offering sanctuary. No big deal, no big theology, no big clout (or even little one). Crimes committed daily in high places; people pushed off the map; power plays succeeding brilliantly; weapons multiplying—all this quite as though we were not in the world, God were not there, Christ were a myth or fetish for the weak" (144f.). It is one of the most moving statements about the church catholic I have read recently. I may misunderstand Berrigan's overall thrust. Again, though, the issue is "control." I find trying to "bring the world under control" to be part of the brash hubris. I do understand Berrigan's pain. The dilemma, though, is that we want to *control* even campesinos in Argentina whereas the dire need is to give it up, to give it all up—to let go and let God—and only then cooperate with God.

46. It is not possible in terms of the usual straightline logic to make satisfactory statements about the church today. We need to clown our way through this time period. Berrigan thinks we will not see significant change in our lifetime. What we might see is more Christian clowning, though. See Conrad Hyers, *The Comic Vision and the Christian Faith* (New York, 1981); from a secular perspective, see Joseph W. Meeker, *The Comedy of Survival* (New York, 1974). For a little clowning in trying to work through the *ecclesia/koinonia* tension, see "Laying the Groundwork at Duke Divinity School," *Covenant Discipleship Quarterly*, 1:3 (April 1986) 4–5. The basic challenge is to develop learning processes of mutual accountability within the framework of any church structure. That includes the context of ministerial education.

47. Whether in Christian education in local churches or in ministerial education in seminaries and divinity schools, we no longer have the luxury of picking between various models of the church: Which church suits us best? For an excellent presentation of models, see Avery Dulles, *Models of the Church* (Garden City, N.Y., 1978). The mandate for our day is discipleship. From here, the priority for reflection is the dynamics of history—with the understanding that God gives us no right to divide up history into two kingdoms. This is especially crucial for the new understanding of the eucharist.

48. From the medieval hymn *Veni Creator Spiritus* of Hrabanus Maurus (776–836) Martin Luther shaped his Pentecost hymn, "Komm, Gott Schöpfer, Heiliger Geist," which speaks of the Holy Spirit as "finger on God's right hand." I understand it to mean that the Spirit is also an agent of Jesus as God's right hand in the historical struggle. Along with God-walk probably a completely new experience of heaven arises. Even today in popular Christianity the notion persists that heaven is the place where there is nothing to do, a life without stress, with great harmony, a realm of

sheer exultation. It seems more true to think that God's finger digs deeply into history, so that the struggle continues, only in a different form. Is this notion too far off as far as the biblical context is concerned? Remember Luke 11:20: "But if it is by the finger of God that I cast out demons, then the kingdom of God has come upon you."

49. If Christ is the human mutant, the Holy Spirit is this human mutant divinely empowering corporate humanity. Holy Spirit as resurrection Spirit reinforces God's presence in history. Where God is being walked with as Spirit, there God relates to us as power, and the images or concepts cease. This is probably what Jesus had in mind: "God is spirit, and those who worship God must worship in spirit and truth" (John 4:24). Basically Christianity is not an image-making religion, but a way of life in the Spirit. If we want to speak of Christianity as religion, we probably need to say that it is primarily not one of the religions of redemption, but a religion of conscience. It is a walk that leads into mutual accountability before God and not primarily into "I am somebody" in heaven. The various older models of religious egocentricity have been awesomely destructive in their function in human self-justification. Even Luther's doctrine of justification by faith has been abused in that vein.

50. Frederick Herzog, "Birth Pangs: Liberation Theology in North America," *Christian Century*, 93:41 (Dec. 15, 1976), 1125.

51. This is probably what the base communities are hearing. We cannot stress enough their importance for jogging our memory in regard to what from our traditions we in North America already know about the *ecclesia/koinonia* dynamics. Especially helpful in this regard is Sergio Torres and John Eagleson (eds.), *The Challenge of Basic Christian Communities* (Maryknoll, N.Y., 1981). As to linking the challenge to our own history, see Guillermo Cook, *The Expectation of the Poor* (n. 45, above). There are many good beginnings in North America in basic reflection on the elementary task. See William K. Tabb (ed.), *Churches in Struggle: Liberation Theologies and Social Change in North America* (New York, 1986).

52. The basic notion of *aufrechter Gang* was the key to many of Ernst Bloch's concerns. Further expression of the dynamics involved is found in Helmut Gollwitzer, *Krummes Holz-aufrechter Gang* (Munich, 1970). *Upright walk* was one facet that immediately gripped me as I saw the picture from South Africa by Constance Stuart Larrabee, now in the Preface of this book.

53. With great limitations of understanding still prevailing at this time, the only way I can see progress along these lines is that we take seriously the very local social location of the issue. So on April 11, 1987, we went to work in a small workshop in Durham, North Carolina, to tackle the

premises for an analysis of Benjamin F. Chavis, Jr., and Charles Lee (eds.), *Toxic Wastes and Race in the United States: A National Report on the Racial and Socio-Economic Characteristics of Communities with Hazardous Waste Sites* (New York, 1987). The North Carolina anti-PCB protest in Warren County in 1982 had a lot to do with the origins of this report. See the above mentioned publication by Jenny Labalme, *A Road To Walk* (n. 34), a social location key. Keeping in mind Daniel Berrigan's reservations with regard to base communities in North America, I am emboldened to think that any future of such communities is rooted around such struggles. We hope against hope. This is the place where eschatology relates to accountable teaching.

54. Our limits here need to be kept in mind very clearly. See James W. Douglass, *Resistance and Contemplation* (New York, 1972), 46f.

55. We need to confront ourselves time and again with the vast story that lies behind this particular tension between eschatology and ecclesiology also in Protestant spirituality. See Frank C. Senn (ed.), *Protestant Spiritual Traditions* (New York, Mahwah, 1986); also Peter C. Erb (ed.), *Pietists: Selected Writings* (New York, Ramsey, Toronto, 1983). For the secular issues that face us in terms of a spin-off, as it were, see Richard J. Bernstein, *Praxis and Action* (Philadelphia, 1971).

56. Quoted in Martin E. Marty, *The Fire We Can Light* (Garden City, N.Y., 1973), 73f.

57. It is utterly crucial not to lose oneself at this point in an eschatological never-never land, but to keep our present history fully before us. See Bertram Gross, *Friendly Fascism: The New Face of Power in America* (Boston, 1980).

58. It is important when we say this to face the harshness of our history time and again—that is, we dare not flinch from it. Since 1972 we in the United States have been facing the lawlessness of state and society in its peculiar clandestine character, whether characterized by Watergate or Irangate. See Morton H. Halperin, Jerry J. Berman, Robert L. Borosage, Christine M. Marwick, *The Lawless State* (New York, 1976); also Robert McAfee Brown, *Saying Yes and Saying No: On Rendering to God and Caesar* (Philadelphia, 1986).

59. *Heidelberg Catechism* (Philadelphia, new ed., 1962).

60. It is inescapable that we develop a new direction for the church to travel in view of the many insoluble problems (with which we have to learn to live) in recollection of the road it has already traveled in North America. Accountable teaching with regard to eschatology is also always a look back. In most respects an unsurpassed account is still H. Richard Niebuhr's *The Social Sources of Denominationalism* (New York, 1957). For the whole issue of accountable teaching in this chapter on spirit-praxis I had

initially also intended to include an analysis of the discussion on the subject in my own denomination, the United Church of Christ. But in putting together the final draft of the manuscript the plan seemed cumbersome. I do need to underline, however, how important my own church is for me in working through the liberation process in context. In *Justice Church* (Maryknoll, N.Y., 1980) that should already have been very clear. For the debate on accountable teaching in the United Church of Christ, see *New Conversations*, 8:1 (Spring 1985). This is a publication of the United Church Board for Homeland Ministries. I am greatly indebted to the attempt to tie all these things together in the overall United Church of Christ polity struggle in Louis H. Gunnemann's *United and Uniting: The Meaning of an Ecclesial Journey* (New York, 1987). Anyone who wants to know more about why liberation theology struggles need to be tied to the accountable teaching challenge ought to read this book. It deserves a wide hearing in the ecumenical church. My personal view is (and I may be wrong) that the ecumenical movement is almost completely ignorant of these struggles.

INDEX OF NAMES

265

GENERAL INDEX